COULD DO BETTER

How can we really look after ourselves and our staff teams in light of everything we face? What if people really valued staff wellbeing rather than staff well-doing? Could Do Better explores the myriad demands upon those working in schools, acknowledging the 'too much' and 'not enoughs' of the climate in which staff work, and considering the impact this has on wellbeing throughout the school.

The book introduces the RESET acronym, which provides a framework for meaningful change: Remember and Reimagine - Examine and Evidence - Safely Speak Up and Share - Equip and Empower - Task and Try One Thing. Each theme inspires hope, encourages self-reflection and equips the reader with practical strategies to support their school journey. Throughout, the author also draws upon her own experiences, as well as a variety of first-hand case studies, to tackle topics from shame and expectations to brave leadership and creating a culture of value.

With an interactive format and space for the reader to reflect throughout, the book is an essential tool to support staff to know their value and to put practices in place to improve their working lives. It will be key reading for teachers in both primary and secondary settings, as well as school leadership teams and those in pastoral roles.

Pippa McLean has been a teacher and SENDCO for many years, working in a number of mainstream primary schools across the South-East of England during her career. She has written regularly for publications including *nasen Connect* and has a passion for wellbeing and inclusion. Pippa loves investing in children and families and encouraging others to do the same, something that is seen in her commitment to school communities and other local community projects.

COULD DO BETTER

A Journey to Improve Staff Wellbeing in Schools

Pippa McLean

Designed cover image: Getty Images

First published 2026
by Routledge
4 Park Square, Milton Park, Abingdon, Oxon OX14 4RN

and by Routledge
605 Third Avenue, New York, NY 10158

Routledge is an imprint of the Taylor & Francis Group, an informa business

© 2026 Pippa McLean

The right of Pippa McLean to be identified as author of this work has been asserted in accordance with sections 77 and 78 of the Copyright, Designs and Patents Act 1988.

All rights reserved. No part of this book may be reprinted or reproduced or utilised in any form or by any electronic, mechanical, or other means, now known or hereafter invented, including photocopying and recording, or in any information storage or retrieval system, without permission in writing from the publishers.

Trademark notice: Product or corporate names may be trademarks or registered trademarks, and are used only for identification and explanation without intent to infringe.

British Library Cataloguing-in-Publication Data
A catalogue record for this book is available from the British Library

ISBN: 978-1-041-07222-5 (hbk)
ISBN: 978-1-041-07201-0 (pbk)
ISBN: 978-1-003-63940-4 (ebk)

DOI: 10.4324/9781003639404

Typeset in Other (specify)
by Apex CoVantage, LLC

CONTENTS

How To Use This Book   ix
Prologue   x
Acknowledgements   xi

Introduction   1

PART I: THE GOOD STUFF   5

1   The Good Things   7
Interlude – Treat Yourself   16
Reflection Activities – Remember and Reimagine   17
Reflection Page – You Are Remarkable   29

PART II: THE HARD STUFF   31

2   The Not Enoughs We Face   33
Interlude – Go Grab a Cup of Tea   55
Reflection Activities – Examine and Evidence (i)   56
Reflection Page – You Are Enough   69

3   The Too Much We Face   71
Interlude – Take a Break   89
Reflection Activities – Examine and Evidence (ii)   90
Reflection Page – You Are of Such Great Worth   102

4   Digging Deeper   104
Interlude – Chat to a Friend   115
Reflection Activities – Safely Speak Up and Share (i)   116
Reflection Page – You Are Seen   127

PART III: DOING BETTER WITH ALL THE STUFF   129

5   Let's Talk About Shame   131
Interlude – And Breathe   149
Reflection Activities – Safely Speak Up and Share (ii)   150
Reflection Page – You Are Not Alone   160

6	**Enough Is Enough**	**162**
	Interlude – Step Outside	178
	Reflection Activities – Equip and Empower	179
	Reflection Page – You Matter	190
7	**Brave Leadership and the Way Ahead**	**192**
	Interlude – Rest	207
	Reflection Activities – Task and Try One Thing	208
	Reflection Page – You Make a Difference	219
	Conclusion	*221*
	Additional Resources	*224*
	Index	*225*
	About the Author	*228*

HOW TO USE THIS BOOK

This book is intended to be an ongoing resource for you. Not just a one-off read, but something you use time and time again to support your wellbeing.

As you go through this book you'll find a series of reflection activities throughout each chapter.

Don't try and do them all at once.

Start with one that catches your attention and sit with it a while. You can come back to others another time.

Be as bravely honest as you can be.

Some reflections might just be for your eyes only.

Others you might want to talk about with other people.

You might decide to do some of the thinking alongside others, together committing to the ongoing journey of your personal development and collective wellbeing.

You might find yourself drawn to particular reflection activities in different seasons.

Create a rhythm of visiting different activities regularly, as a tool to help you reflect.

Return to the reflection activities in the first chapter frequently as a way of resetting the balance.

Practise the built-in breaks (interludes) throughout and build them into your regular routines.

Think, write, draw, doodle, colour in and scribble in the margins.

Make this book yours.

PROLOGUE

We were sat in a small courtyard wrapped around by classrooms. The wellbeing garden had been a year in the making. Planned and brought to life by staff, with careful attention paid to detail. Details that meant something to the people who worked in the school. A handwritten note here, a carefully selected picture there. A stained-glass feature hanging from a branch, specially chosen art and flowers and plants, tables and chairs to gather round. The sun was unexpectedly shining, and you could feel its warmth on your face. And there was cake.

We were all there to remember a boss, a colleague who for many had also become a friend over the years. A life well lived, yet a year ago almost to the day, one that had unexpectedly been cut short. And as the sun shone and we celebrated with chat and cake (she would have loved the cake!), we remembered. Staff still at the school, and others like me who had been invited back for the occasion.

We remembered and laughed, and welled up, and it felt like something precious. You do so much life with each other when you work in a school. School teams are not just functional; they are relational. You weep together and do side-splitting laughter together. You do the mundane ordinary everyday, and the utterly extraordinary, side by side. If you're part of a school community, you share a journey that builds trust and goes way beyond the confines of the classroom. I think part of the bonding is because it's not easy working in a school. It's wonderful at times, but it's also really hard. But that's what grafts us together.

This book is about all those things: the good things and the things that take their toll, and a wondering if we could somehow do things better. My friend would have loved that. She wanted to do things better. She wanted to do things that would make it better for us, the people she worked with, and for the children and families in our school.

ACKNOWLEDGEMENTS

Huge thank-yous especially to family, friends and colleagues for all the time and conversations around this book. Thank you for knowing my heart behind it and giving me the time to bring it to life. Huge thank-yous to Caroline Hare and Anna McLean for the illustrations. You are all so kind.

To all those who have spoken value over me in my life and do so to this day, thank you . . and to the One who knows me and shows me my worth more than any other, thank you.

To all those I've worked with over the years, and to all of you who give your all to the task, my hope is that you would deeply know how valued you are, and that this would feel like solid ground beneath your feet and sure hope within your heart . . .

Introduction

Could do better. In one sense, these words might have echoes of a teacher's remark from days long ago, with 'See me' kinds of overtones. It smacks of not right. Not enough. And the words have a weight to them that somehow sinks into your bones. It's a felt thing. Not just in your head but in your body. Sometimes that's how we can feel when it comes to teaching. That what we're doing is never quite enough, and someone somewhere is always out there saying we could do better. When it comes to those who comment on how we're doing, the ones who say we're doing well can seem to have a much quieter voice than the others. And sometimes all that talk of not doing so well leaves us not doing so well. So, when it comes to wellbeing in schools, what if we actually *could* do better? Not just having wellbeing on the agenda for the children and students, but genuinely having it as a priority for us too? If we could do this better, and by that, I mean if we could *be* better (as in, *be more well*, or at least aware of when we're not doing so well), then that in itself has got to lead to better things for us and the children we teach.

We know that when it comes to wellbeing it's important to take a holistic view. Lots of different factors impact on our wellbeing, and many of these are outside the control of life in school, but other factors like our sense of purpose and safety, and the quality of our relationships are impacted by our school environments. We know that wellbeing is a personal and collective responsibility, with elements of self-care as well as looking out for each other, and working together to shape the environments in which we work. Collaboration between the Department for Education (DfE), Ofsted (Office for Standards in Education), Education Support Partnership, teaching unions and a variety of independent and state schools from primary right through to colleges created The Education Staff Wellbeing Charter, first published in 2021, and then updated in 2024 (2021). Its purpose is that schools sign up to the commitment to prioritise wellbeing practice and open up discussion and accountability around wellbeing. Education Support's annual Teacher Wellbeing Index seeks to monitor the impact from all partners on wellbeing outcomes, and changes in inspection guidance in light of the Beyond Ofsted report (2023) also has a strong thread around wellbeing. So, wellbeing is on the agenda. Even so, McBrearty, introducing the latest research statistics around wellbeing in schools, states in the introduction of the Teacher Wellbeing Index of 2024 that

> The mental health and wellbeing challenges in the workforce are chronic, and require urgent action. Children who were born during the isolation of the pandemic are now entering schools. More than ever, our children and young people need the very best quality of presence and attention that we are capable of offering them.

So, we're moving in the right direction, but we're on a journey and we've still a long way to go. There's a lot of catching up to do.

When it comes to staff wellbeing and emotional and mental health in schools, what we do can sometimes feel like a drop in the ocean. You don't have to be super close to someone in education to realise the demands of the role. The daily challenges we face are immense. So, when it comes to supporting staff wellbeing, do any of our changes to practice actually help, when the system we're working in demands so much more than we can sustainably give? When points on action plans about staff wellbeing can sometimes still feel a bit tokenistic, even though the motivation behind them is far from it, I wonder if somehow, we might be missing something. Perhaps we need to look beneath the surface, beyond all the externals that are visible to the naked eye? Beyond the not enough time, not enough resources, not enough funding, not enough this or that, beyond the endlessly high and some might say unrealistic expectations. What if other things impact us and have the power to undermine, deskill, overpower and sap energy, and yet go unmentioned? My intention is that we explore some of these things as we go on a journey towards better wellbeing in our schools.

I want to suggest that perhaps one of the biggest things that impacts school staff is when you feel like not just *what you do* is not enough, or can never be enough, but that *you* are not enough. You are the one who just needs to do better. For many of us, our sense of wellbeing is closely linked to how we think we're doing in the job. Well-doing, if you like, or our perception of this, affects our wellbeing. We're measured all the time by how well we're doing. But I'm interested in how well we're being.

Maybe you're doing (or being) well at the moment. If so, that's a cause for celebration. Maybe you're not so sure or you know for sure that you're not. This book is for you all. Sometimes things can get out of balance, and we need to find a way to reset. My hope is that this book can be part of that process. As we look together at some of the things that can impact us in the job and how they can leave us feeling, this book may be something of a journey of discovery. Maybe you'll come across things you've not thought of before, but there'll be a deep-down sense that they ring true. I think you have to be able to see what's at play before you can begin to grapple with it.

I come from this from being on the ground as a practitioner for many years, first cutting my teeth in the job in East London, followed by teaching and then being a SENDCO (Special Educational Needs and Disability Coordinator) in different schools in the Southeast. As a teacher I've felt a whole range of emotions in the job. The highs of a real sense of achievement, compassion, relief, elation and a lot of laughter, as well as frustration, exasperation, helplessness, anger, sadness and tiredness that feels like it's literally in your bones. Sometimes it can feel like you can feel them all in one day. Hewett (2019) says

> As a teacher you will have good days; you'll have bad days. Days that are overwhelming and tiring and days that leave you feeling awesome and euphoric. Days that make you believe you are the best teacher in the world, but also days that will leave you feeling like the worst.

We've all been there, right? There are days when I have loved my job, and days when I have found it hard to even walk through the door, just anticipating the demands that will be on me and the stress I might be under. Some lessons, conversations or interactions have left me with a sense of knowing this is what I always wanted to do, and at other times I've literally been counting the days to the end of term.

In talking and working with teachers and support staff over the years, and in having conversations with school counsellors who counsel staff, life coaches who coach and provide supervision for staff, professionals who train trainee teachers and educational psychologists, it's clear that staff wellbeing is a significant area of concern. The pandemic played a part in raising the profile of wellbeing and mental health for all, but in its wake there's still a sense that we need to wake up to the ongoing challenges we face in schools. There is so much good stuff about the job, and this often keeps us going when the hard stuff comes our way. The premise of this book is that when it comes to the hard stuff, it's the surface things we often talk about. The obvious things, the things we can see, the things that we don't have enough of . . . time, resources and the like. What we don't often talk about is how these things can leave us feeling. Sometimes we find ourselves thinking we've just got to push on through and hold it all together (well, at least until the end of term). Because everyone else is . . . Or so we think. What if we could do better with it all?

As we go through this book, there'll be opportunities for you to reflect. There'll be journal pages that you can use to explore what you're thinking and feeling about the different questions that are posed. You might think that you're not the journaling kind, but for sure you'll be used to doing a lot of reflecting. It's our bread and butter as teachers. So, if it helps, just think of it as reflecting, with intermittent stops along the way, to pause and breathe. I believe that the time you give to it will be time well spent. What I'm wondering is, if enough of us could venture along this path, then maybe, just maybe, it could lead to a healthier way of us *being* and *doing* in schools. My hope is that as we go on this journey together, we'll become more aware of what we're up against, we'll be better equipped to respond and that this process in itself will help reset the balance and do well for our wellbeing. Because when it comes to teaching, we have to find some kind of balance with the good stuff, the hard stuff and everything in between. I mean, what do we do with all this stuff? My hope is that by calling out some of these things, we can journey towards healthier school environments for all, and in the doing of it, we Could Do Better.

References

Beyond Ofsted Inquiry. (2023). *Final report of the inquiry*. NEU.

Department for Education. (2021). *The education staff wellbeing charter*. https://www.gov.uk/guidance/education-staff-wellbeing-charter

Education Support. (2024). *Teacher wellbeing index 2024* (p. 6). Education Support. https://www.educationsupport.org.uk/media/ftwl04cs/twix-2024.pdf

Hewett, V. (2019). *Making it as a teacher: How to survive and thrive in the first five years* (p. 4). Routledge.

PART I
The Good Stuff

1
The Good Things

I went into teaching for the people. The children. They are the good things about this job. They can be the hard things too (the challenges they present, the challenges they represent, the challenges they face), but fundamentally they're the reason most of us come into this thing in the first place. For me, it's always been about the people. Sat in an interview chair as a fresh-faced 18-year-old school leaver, trying to put words to why I wanted to teach, I remember it coming out of my mouth. 'I want to be their friends'. It's pretty cringeworthy I know, and even now it seems like such a naïve thing to say. Fortunately, the university Education course team was able to pull more out of me on the day, and I went on to study for four years in order to teach. It's what I'd wanted to do for a long time. I love working with children. I love seeing their play, their spark and their interest in the world around them. I love seeing their minds grow. I love their sense of humour, their sometimes straightforward perspective on life. I think the whole 'I want to be their friends' thing was just a poor attempt at trying to say I thought they had value. Every single one of them, and I wanted them to know that and to be able to trust that I wanted the best for them, that I wanted to be part of somehow drawing out the gold in them, so that they could know and grow into being the marvellous human beings that they were. That's why I wanted to teach. I mean, what a privilege to be a part of something like that.

And truth be told, decades down the line I still think that. Different children come to mind: those who had a passion for justice and showed extraordinary kindness even from a young age; those who showed breathtaking artistic flair, or had incredible natural talent when they wrote; those who loved listening to music and practised long and hard to become skilled with an instrument; those who had natural wit, and those who pursued things with a passion; those who found learning so very hard but kept on trying; those who showed unimaginable resilience in daily life; those who struggled with friendships; those who had breakthrough moments and those who didn't; those who were so messed up by life you weren't sure if they were going to make it (whatever that means), and there are those who of course just stay with you. It has been such a privilege to invest in the lives of so many. All the children I've worked with, all the families I've known, all the staff I've worked alongside who have given above and beyond for the sake of others. It's been a good thing.

DOI: 10.4324/9781003639404-3

Maybe you need more than just my word for it. If you're wondering 'Why teach?' it doesn't take very long to come across some inspirational quotes out there. To be honest, I think some of them just sound a bit mushy, or fluffy (think of over sentimental words inside a birthday card), like they've been dreamt up by someone who's never set foot inside a classroom, but they think it sounds kind of good and that it'll encourage you if you glance at it every now and then on a magnet stuck on the fridge door. The reality of working with children has a bit more grit about it. The other motivational things you'll find are words from famous educators or leaders who speak about the power of learning. These have far more weight about them. In the fight against the apartheid regime, in a high school speech, Nelson Mandela, former president of South Africa, is famously quoted as saying 'Education is the most powerful weapon which you can use to change the world' (2017). Learning can shape the thinking of individuals, communities and nations and contribute to the work of reconciliation and the greater good. John Dewey the American philosopher, educational and social reformer believed education was integral to social and moral development in society (Williams, 2017). Paulo Freire the Brazilian educator and philosopher encouraged critical thinking and talked about the place of education in bringing about peace and liberation from oppression (Freire, 1985). I could go on. We know the value of education. But do you know you are valued? Do you know you are valued in the doing of it? Because in the normal day to day, it doesn't always feel like that.

So, what has it been for you? Why did you want to teach?

We do a really important job. A people kind of job. In one Michael Rosen poem, he looks back on his time at school and remembers all the time he spent rehearsing for school plays, reminiscing on how one particular teacher invested in him.

> I wanted to say that those hours . . .
> mattered then
> mattered again and again
> and still matter.
> Well, they matter to me.
> But did he know that?
> Did he know that they would go on mattering?
> (Rosen, 2022)

What we do matters because it's about people. At the end of the day, it's not about numbers or data, or the latest project or idea or government initiative; it's always about the children (Zafirakou, 2022).

We've probably all heard stories of when someone in the public eye thanks their teacher for their part in making them who they are, the teachers who encouraged them, stood with them, inspired them or lit a spark. You and I are part of that. You and I are part of that with all those who will never be famous, but who now impact lives and communities for the better in a whole host of different ways. There's a sense of real purpose about what we do, and that feels good. For some of us it even feels like this is what we were made to do. This is where we come alive. This is where we feel most at home. Sometimes it even feels beautiful, and that can feel like homecoming (O'Donohue, 2005).

Whether you're at the very start of your career or a good few years into it, there will be so many good things you can say about working in a school, about doing what you do, teaching and supporting children and young people. Think about it for a minute. Ground it in your own practice. Think of the difference you've made, the learning you've facilitated, the minds you've inspired, the passion you've stirred up, the young people you've nurtured, the children who against all the odds you've helped begin to find a sense of trust in others. I expect names and faces come to mind. Real-life children and young people with flesh and bones and hearts thumping and blood running through their veins. Children with parents and carers, grandads and cousins and aunts and uncles, younger and older brothers and sisters, all of them knowing your name and you being in some way a part of their wider lives too. It's the personal stories that ground us in the good things. The things we see and hear and put our fingertips to every day.

But it's not just about the individuals. It's about community too. Think for a moment about you and your colleagues and allow yourself to feel a sense of satisfaction and pride. Think of the team you've been a part of and the challenges you've overcome. Think of the standing you have as a school in your local community and the consistent presence you've been to those around you. Think of the lead you take on local issues and the part you play in building wider community. The list could go on. When you stop to think about it there are so many things that we are a part of in the life of our schools that are incredible. They're good things. They're literally life-changing things. It's just sometimes we get so busy that we forget them. We forget what we do, day in, day out. We forget what we achieve. We get so focused on all the things we have to do that we assign the good things to the past, just so we can get on with the present. The problem is in doing so, we often forget about them altogether.

What if we remembered all these good things? The monumental and the daily ordinary, the small and even the teeny tiny, and we lined them up in all their shining glory like in some kind of trophy cabinet. Not even for everyone else to see, but for our eyes only. It would be a place we could just pop back into and take a look at, from time to time. A place to help us remember. My hunch is there wouldn't be a cabinet big enough to house all the gleaming silverware if we were to collect every single piece of it. Every single moment.

So many good things.

The DfE (2023) says 'Teaching is a job like no other' – (we can all vouch for that, I'm sure!) – 'It's unique in combining a rich range of professional skills with creativity, excitement and personal satisfaction – and a sense of making a real difference to the lives of children.' This is all true. Speak to teacher friends and colleagues and you can bet your

THREE THINGS

№.3

Think of a child . . . Then think of a moment or a conversation that was good with them . . .

What did you feel and think in that moment, and why did this moment matter to you, them and any others involved?

TROPHY CABINET

What do you have in yours? Which of your achievements in school are worthy of celebration in your eyes? Why?

bottom dollar that someone will talk about making a difference and the sense of satisfaction that can come with it. We can have such a personal sense of achievement in what we do, and we use so many different skills in the doing of it. I could never imagine myself doing a deskbound job, where perhaps I'd feel like I was doing the same kinds of things every day. Teaching and working with children and young people are rewarding. I get to use my brain and my hands and my heart. I am surrounded by diversity and get to work with so many different people. There's a real sense of variety about my day and I never know quite what each day will hold. There's often a very real sense of challenge, as well as fulfilment that can come with it. If you're in a secondary school with a specialist subject, you get to talk about that thing you love and teach it and inspire others about it with your passion. If you're in a primary or early years setting you get to explore a whole range of subjects in a whole variety of ways. For me, the biggest reward in teaching is simply the being with people stuff, investing in people and seeing them grow. It's a good thing.

Remembering good things is a good thing to do. Some might say it's a means of escapism or avoiding difficult things in the present, but studies show that recalling good things can have a positive impact on our wellbeing and developing our resilience. It doesn't just lift

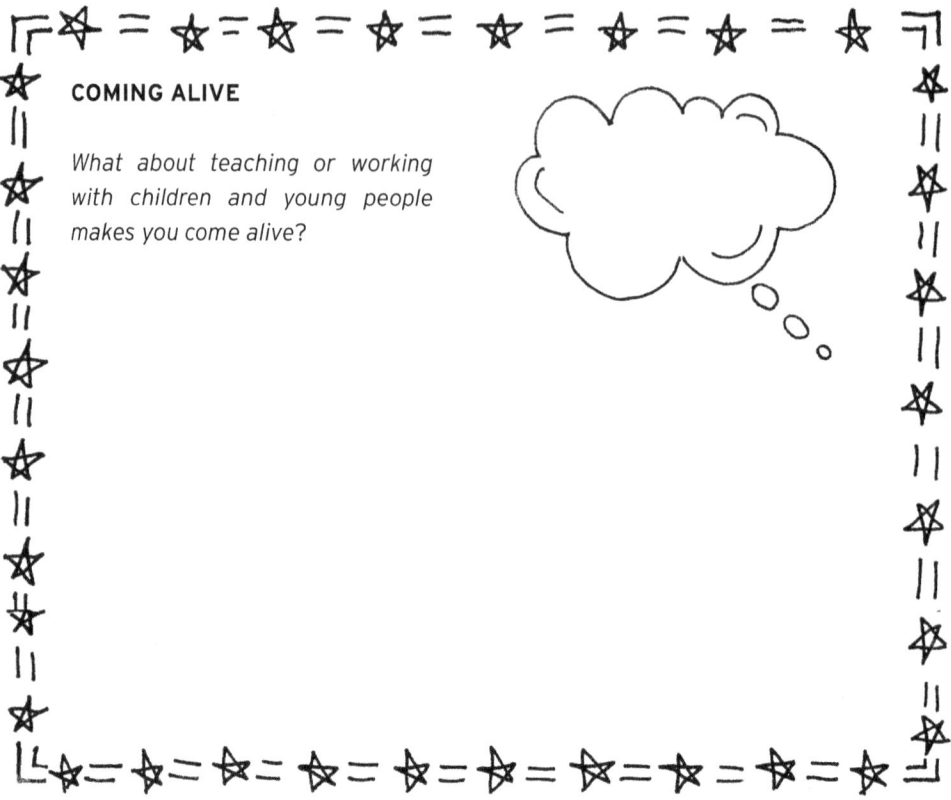

COMING ALIVE

What about teaching or working with children and young people makes you come alive?

our spirits in the moment. It can increase our self-esteem, flood our bodies with positive emotion, lower anxiety and counteract negative thought processes (Bryant et al., 2005). With our ever-increasing understanding around the neuroplasticity of the brain, and its ability to change its structure and function in response to life experiences, recalling positive memories is not just a good idea but it does us good. We find that what we are mindful of impacts our minds.

Sometimes we get distracted with all the other stuff about teaching and working in schools that we fail to see or remember the good things. Or we fail to remember them enough. For some of us, maybe we're just not very good at doing this and we need to practise. We literally need to learn how to see the good, to begin to fire new neural pathways that over time become more attuned to noticing the good things we experience in school. Maybe we could work more on doing this together, to share the trophy cabinet with others or even put it on public display. This could be an act of powerful collective remembering. Look what we've achieved this term, this year, with this class, this cohort, in this climate. At the moment, perhaps the closest thing we get to this is having a hastily grabbed moment at the end of a lesson where we pause briefly and smile at what's just been achieved. Or maybe at the end of term we think back to a special occasion or a performance, where the culmination of weeks of rehearsing and the overwhelming sense of communal pride was felt by children, staff and parents alike. Or maybe your remembering is looking back at the results that came out in the summer, and you're all still staggered as a team that it was even possible this year, and those numbers or letters on a page show your sheer grit and determination and commitment to the task and the people.

As we recall good things, we stumble upon being grateful. Psychologist Reivich's definition of gratitude is 'hunting the good stuff' (Reivich & Shatte, 2002). In everyday school life we can forget to see things we're grateful for. Maybe they're just things we take for granted, the things that go unnoticed to the general eye, or things we think should just go without saying . . . But let's say them. I'm grateful for colleagues who lighten the load, who make me laugh, who step in to help, who help me see the bigger picture. I'm grateful for senior leaders who have my back and know the pressure I'm under right now. I'm grateful for that parent who said thank you, and that parent not getting rattled. I'm grateful for that child having an unexpectedly easier day; I'm grateful it wasn't a wet dinnertime today and the children got out to let some steam off; I'm grateful for Ofsted not coming this week; I'm grateful for my reports being done . . . and I am beyond grateful for my family and friends who are there for me. In being grateful for things, more often than not, we realise we are grateful for people.

There is neuroscience behind it all, because when we are present to experience good with others and receive good from others, we experience connection and community. Gratitude is important for forming and maintaining our everyday relationships (Algoe, 2012). Being grateful literally helps us (Humington, 2023). In their research, Emmons and McCullough (2003) found that those who focused on gratitude had an improved sense of wellbeing, with greater increases in determination, attention, enthusiasm and energy compared to others. When we focus on the good stuff, it is harder for our brains to focus on the negative stuff. Being grateful forces us to focus on the positive (Korb, 2015). So, let's make it a practice to collect up all the good things.

But of course, work is just one space and place that we occupy. What we do is just one facet of who we are, and it's good to be able to separate our worth from just what we do (Stolzoff, 2023). So how about we change the angle a bit and look outside of school at other good things?

Like us.

What about you? If that feels a bit awkward, like you're trying to big yourself up in an interview, all the while wondering if you're really a fraud for even sitting in the chair, maybe it's easier to think about what someone else might say about you. What good things does a good friend say about you? What about someone you love? What do they say about the kind of person you are? When you walk into a room, what kinds of things do you bring into that

GRATEFUL TO...
GRATEFUL FOR

Make a list

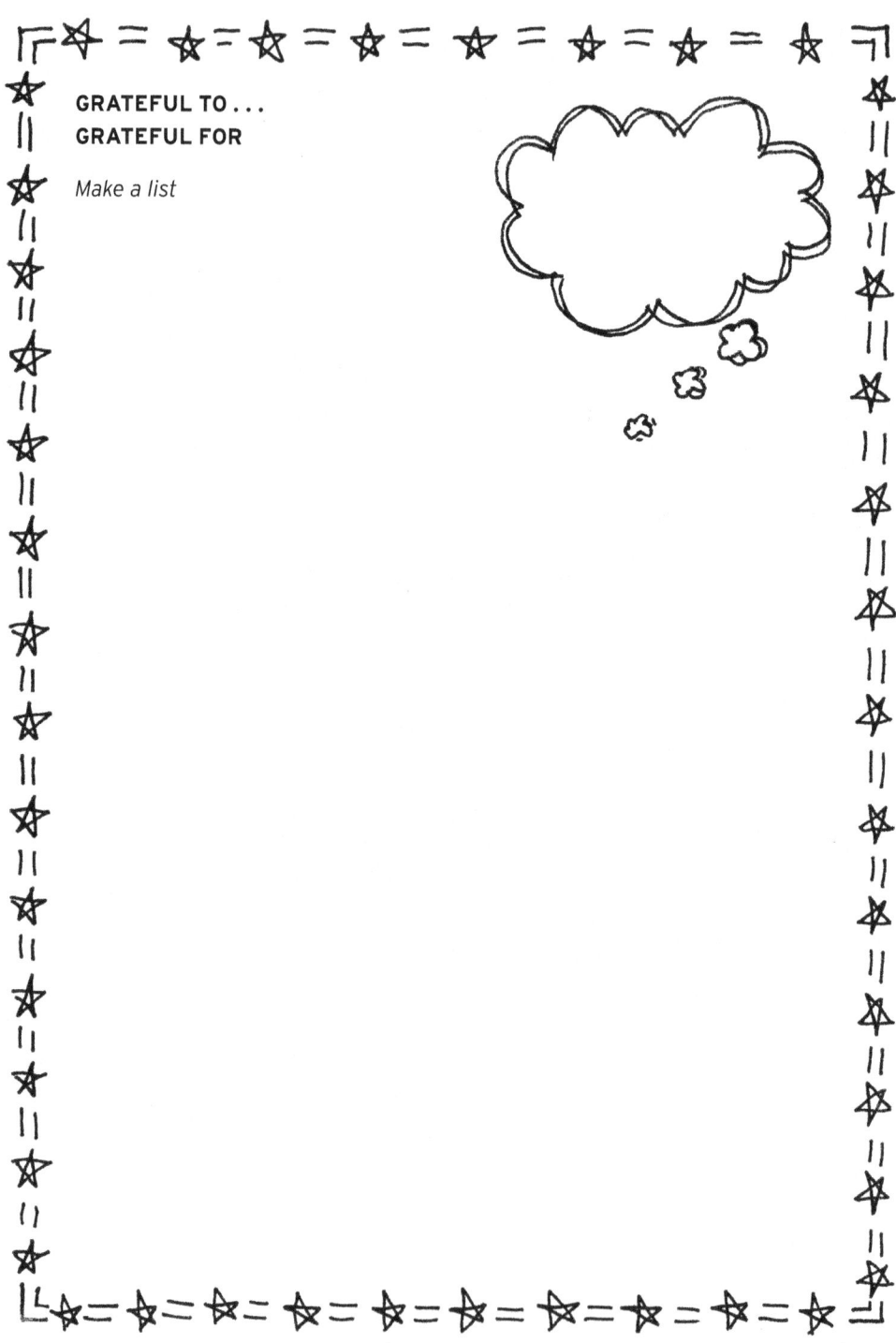

SPOTLIGHT

What good things do children, colleagues and parents say about you? What about people outside of school?

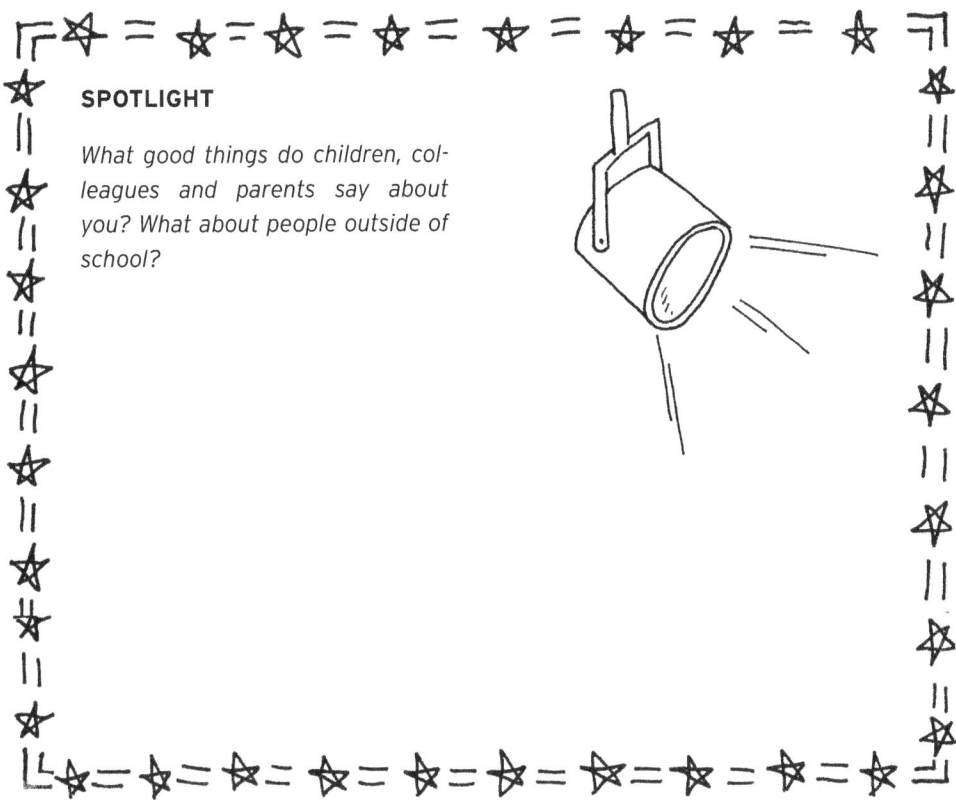

space? Most of us are not very good at doing this. It can feel kind of uncomfortable. But let's remember these things. Let's not rush past them, in a keeping-it-humble, embarrassed kind of way. Think on them. You're not bragging. You're just giving yourself a bit of time to know your value, the good things about you. Remember who you are. If you've lost sight of that a bit, you might just need to pause there a while.

The truth is each and every one of us is of inherent worth. You, your colleague, your boss, each and every child, each and every family member connected to your school community. If we look to our job for our worth, we might have moments where we experience a sense of value, but in another moment, it can come crashing down around us with just a word. Only you can bring the unique you-ness that you bring to your setting at this time, with these children, with these families, with these colleagues, in this climate. Your worth is not found in your job, but you do bring worth to those around you. You do it in your daily showing up and in your being present to people every day, let alone what you speak or nurture into being. What's the value added regarding this intervention? It's you. What's the value added regarding this pathway? It's you. You add worth just by being in the room. You are the treasure in your room because you bring out treasure in others. So, remember the good that you bring.

Perhaps you're in a place where remembering good things about work feels just a bit too hard, like you're foraging around in your memory trying to find something to say, but you can't quite come up with anything that'll sound convincing. You could maybe make something up, but it would just be to fill in the blank, rather than being anything meaningful or genuinely felt. Sometimes it can feel like that. We can lose sight of the good for a while. We get distracted by other things that feel more pressing. It can be hard to remember the good if things are feeling bad. So, if this is the case, maybe instead we could try to reimagine. Reimagine what we hoped for in the job. Reimagine what we wanted to achieve, the difference we wanted to make. Reimagine the hopes and dreams we've had, for ourselves and for those we teach. Have you ever thought of a child you've taught in the past and wondered what they're up to now? Wondered what kind of person they are? Wondered what kind of impact you might have had on them? Have you ever wondered if your love for a subject ignited passion in them that they still carry around today? Have you thought about how you hope to have encouraged them, or given them the skills to go on and do great things or ordinary things, but things that make them come alive? Have you ever thought about all the young people and adults walking around today, where you have had some tiny (or huge) part to play in their lives? You are remarkable. It's good to remember and reimagine the good things.

So...

*****Treat Yourself*****

Remember and Reimagine

THINGS TO CELEBRATE

Take an interval of time – today, this week, this half term. Describe a success during that period.

Why was it a success? Was it worked hard for or something of a surprise?

What are your feelings and thoughts as you remember?

CAPTURE THE MOMENT

What was the golden moment?

Why is it important for you to capture this moment in particular?

INTERVIEW

Think back to your interview for your job (or course). Why did you want to go into teaching or working with children in the first place?

What did you want to achieve? What did you feel you had to offer? What personal goals have you achieved?

CONFETTI

What can you celebrate with others today? What kind of light and colour do these thoughts bring?

LEGACY

What legacy do you want to leave? What do you think you'll be known for?

If you were to up and move from your school today, how would you most likely be remembered?

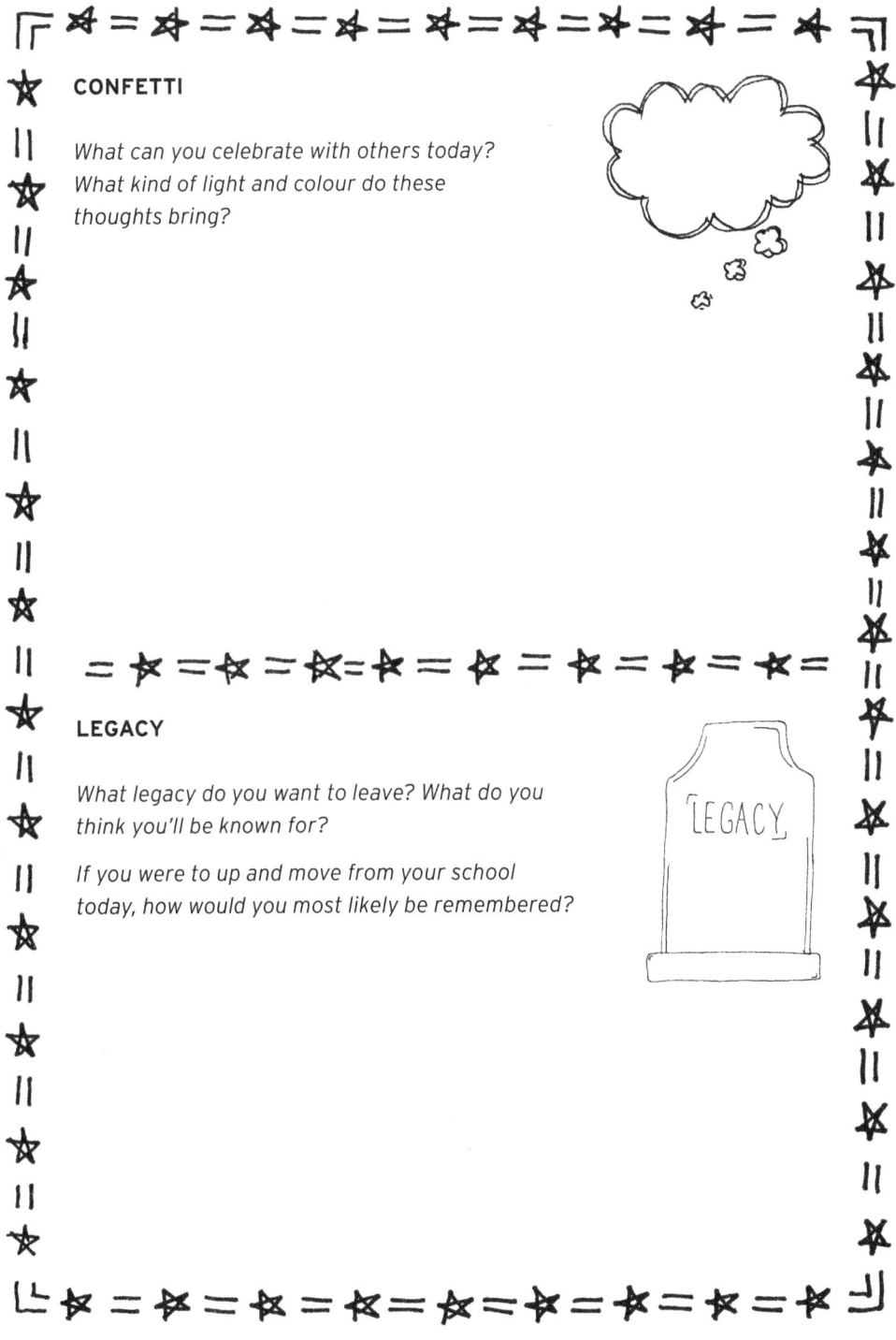

SPOT THE DIFFERENCE

What difference have you made to the children/ young people you have taught?

Think of three specific children where you know that you being part of their lives has been a good thing. Describe what you think those things might be.

PARACHUTE GAMES

If you could catch all the fun/good things and scoop them up, what would they look like?

How much joy would they bring and to whom?

REMEMBER WHEN...

Take a look back through the school calendar and recall different positive experiences in school this year. What was so good about them?

END OF YEAR

Remember an end-of-year note/card/ present/conversation which meant a lot to you.

What was said? How did you feel in that moment? And how do you feel now as you recall it?

UPDATING YOUR CV

Rewrite your CV stating all your credentials, skills, recent learning, passion and achievements when it comes to being in school. As you make the list, does anything take you by surprise?

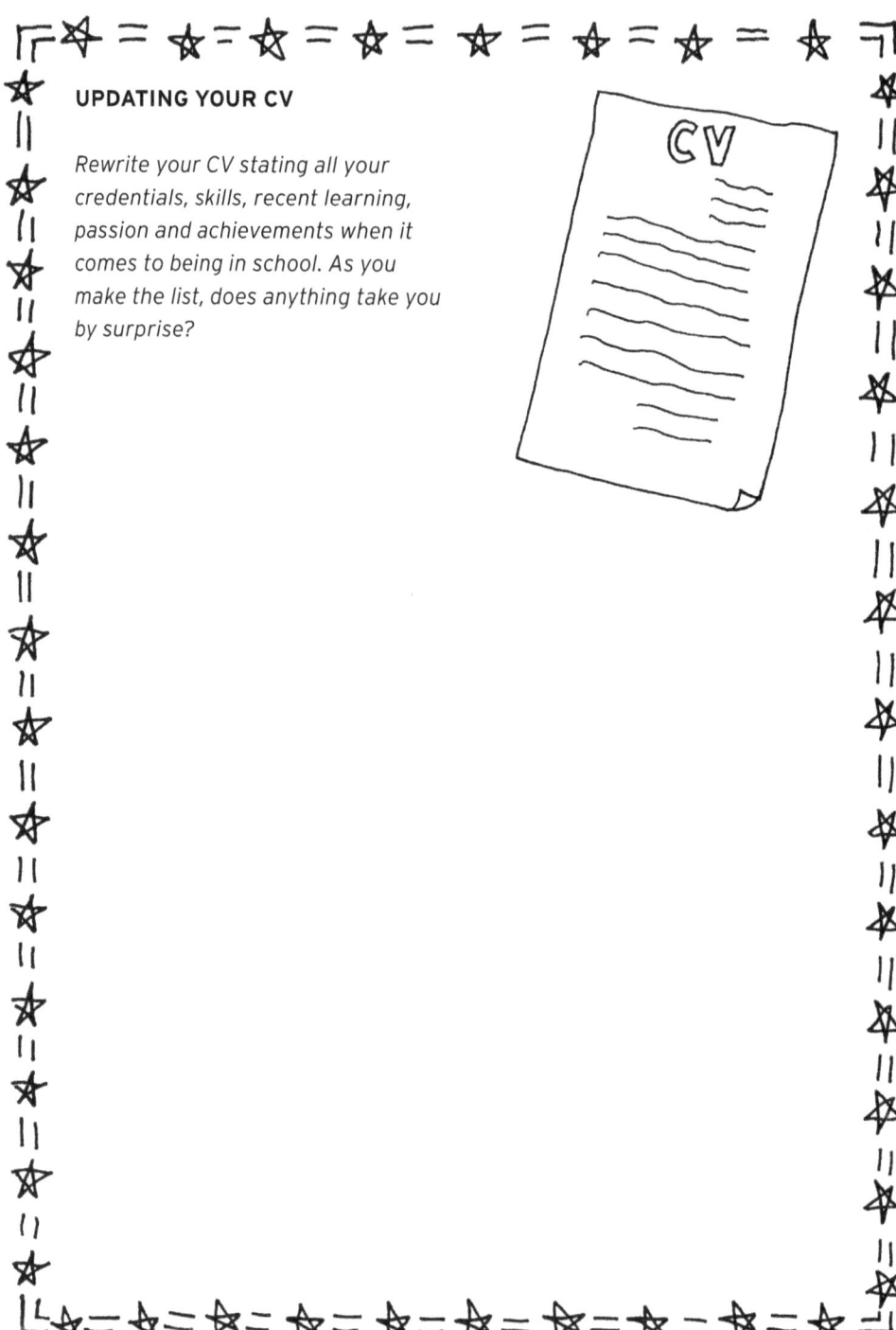

LIFE LESSONS

What good things have you learnt about yourself and others through being in school?

HIGH HOPES AND DARING DREAMS

What are your hopes for your current class/cohort? What are your hopes for your colleagues and team? What are your hopes for yourself?

PIE IN THE SKY

If there were none of the constraints you sometimes feel in your job, what would it look like? And how would you feel?

THINK BIG

Close your eyes and imagine where you'd like to be or what you would have liked to achieve in teaching five years from now.

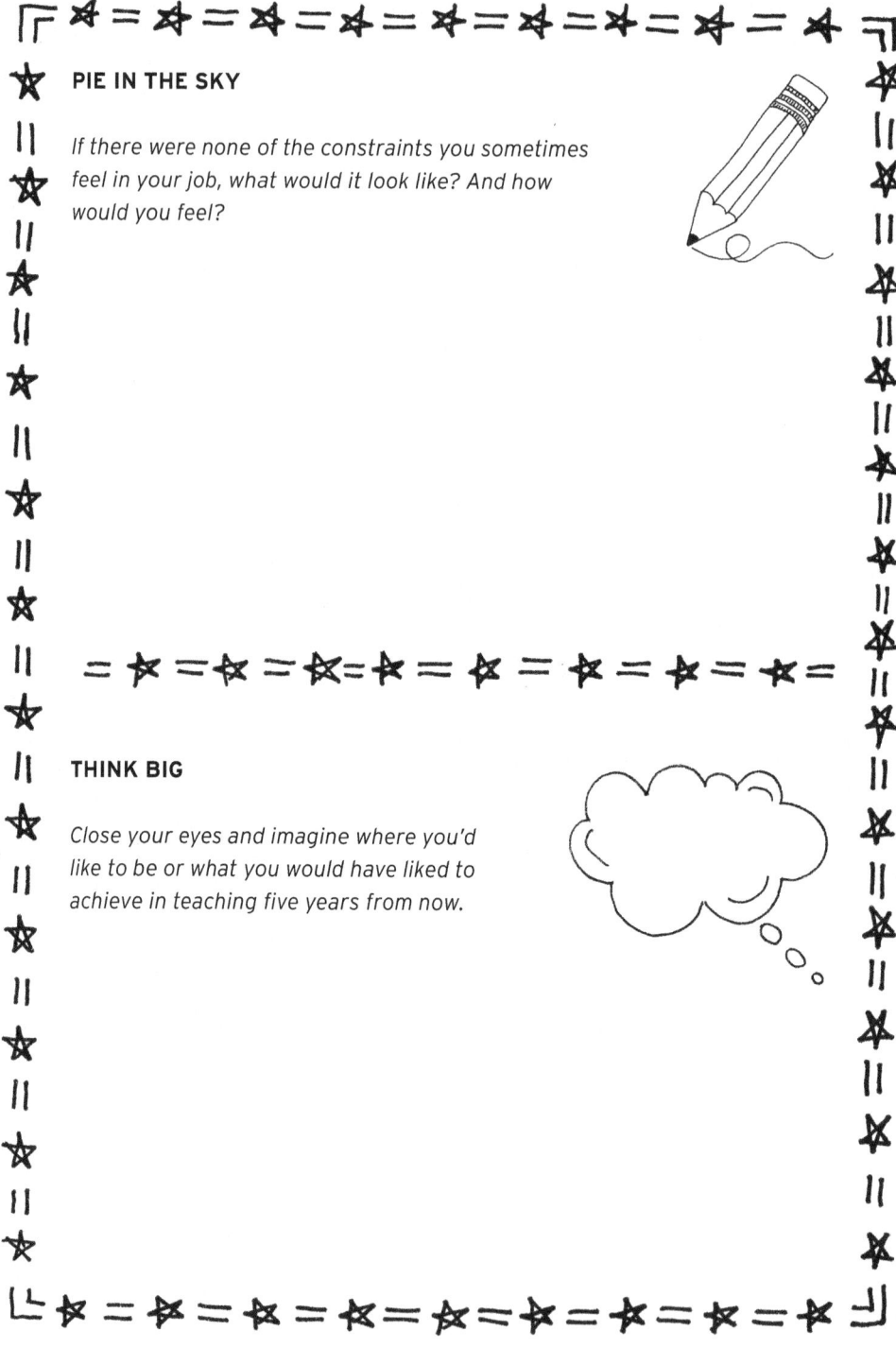

REMEMBER WHO YOU ARE

List things that trusted friends and family say about you. If you're not sure what they might say, ask them.

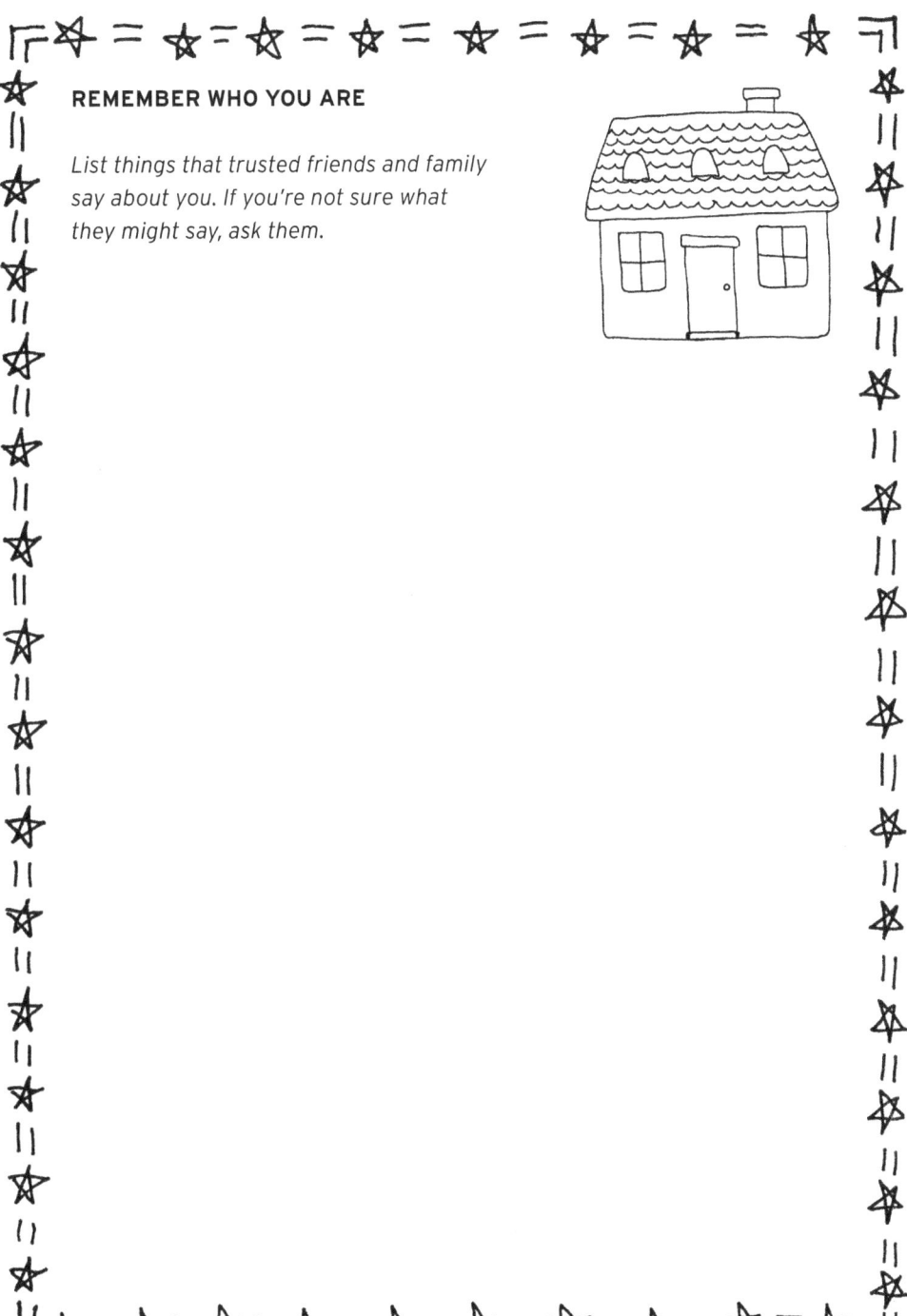

BRAIN DUMP

What are you thinking? What are you feeling?

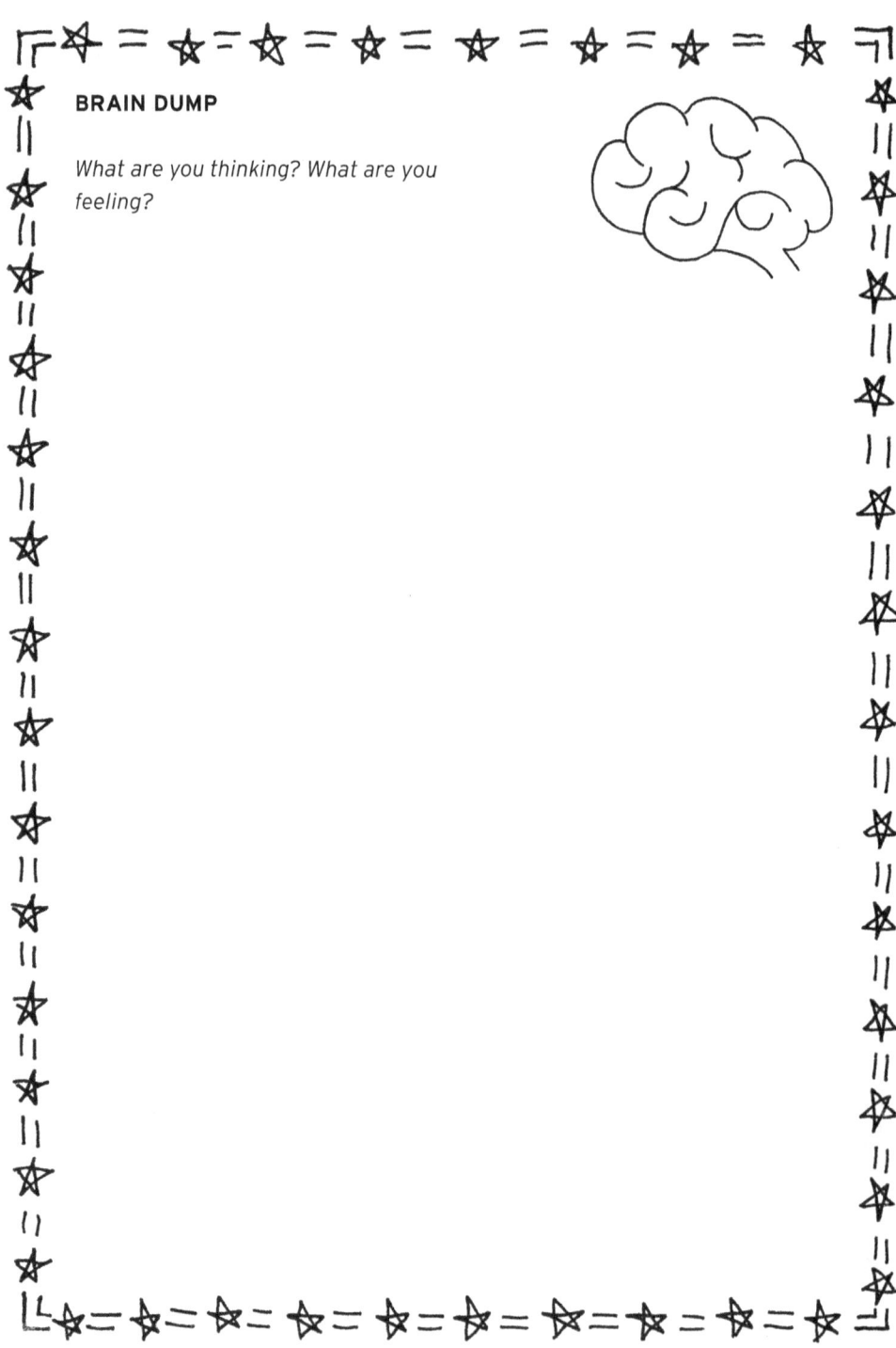

YOU ARE REMARKABLE

References

Algoe, S. B. (2012). Find, remind, and bind: The functions of gratitude in everyday relationships. *Social and Personality Psychology Compass*, 6(6), 455–469.

Bryant, F. B., Smart, C. M., & King, S. P. (2005). Using the past to enhance the present: Boosting happiness through positive reminiscence. *Journal of Happiness Studies*, 6, 227–260.

Department for Education. (2023, January 11). *Why teaching is a rewarding career*. https://educationhub.blog.gov.uk/2023/01/why-teaching-is-a-rewarding-career/

Emmons, R. A., & McCullough, M. E. (2003). Counting blessings versus burdens: An experimental investigation of gratitude and subjective well-being in daily life. *Journal of Personality and Social Psychology*, 84(2), 377–389.

Freire, P. (1985). *The politics of education: Culture, power, and liberation* (D. Macedo, Trans.). Bergin & Garvey.

Humington, A. (2023). *The neuroscience of gratitude – Why self help has it all wrong*. NeuroMastery Lab.

Korb, A. (2015). *The upward spiral: Using neuroscience to reverse the course of depression, one small change at a time*. New Harbinger.

O'Donohue, J. (2005). *Beauty: The invisible embrace: Rediscovering the true sources of compassion, serenity, and hope*. Harper Perennial.

Ratcliffe, S. (Ed.). (2017). *Oxford essential quotations* (5th ed.). Oxford University Press. eISBN: 9780191843730 Speech, Madison Park High School, Boston, June 23, 1990; reported in various forms.

Reivich, K., & Shatte, A. (2002). *The resilience factor* (p. 125). Broadway Books.

Rosen, M. (2022). English teachers. *English in Education*, 56(2), 106–107. https://doi.org/10.1080/04250494.2022.2028500

Stolzoff, S. (2023). *The good enough job: What we gain when we don't put work first*. Ebury Edge.

Williams, M. K. (2017). John Dewey in the 21st century. *Journal of Inquiry and Action in Education*, 9(1), 91–102.

Zafirakou, A. (2022). *Those who can, teach: What it takes to make the next generation*. Bloomsbury.

PART II
The Hard Stuff

2
The Not Enoughs We Face

So, there's all this good stuff out there, but the conditions around us are tough. We live in a culture of scarcity, of there not being enough. We are bombarded from all sides with this idea that we need more to be able to live, function and certainly if we are to thrive. We need more, we get more, we acquire more. This is the narrative of our culture. In schools it's quite easy for us to talk about all the things we don't have to do our job to its best, to talk about the more that we need. These are the obvious things. What's more difficult to talk about is what this sense of lack does to us and how it can leave us feeling. So, let's look at some of these things.

Not Enough Time

We face inordinate pressure on our time in schools. Time is so limited in the face of everything we have to do. There is so much to squeeze into, so much to squeeze out of a finite amount of time. Let's think for a moment about some of the time pressures we face all the time.

Picture the scene:

> Sometimes you know you aced a lesson. You know everything went to plan and the way you caught their attention was everything you'd hoped it would be, and it just worked. All your hard work and planning paid off. It's just no one saw. No one was watching. It was just you. No one caught it on camera or said, 'Well done!' or patted you on the back. But you know it went well, and that's what you hold onto. The children grasped something they hadn't done before, and you had this inner sense of pride that you did a good job. It's a bit like when you reverse into a tight parking space. No one ever seems to be watching when you do it well... But when you cock it up and have to pull out and do it all over again (and maybe again and again?!) that's when you always seem to have an audience.
>
> So sometimes you ace a lesson...

But sometimes you don't. Sometimes it's mediocre, unmemorable, un – (dare I say it?) satisfactory … and sometimes it's a full-blown flunk, a let's-gloss-over-it, wish-the-ground-would-swallow-you-up lesson. And if you're feeling resilient you pick yourself up and dust yourself down and just get on with the day, knowing that next time you'll do things differently. But if it's a less resilient kind of a day, that can be harder to do.

Sometimes you know you just rushed it. You rushed the delivery. You rushed the content. You rushed the examples, the explanation, the time for questions, the breaking it down, the going over it, the practising it. You rushed the recall of previous learning; you rushed the feedback. You moved on too quick. Because the pressure to get on to the next thing is real.

There is so much content to teach. There are so many concepts to learn … that if you miss the timing of it all, it's like you have no time at all. You'll literally run out of time. There is no time to slow things down, or take your time, because time is this finite thing and we have things to do and places to go and people to see, all in the name of work.

Sound familiar?

Time and the Curriculum

When it comes to delivering the curriculum, time and timing are crucial. There is so much curriculum content and there are so many learning objectives to cover for each year group, catch-up group or intervention. Most of these objectives are set by others for us to do (think year group expectations), and some curriculum content and learning objectives are set by us in our local contexts, such as when delivering an intervention. Expectations about what needs to be covered in a year equate to this much this term, this much this week, this much today and this in this lesson. We're good at planning because we have to be, or we'd never be able to even try to fit everything in.

The fast pace and vast amount we have to deliver can leave us (and often children) floundering. At times we feel that we're racing through content, when what we really want to do is take a bit more time. At times we feel we're not actually doing a very good job of supporting children to learn particular skills or assimilate information or deepen their knowledge and understanding before having to move on to the next thing that has to be taught. We're aware of gaps in children's learning, and for some children we're especially aware of the extra time they need to be able to process information and practise in order to understand, but even so, there is this external pressure to just keep going. At the same time, we know that at the end of the day, the children in our classes will be measured on what they have learned, on how well they know, understand and can use the content we have covered. We know that what they have learned will be a building block for further learning. Secure foundations first, not rushed. Brick on brick for the walls, and then the cement has to dry and breathe before you can layer on the plaster. The plaster has to dry before you can paint the walls or decorate and furnish the room. It all takes time. But we also know that the measuring of the children will be the measuring of us. It's a tension we hold, but crack on we must.

Interruptions to the timing can happen all over the place. We get ill or our children get ill, which means we can't get into work, or we drag ourselves in because we know that if we don't, there'll be more for us to do when we get back. If we take a day off, we feel guilty. Guilty that we're landing more on the plate of our colleagues, that they'll have to pick up the slack when they're already snowed under, whether that means them mucking in to cover our playground duty, or taking our class or them helping that child who is more likely to be dysregulated because we're not there. If we're year group leads, subject leads or Key Stage leads we can feel the pressure of staff absence all the more. So much depends on us being in the room. It's not that we can't be replaced, but there is something about the consistent relationship between adults and children in a classroom which creates the dynamic for effective learning. We're up against it when it comes to time.

Aside from illness or absence, we feel the pressure of time slipping through our fingers if we're interrupted by children with challenging behaviour. We feel the pressure of what we are supposed to be delivering in the lesson, as well as the weight of these interruptions on other children's learning. And if managing pupil behaviour is an ongoing challenge in a class or a year group, we can feel a sense that we're letting children down, that they're missing out on what they should be getting, that what's happening is not fair and perhaps that it's our fault. Maybe we can't remedy the situation quickly enough or seem to get on top of it. When it gets into a cycle of recurring disruption, we know the pressure of parent and senior leadership views about it all. All these things weigh in on us perhaps without us even realising, and it's all about time. About time that we acknowledge these things and how they can leave us feeling. That sometimes feeling of maybe we're not quite up to this or we're not sure how long we can keep doing it for. Have you noticed how it's often that one lesson where something went a bit wrong that somehow sticks with you at the end of the week, more than all the others that were ok or even good?

Time and Meeting Children's Needs

We have a holistic approach to meeting children's needs. We're concerned about the whole child and their wellbeing, their cognitive and learning needs, communication and interaction needs, physical and sensory, as well as their social, emotional and mental health needs. And whilst there are significant challenges when it comes to resources and meeting pupil needs, which we'll come onto later, there is also a challenge around meeting them with regards to the time that we have. How are we supposed to fit in looking after the children in our care in this wholehearted way within the time constraints we have, when some of these children need so much more to fit in? Inclusion shouldn't be about children fitting in, but with multiple constraints upon us, it can still sometimes feel like that. Children are learning to sit and take turns and wash their hands, to take risks, to trust, to try again, to recognise their feelings and make friends and a thousand other things as well as all the academic stuff. We know from Maslow's hierarchy of needs (Maslow, 1943) that the really important things have to happen first so that a child feels safe, because only when these needs are met is it safe enough for a child to engage in the risky business of learning. The other needs are not lesser than the academic ones, but it can feel like the academic ones are given more importance because they are the ones that are routinely measured throughout a child's life in school. But we have to meet them all.

Sometimes you have a child you are working with who has a language processing need, who literally needs more time to process what you say, before they can respond. If you rush, they miss it. They won't be able to grasp, understand, let alone consolidate, any learning. This can be a pressure, a tension you have to hold, when the system says all these things need to be covered now. What about the pressures on time when we're working with children with specific medical needs? If you have to regularly support a child to check their blood sugar levels and monitor and administer insulin, this takes time, especially when children are learning how to do this for themselves. Some medical needs can be met in the classroom, depending on the level of privacy needed. Other medical conditions need to be met outside the classroom, which takes time from the child's curriculum learning day. If a child needs support around intimate care routines, these impact on the time the child has in class. We get very creative in a bid to maximise children's learning wherever they are, but there is often a generalisation from outside that one size fits all, when we know that not to be the case.

When it comes to meeting children's needs the bigger picture also comes into play. You can't look at children's needs without looking at the needs of the family, and sometimes you have to go some way to meeting community needs as well as school-based ones, because the one often affects the other. Issues such as poverty and prejudice impact on individual pupil needs, and to even begin to meet these kinds of needs takes time. And so we take time, for that extended conversation with a child or parent. We go the extra mile and make sure this child feels seen and heard. We go over and above because we know this is what this child needs. Even when the time we take is our own. But there's never enough time to do it all and this can leave us wanting. This can leave children wanting, needing more. The child feels this, and so do we.

Time for Training

Picture the scene:

> It's your weekly staff meeting and you're delivering (or listening to) the training on a new initiative that's coming in, and you need to be ready to run with it in the next few weeks. The only problem is that for you, it feels like it throws up more questions than it answers. It leans towards something that might be helpful for you in your school setting and looks like it could improve outcomes for some pupils, but maybe not all, you wonder. And you also wonder about all the time it's going to take you, outside of this training time, to really get your head round it in such a way that you'll be able to confidently deliver it. It's already been decided that it's happening (maybe you've

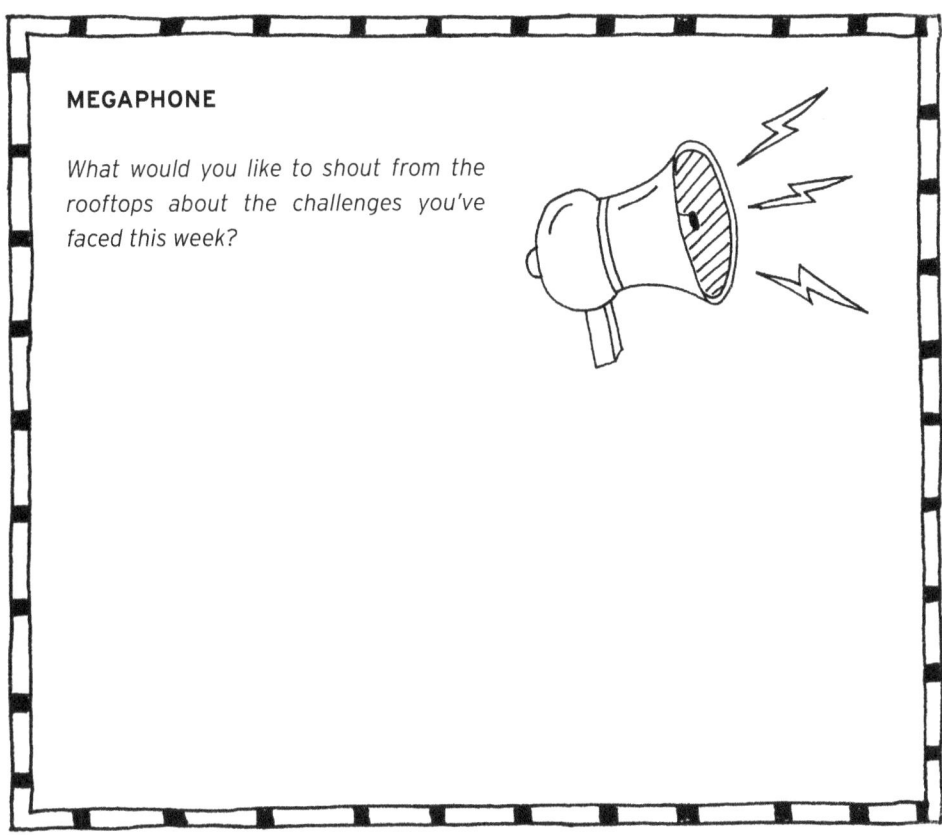

MEGAPHONE

What would you like to shout from the rooftops about the challenges you've faced this week?

been in on that conversation or maybe you've not), but now you're a part of doing this thing, of bringing it into being, whether you're fully behind it or not, and the clock is ticking.

You just feel like you need a bit more time, to assimilate new information, to understand the thinking behind it, to upskill your skill set, to practise before you hit the ground running, but there is no time for all that.

And the difficulty is that it leaves you feeling a bit vulnerable, like you're being thrown in at the deep end a little. You're left wondering if you'll be able to pull it off or if you even believe in it at all?

Sound familiar?

It's ok to have mixed feelings about training. Sometimes training helps consolidate our understanding and practice. Sometimes we're inspired by new learning and can't wait to try new things. But sometimes, we have this niggling sense that there'll be no time to invest in it fully. On the one hand we're enthused and excited about all the opportunities this new thing will open up, and on the other, we know that to actually make it happen, for it to be fully owned by everyone and be all that it is intended to be, it is going to require a lot of work and a lot of time. If training sometimes doesn't have the time to get any real traction, after a few times, it can leave you with a sense of hesitancy (or maybe it's disappointment?) that might mean you invest less fully in the training next time. You rock up, but you're not invested. You listen but you don't give your full attention. After all, you've heard it all before. You've been here before. You've seen new ideas come and go a thousand times before and they always fizzle out. But surely that can't be right? Surely that kind of does something to us over time? Maybe the checking out is so that we don't feel overwhelmed, but might it leave us wondering if we really care anymore? Or maybe we just care too much and that's why it all feels a bit hard.

When it comes to meeting the needs of children, one of the biggest constraints we experience is not having enough time to comprehensively train staff teams. We prioritise who needs to be trained in what, and we use every pocket of time we can, but there is always more training needed than we can possibly deliver. Training might be around new government initiatives or guidance, a new focus within an Academy Trust or Local Authority, a policy or practice that needs to be developed within a certain timeframe. Training links to School Development Plans or our School Improvement Plan cycles. We are a people of action, and we have action plans coming out of our ears, but it can sometimes feel like we're just squeezing things in and ticking things off. In the squeeze, sometimes important things are rushed, and then they don't have the impact they could if we were just able to take more time. It takes time to develop and embed skills and expertise in a staff team, especially if teams are more transient. Things grow over time. The ticktock of a clock has a steady rhythm about it for a reason. When action plans are too full, items spill out all over the place, and that's when things can get a bit messy. Spillages always need mopping up.

If you lead a subject area, have you ever felt like you almost have to fight your corner to secure the time and space you need to deliver training? With the drive for training being around improving outcomes for children, there's an element in which we sometimes feel we need to compete to gain our slot. We come up with ingenious ways to try to create time and space for training to happen for the people who need it. We bend over backwards, cover each other, cram things into training days, arrive early, stay late, learn things before the school day starts and after the school day ends, cut short lunch breaks, have working lunches. We research things in our own time, make resources in our own time, do online learning modules in our own time, because there is not enough time to do what needs to be done in school when it comes to training. Even when we've got our training plans in place, things like staff absence or staff shortages often come along to scupper it. If high-quality training is something we value, we need to try to protect the time to make it happen. I know that's a hard thing to do in the busyness of our school days, but it is so important. If training is irrelevant, mediocre, snatched at, rushed or a hotchpotch, fill-in-the-gaps approach it can leave us feeling frustrated and unprepared. Untrained. Undervalued, even. If you don't feel trained enough, you can very quickly feel like you're floundering. It can feel like you've been thrown in at the deep end and left to sink or swim. Or left for dead. It doesn't feel very cared for. It doesn't feel like you're worth much, or that you count for much. And if people don't have the time to say this is how they feel, it can impact on the trust we have for each other, and the safety of the environment we create. It ends up affecting everyone. Just ask a learning support assistant if they've ever felt like this. If they've ever felt they've been given little to no support and have been hastily sent off to do a task or work with a child that leaves them feeling undone. You can feel very alone when that happens. I've been there, on both ends. I've been the one who's felt like I'm completely disqualified for the task, and I've been the sender off-er, offering some quick instructions or strategies to a bewildered other. It's not good enough when we do this. Carefully prioritising training and time for feedback communicates what we value and who we value.

Time for Paperwork/Administration

In the DfE's Working Lives of Teachers and Leaders survey of 2024, 80% of participating teachers cited high workload, and 74% stress or poor wellbeing as reasons to quit the profession (DfE, 2024b). Think for a moment about all the administrative things you do in a day, in a week, in a term, in a year, to make your job just tick along, all the 'paperwork.' Marking, planning, recording, checklists, pro formas, observations, feedback, evidencing, data inputting, case studies, report-writing, resource-making, to name but a few. It can easily feel overwhelming if you sit down and think about it. We have a really long list of things we do just to make the teaching and learning stuff happen.

We recognise the pinch points in the school year, the times of year when we particularly feel the stress perhaps more than other times. Have you ever felt like you're struggling to meet the deadline of getting reports written? Have you ever felt like you're not on top of your marking? Have you ever just drawn a blank when it comes to planning how to teach that concept in a fun and creative way? Have you ever felt like you're just going through the motions and have lost sight of the magic, the spark? Have you ever felt like you're just falling back on tried and tested ways of doing things because you've done it that way so many times before, and although there's no point in reinventing the wheel, today, just taking that path feels somehow mediocre, like your creativity dies a bit inside, like you're not giving of your best, and what you really deep down want to do is come up with something that's a bit more innovative that might really capture that child's interest and heart, but you just don't have the time (and maybe energy) to come up with it? And we gloss over any uneasy feelings that start to rise, because there's no time to dwell on them, but somewhere far off we also wonder that if we were to let ourselves sit with that sense of unease long enough, it might feel like we've not done enough or that we've let someone down. If you've felt anything of this, you're not alone. You might think you are, because we can all do a good job of trying to hide it, but you're not. We have all been there. We have all felt the weight of a never-ending to-do-list and not enough time to even make a dent in it.

Picture the scene:

> Your desk is a mess. A working mess you say. You kind of know where everything is but it still takes you a little longer to find that bit of paper, a bit longer than the person next door, whose desk is always pristine with factory-like precision, everything having its own place. You start off with good intentions, you mean well. It's just in the busy-ness of the day things just get dumped, to be rehoused later, but by the time 'later' comes you've too many other jobs you're in the middle of doing and your reserves are pretty low so you'll sort it in the morning, but that just plays on repeat for the rest of the week and before you know it you have the apocalyptic scene that is before you now.
>
> We have a 'tidy desk' policy in school, so if my week has been like this (and most weeks are), come Friday afternoon it's sometimes a case of shoving the extras that are splattered about the place like some kind of carnage into a drawer, which I then lock. Shoving (loosely known as tidying), out of sight out of mind. It's just that's the problem, because come Monday I'm quickly so busy that the same entire thing happens again, until one day the drawer is full and I'm literally pushing things in by my fingertips so that I can shut the damn drawer on my to-do-list to at least try to give a semblance of tidiness, which means 'order' to some and 'competence' to others. Well, that's what goes round in my head anyway. I know it's all superficial surface stuff; it is, until you suddenly realise it isn't. Appearances are, as it happens, important. Judgements are made on them. Belief systems are built on them. Reputations rise and fall. So, others see the mess . . . but I 'feel' it. I literally feel it in my body. The tightness in my chest. Like I've been found out. Like my mess is out there for all to see.
>
> The thing is, I say, I'm good at my job. And I truly believe I am, or at least I hope I am (at least some of the time.) It's just it might not look that way if someone just looks at my desk. When my desk* gets messy, I feel bad. It's like I feel this need to prove myself.
>
> (Substitute desk* for bag, cupboard, drawer, classroom, life, as necessary.)
>
> Sound familiar?

If we let ourselves feel these kinds of feelings, we can quickly feel undone, and the problem is there's no time or space for things *not* to be done. That's how schools work. There's no buffer of spare time or space for anything. Time is this precious commodity. Every minute of every day is important; every second has value. We don't waste a drop. When a community is living with drought, when there are seasons of prolonged shortage of water, everyone knows it, everyone feels it. You feel the dryness in your mouth. It inhabits every conversation until your mouth is so dry that you don't mention it anymore. You make sure taps are turned off so that not even a drop is wasted. You utilise what you have to its utmost. There is a concerted community effort to protect and sustain the little that you have. You become creative in how you do things, altering practices to maximise the thing that is scarce. We

do this in schools, and we have been doing it for a long time, because we have had to. We use every moment of the time we have to meet the needs of the children in our classrooms. Every moment is accounted for, and we feel parched, because there is just not enough time to fully meet the need before us.

Let's move on. Let's think about resources . . .

Not Enough Resources

School budgets are squeezed. Speak to most people in education and they'll say it's been chronically underfunded for years. This is not a political comment, just a descriptive one. All kinds of schools in all kinds of settings, contexts and communities have faced a lack of resources in so many ways for a very long time. We've just got used to the lack, got used to not being able to do all that we want to, got used to juggling budgets and scrimping and saving with the one hand so that we can do a bit of something else with the other. We've got used to buying resources out of our own money, of picking up something cheaply, of recycling anything we can that might just do the job further down the line. We've just got used to the lack of resources everywhere.

Now let your mind wander if you dare. Can you imagine what it would feel like if the budget was genuinely not an issue and you could really do all that you wanted to in your school community, in your school building and grounds, for your children and families? Can you imagine what kind of provision you could have and what kinds of needs you could meet?

Close your eyes. Think big. Dream big. What would that look like? What would that feel like not only for you and your colleagues but also for the children and families in your setting? What images and words spring to mind? Stay there a moment. Can you feel the hope?

Pause.

And then come crashing back to earth to see the reality we face on a daily basis. And in that coming back, notice the gap between the two. The reality and the dream. And notice the accompanying feelings. Because when we notice the distance between the two, we begin to notice that we might be carrying the weight of this 'gap' around with us all the time, without even realising.

Let's look a little closer at the lack, and begin with the physical environments we work in.

Resourcing School Environments

Run-down areas, leaking rooves, suspect old building materials only now coming to light, things patched up with a new lick of paint ... The condition of many of our school buildings is a telltale sign of the leanness of our pockets. Some of us have got used to layering up in cold weather just to try to keep warm in draughty demountable classroom blocks that were supposed to be temporary 20 years ago but are still fully functioning classrooms for 30+ children each day yet are not really fit for purpose. Site staff do an amazing job of maintaining our buildings, but having to prioritise repairs, when in an ideal world you'd want it all to be fixed and in good working order, can be a challenge. We want our schools to be welcoming spaces. We want them to be spaces that invite people in and become thriving places of learning and play, spaces that the community feels at home in. That requires a certain level of heating and lighting and furnishing and landscaping, creativity and colour and life. If you're working in an environment that is unpleasant or uncomfortable, bare or just plain tired, sometimes you can just feel a bit tired of it all. Working conditions matter. They convey value to the people working within them. Granted, the light and life of a place often come from the people within it and the culture you create, but the conditions around you help.

We want to have the resources we need to be able to teach the children in our classes. We want footballs that bounce, and glue sticks that stick. We want the basics and some of the frills too, but even the basics are not always possible. So, we recycle books and props, we share laptops and whiteboards. We get creative and thrifty, and we live and work with the not enough. But if we stop and think about it, doesn't that sometimes feel like it's not quite good enough?

Not Enough People

The biggest resource we have in schools is the people, and we are in a climate where there are not enough teachers, subject specialist teachers or trainee teachers. Not enough people are coming into the profession or staying in the profession. There are not enough support staff, and sometimes there are not enough site staff, office staff, midday staff or after school staff. And that's just the people *inside* the building. We'll come onto the not enough of other people outside the building in a moment.

If you're in a mid or senior leadership role in school (or involved in overseeing staffing), you'll know the stress that covering staff brings to a school on a daily basis. Schools can't turn children away if there are not enough staff. Come rain or shine they'll be waiting at the door when the bell goes. Pupils still have to be taught within legal ratios, and pupil needs still have to be met. That feeling of trying to conjure something up, (someone up) out of thin air, all before the school day starts is stressful, and doing that day after day is a strain. There's that sick early morning feeling of going through the staff answerphone picking up the messages that have been left and praying that so and so will be in today. It's not as easy as just finding a body, a someone with a pulse to do the job. All the while you're thinking about what will be best for the children, and what will cause the least disruption to their learning and wellbeing.

The current reality around the recruitment, training and retention of staff paints something of a bleak picture here in the UK. Long and Danechi (2022) reported that in England, 12.5% of teachers had left the profession within one year of qualifying, and 31.2% after five years. Education Policy Institute (2022) talks about a prospective increase in the number of experienced staff leaving teaching before retirement. Perryman (2022) speaks of the negative impact on health and wellbeing as issues that are impacting on staff retention. Whilst different incentives are being offered to try to draw people into the profession, staff shortages undoubtedly impact on the quality of teaching and learning, and therefore pupil outcomes in schools. Experienced staff are expensive staff, and budgets have to be balanced accordingly. If less experienced staff are employed so that they can be trained in situ (it's cheaper that way), sometimes the lack of experience they have during the ongoing process of training can lead to other pressures being felt by staff teams if they have to pick up any slack or spend more time coaching and mentoring others.

When it comes to absence and covering staff, if you're having to teach a subject you're not qualified in or confident in, that's going to make a difference as you deliver unfamiliar material and interact with the class. If you're a teacher who's doing the last-minute unexpected covering, you'll know how that feels in that moment. You'll feel inconvenienced for sure, and maybe inadequate too. Maybe there'll be an anxious sense of 'I don't know these children,' or the words 'I feel out of my depth' might run through your mind, as well as 'but I'm supposed to be doing something else!' If your school is under pressure around staffing, you'll feel it in the air. Bodies hurrying through corridors, stray flippant comments. Things can

sometimes feel strained when people are taking the strain, and we can feel the not enough-
ness all around.

When it comes to the amount of support staff in schools, it can feel like there are not enough people to help with the level of need in our settings. We have to be accountable for the way we deploy staff, to ensure that we all effectively add value to our provision, enhancing teaching and learning and improving pupil outcomes, but the long and short of it is we are crying out for more people. Support staff who might be delivering a specific intervention speak of delivering it for more children, squeezing more into the allocated time. Support staff who are supporting children around their learning or significant social, emotional and mental health needs speak of the challenges that come when they are deployed elsewhere due to staff absence. Sometimes it can feel like we're operating with an almost skeleton staff, just skin and bones, with the bare minimum to get by. It doesn't make for a stress-free, productive environment. You can feel a sense of personal and collective anxiety, and some-times it can feel like there is an element of risk. When people are stretched, when people are stepping in and out of different roles, that's when things can go wrong. Even with all the procedures, policies and planning in place, things can be overlooked or missed, and that can have consequences that can impact on individuals and families as well as the whole school community. If that very real prospect is hanging over you, that's a weight you carry, and if it is something you face regularly, that becomes a sustained, often unspoken pressure.

Not Enough To Meet the Needs of Children With SEND (Special Educational Needs and Disability)

Where do we even start with this one?

Picture the scene:

> It only takes one child, one situation, one 'event' for you to feel unravelled. Sometimes the unravelling is only a little and it doesn't take too long to put everything back in its place and get good to go again. But sometimes the unravelling is on an epic scale, catastrophic in nature and you feel de-skilled to the point that you wonder if you can do your job at all.

> I'm walking towards a child who is highly dysregulated, ready to offer to help in some way. And if it was just me and the child that would be different, but I know that other people are around too, so they'll be watching . . . and it's the watching that makes it harder. I have no idea if I'll be able to make a difference. I hope I can. I have tools in my toolbox; my teaching and SENDCO experience of goodness knows how many years, but there are still no guarantees. People will be watching and so somehow the pres-sure will feel like it's on. I trust the people around me, so I know we all want to de-esca-late what's happening. I know we're all on the same team, but somehow my reputation still kind of feels like it's on the line. After all, this is what I'm supposed to know how

to do. And then suddenly a parent walks past and the stakes just got higher, because in their glancing over at all the noise, now they're watching too – just in passing, but in that micro moment they'll have views and opinions, they'll make judgements about me, the child, the situation, and possibly the school. And if things go well and peace is restored then everyone's happy (and we're good at our jobs), but if it takes longer, or if things escalate a bit more, then what does that say? And the discomfort feels real. And if I name the discomfort in that moment, it can feel a bit like shame. It's the possibility that this is what they'll think – that I'm not good enough.

Sound familiar?

Not having enough resources (whether that be people or other kinds of resources) to meet the needs of pupils with additional needs or SEND is a huge area of 'not enough' in our schools. The number of pupils with SEND is unquestionably growing (DfE, 2024a), and with this comes the need to meet their needs. There are all kinds of needs to meet, and if we don't meet them, we know about it (and of course, so do the children themselves). We feel the effects of unmet needs. They can lead to all kinds of challenges for children, families and staff. The needs we encounter broadly come under the banners of: communication and language needs; cognitive and learning needs; social, emotional and mental health needs; and physical and sensory needs. Whilst there is more awareness of lots of needs and conditions, and with that comes sometimes earlier diagnoses, with or without a diagnosis, children's needs present themselves in the classroom and at home. They may be lower-level needs met entirely through High-Quality Teaching; they may be needs that require support that is additional to or different from the universal or ordinarily available provision in place, or they may be high level needs where individuals require significant resources and levels of funding and provision. Not just the number of children with needs is on the increase, but so is the number of children with Education Health and Care Plans (EHCP), the highest level of need (DfE, 2024a). The government's 2022 consultation and green paper SEND Review highlighted the need for the right support, in the right place, at the right time. Oh, for this to be the case, we might say. The green paper was followed by the SEND and Alternative Provision Improvement Plan in 2023, which acknowledged many of the challenges families and professionals face, with a cycle of 'late intervention, low confidence and inefficient resource allocation' (DfE, 2023b). It announced the plan for National Special Educational Needs and Alternative Provision Standards to set clear and ambitious expectations of what good looks like when it comes to identifying and meeting children's needs. Regardless of the shape of any incoming future SEND reforms, the resourcing of supporting children with SEND is a felt need for all. We're on the same side, we try to remind ourselves.

We know that many children with EHCPs thrive in mainstream settings. However, sometimes, when a child with complex or severe needs is part of a mainstream setting, we try our utmost to meet their needs, but there are times when everyone – the child, their family and staff – feel a sense of lack. For some children, what we have in our settings will never be enough. For some children who need extra specialist resources, equipment, flexibility of curriculum or environment, who need the daily input of other professionals – however hard we try to meet the complexity of their needs it won't be everything that they need. For some children with more complex or severe needs, a mainstream setting isn't the best fit. They require specialist provision, but often the wait for this is a long, frustrating and painful one. If you know that a child requires not just a makeshift sensory room and technologies but a state-of-the-art one with in-built therapies and therapists on site, it is hard when all you can keep offering them (and their parents) is what seems to be second best. That doesn't feel ok. It feels like you're complicit with a system that's letting people down. Yet this is the position we sometimes find ourselves in. What we can be left with is a sometimes uneasy feeling of making do, a lack of expertise, confidence or experience, even though we've had ongoing relevant training. We keep doing our best, but sometimes we feel responsible for that lack, knowing that better resources would mean better provision, and therefore better outcomes, for the child.

We also keenly feel the gap in provision from external services. Services such as Speech and Language Therapy, Occupational Therapy, Physiotherapy, Paediatricians, Educational Psychologists, Specialist Teacher teams, Mental Health teams and Social Care are also under huge strain, with long waiting lists and high demand (NHS, 2023). So, accessing the expertise and support of these teams in a timely manner for children and families in school can be tricky. We know that detailed assessments and information from other professionals can lead to more focused interventions and better outcomes for children, so there's a level of frustration when things don't always happen as quickly as we would like. We work collaboratively and creatively with so many different professionals across different sectors to meet the varying needs of children, but what is felt across the board is a sense of scarcity, of being stretched thin . . . and in the thinness it can feel like you're only just providing what is needed, if you're lucky, and you know that if you had more, you could do more. And all the while it can feel like you're not quite doing enough.

If you are working with a child who is not thriving in your setting, the likelihood is that you might feel the same. Maybe you feel a sense of lack and not enough-ness around the child. When the level of funding for meeting a child's needs feels like it's not enough, even if everyone says it should be enough, you're left with what feels like a gap. If everyone else thinks there isn't a discrepancy, then it doesn't take long to sometimes think that maybe the problem, the fault, lies with you. And maybe you carry the weight of that sense of fault whenever the child is highly distressed. Maybe it sits on your shoulder when you talk with senior leaders about the child's needs not being met and the impact of this on others. Maybe you feel it when you notice the glances between parents at the end of the day. And if you try with all your might to evidence the gap, in the hope that you might be able to plug the gap but there is nothing out there to plug it with, what you can be left with is this gaping hole and a sense that your voice is not enough to change things. If you were enough, if your professional opinion counted, if you felt heard, someone somewhere would believe you and see that this child and you need more resources, and they would give you what you need. Sometimes we can feel like a Dickensian Oliver offering up our empty bowl, asking 'Please, sir, can I have some more?' We ask because the child is hungry, and we are hungry. We ask because they haven't got enough and neither have we. We ask because we want something

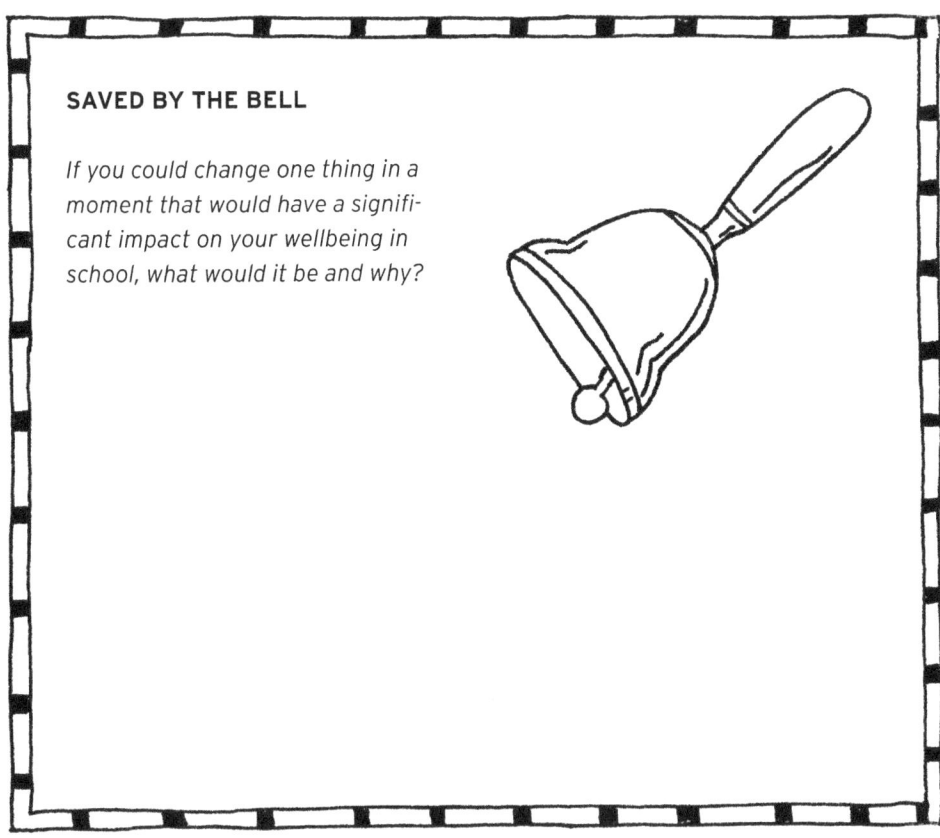

SAVED BY THE BELL

If you could change one thing in a moment that would have a significant impact on your wellbeing in school, what would it be and why?

more to sustain us. When the more doesn't come, that's a hard place to be. It can feel like no one cares (except of course you and the child and their parents, and the other children in your class and the other staff and parents and those who observe and track data and progress). No one sees except everyone sees, and so it seems that no one cares ... and that can feel a bit lonely. When we're faced with immense challenges, this is sometimes how it feels.

I'm not trying to lay it on thick, looking at all these layers of lack. It's just important to really see what we're often up against, because often we kind of feel it, but don't think about the extent of the challenges we face and the resilience we have. So, stick with me ... with just one more area of not enough.

Not Enough Trust

Public and Parental Perception

Let's think for a moment about the perception of the teaching profession amongst others, and possible differing schools of thought. There are some who value the work that we do and appreciate all the good stuff about the job. Maybe that comes from a place of personal appreciation for the investment in their own lives or the lives of those around them. Others perhaps major on (or just quip about) the short days, term-time hours (aka. flexibility for childcare), long holidays, job security and good pay. There are others, who are perhaps a little closer to the job, who may see something different. Workload, long hours including evenings and weekends, pressure, the demands of managing children's behaviour etc. The idea that there are such differing opinions might conceivably lead to an undercurrent of suspicion. How can all of these be true? So, which is true, and who is telling the truth? Who do we trust? And some might say, if all you keep banging on about is how hard things are, or how you've not got enough of this and that, but it looks to me like you've already got it so much better than some, then can I really trust you? Maybe that's the view of some, and maybe that feels hard to take. Kim et al. (2023) discuss possible reasons for the decreasing levels of perceived societal appreciation (PSA) among teachers in England, including the impact of the pandemic. It matters what we think others think of us. Gavish and Friedman (2010) found that new teachers who felt a lack of recognition and appreciation from the public and the students they taught reported increased levels of burnout. Let's bring it closer to home . . .

Picture the scene:

> Parents Evening. In person or online, it doesn't really matter, although the stakes can feel upped if you're sitting face to face with someone in the same room. You have back-to-back ten-minute slots to say everything you need to communicate to the parents about their child. So, there's everything you want to say, but there's also everything the parents want to say. And rightly so. And you make room for this to happen. You welcome questions and answer them to the best of your knowledge. And you also have this unease. This 'not knowing' if anyone will suddenly throw you a curveball. The anticipation of the unknown can often have an unpleasant taste about it. Most of the time it's ok, but right now this parent says they're disappointed that something hasn't happened. And although they're talking about the 'something,' what you actually think and feel in that moment is that they're disappointed not just with something you've done or not done, but that they're somehow disappointed in you. Like it suddenly gets personal.

> So, I'm sitting ready for Parents Evening to start, looking down at my list of people, and I know that some of the discussions could well be tricky, because some of what's going on for this or that child is a bit tricky at the moment. And when things feel tricky it's not just one person that feels the trickiness. It's the child, the parent, the family and me, and sometimes also the rest of the class and the wider school community.

> Sound familiar?

Sometimes when working with parents, it can feel like you're walking a fine line . . . that at any point a parent's trust in you can change if you get just one thing wrong, or something they perceive to be wrong. 'It's not good enough. You've not done enough for my boy,' they might say. There can be a sense that with some parents, any trust you build is fragile ... that with just a word or a minor mishap it can be broken and everything you've built together can come crashing down to the ground. With some parents maybe you have a bit more credit in the bank, and if something goes wrong one day, you've still got a good working relationship with them because of the trust you've built over time. Maybe just a bit of repairing needs doing, but it's not like the whole build is at stake. But with some, it comes tumbling down and you have to start all over again, and because you're starting again there's some mistrust-shaped rubble to clear away at ground level, so the build feels harder. Sometimes the hardest thing is not knowing how a parent will respond when something happens, and sometimes the hardest thing is knowing without a shadow of a doubt how they'll respond, because you or someone else has experienced it before. No one wants to be the teacher that all the parents are talking about or hoping their child doesn't have next year. No one wants to not be trusted. It doesn't feel nice.

In potentially difficult conversations with parents, it matters how we say things. It matters what words we use. It's important that we consider different perceptions or perceived positions of power that might be at play in the interaction. It matters that both sides can express their views and be heard. It matters that we have shared goals to aim for that have been worked on collaboratively. It matters that the child, their best interests and outcomes are at the heart of it all. It's important that we talk about what's working well, as well as what might not be working quite so well for a child, and it's important that we avoid loaded words. If you use the word 'incident' when relaying something that's happened in school, it can immediately conjure up images of threat or police tape and can be unhelpful. Using clear language to describe what has happened leaves less room for interpretation. We want parents to trust and respect us and the language we use is vital in building those things, because trust makes for a more secure parent-teacher relationship and a safer, more nurturing environment for the child. It is a powerful currency, and you feel its absence when it's not around. If you work in a school where parents don't trust you it can feel unsettling for everyone.

Not Enough Trust in Professional Judgement

Big policy decisions about education are made by others (politicians, strategists and the like), and often some of these others haven't set foot inside a classroom since they were at school. It's understandable then that it sometimes feels like they might be a little out of touch with the current reality of day-to-day life in schools. You can listen to all the reports on how things are going, but if your feet have not actually been on the ground in the classroom it doesn't always feel like it counts for much. So perhaps from the outset, there's an underlying sense of them and us. A sense of us having to prove ourselves or show our credentials, a sense of mistrust. Where might that seep into our day-to-day work? Let's think first about the curriculum. The curriculum we teach is set out clearly, with emphases and expectations that children know certain things by a certain age, with little wiggle room for other things. If we're teaching something that we're not sure really has much point or value, but is just some distant person's idea of a good thing, could this sometimes feel like decisions are being made elsewhere and we don't really have a say in the matter, that somehow our voice isn't heard and that our professional judgement isn't counted? Sometimes the curriculum content we have to teach can feel so full that there's no room to breathe. Sometimes it can feel so full that it squeezes any creativity from other places.

When you don't have enough space, you stifle growth. A plant fails to thrive when it is pot bound. There's nowhere for it to go, nowhere for it to grow. All that life running through it somehow kept in, kept back, kept from flourishing. If we're asking ourselves if we're really giving children the life skills they need, the interpersonal skills they need, the resilience they need, the emotional health they need, the joy they need – if we're not sure or we're sometimes asking questions about the validity of what we're currently delivering, it can sometimes feel like another not enough. If we're passionate about the arts but feel these are being marginalised in our schools, that can do something to us inside; if we could respond quickly to things that are more pertinent to our local areas and communities, that could feel like something really important; if we could drop some of the jargon and vocabulary that can feel superfluous, if we could be trusted to use the curriculum and adapt things as we see fit, to create space when it is needed, perhaps that could feel a lot like trust in our professional judgement.

If we're in education, we're all on the same side. We're all in it for the children, striving to gain the best outcomes for each child that comes our way. There's a lot at stake and just like in any other job, we know that being accountable for what we do is important. We work hard; we have expertise and experience that we develop over time and what we do needs to be measured. Sometimes what is measured leads to celebration, where targets that have been set are met or exceeded. Sometimes where the outcome is less favourable or clouded by other factors, the measuring can feel more awkward, and no one likes feeling awkward. But being accountable is a healthy thing. It conveys our sense of responsibility and commitment to the cause. It helps to identify strengths and areas for development, both for us as individuals and as a collective school community. Take some very normal accountability practices that happen in schools. Monitoring, moderation of work with colleagues, peer reviews, performance management target setting and reviews. If these are done within a context of trust, respect and professionalism, they are an effective tool for personal and whole school development. If there is less trust in the relationship, whether that be felt or perceived, the experience can feel very different. Conversations with clear expectations, boundaries and timescales feel very different to those that are loaded or biased. Things that are planned feel very different to things that take you by surprise. When things are not done well it can feel like people are looking to catch you out, to pull you up, to expose you, and if you're feeling under pressure, sometimes with all that measuring, it can feel like you're not really trusted with it all.

Picture the scene:

> Sitting there, sweaty palms, all your prepped paperwork and files to hand, just waiting for it all to start. It's a peer review they say. All these leaders from other schools are

GROW

In what areas would you like to grow deep-down roots that nourish you? Both in school and outside of school?

on your side they say, it's to improve your practice they say, it's good practice they say, it's just deep down you're not sure you totally believe them. All you can feel is not just a deep dive into your subject, but a deep dive into your soul, into your very being. This being publicly cut open and dissected. Not just the thing, but you. Not just what you do but who you are.

It would be alright if I didn't feel so under pressure. In this moment scrutiny feels like them and us, them pointing the finger or a shifty look between others at the expense of me. Scrutiny. Sometimes it feels like 'Screw tiny me.' Whereas I want more 'Scrutinice - me'. Like, be nice. Be thorough but be nice. Encourage. Build up rather than tear down. Acknowledge the intent even if there are things that need tweaking. Recognise the expertise. See the passion. It would be alright if any shortcomings were genuinely communicated with support. Support without shame. But that doesn't always happen. And it's the uncertainty of how things might play out that unsettles.

Here I am, in a meeting with local head teachers poring over redacted case studies, and me telling the story, giving the context of the data before them, not as an excuse but as an explanation. I've prepped hard for the moment, knowing it will be a high-level examination of my work. And then this thing happens, and suddenly the pressure is off me. For in a moment, my colleague who is doing the very same thing as me at this table, fighting her corner (I mean 'presenting her information'), seems to slip up. Not everyone notices but one person just seems to pounce. It's just a slight misuse of language. Nothing wrong, just not the most up-to-date word, not the language of the moment, and in that moment, it seems to cost her points. She doesn't even realise, which kind of makes it all feel worse, but I see the shift in the room, I feel it in the air, and this one person just calls it out, blurts it out, shouts it out. Well, not really . . . but that's what it feels like in the room. In a bid to coach and teach, the scrutineer says something like 'It's better to phrase it like this instead,' and it all just feels a little laden with something else, and it's all just so public and uncomfortable. I sense something of my colleague's discomfort, but in that moment, I also feel this strange sense of relief that the focus is now off me. It's almost like I'm now winning and she's losing, which is an ugly thing to admit, because we're on the same side, but I'm just so relieved I've passed the test.

Sound familiar?

How can it sometimes feel like this? How can there sometimes feel like there's not enough trust around our professional judgement? But all this happens within a much broader context and in a society that likes to expose anything that is perceived as less than and likes to trip people up. Language, as we've seen, is important, and sometimes the language that is used more widely around education is not helpful. Politicians speak of driving up standards, which can sometimes feel like they're saying what we've been doing up

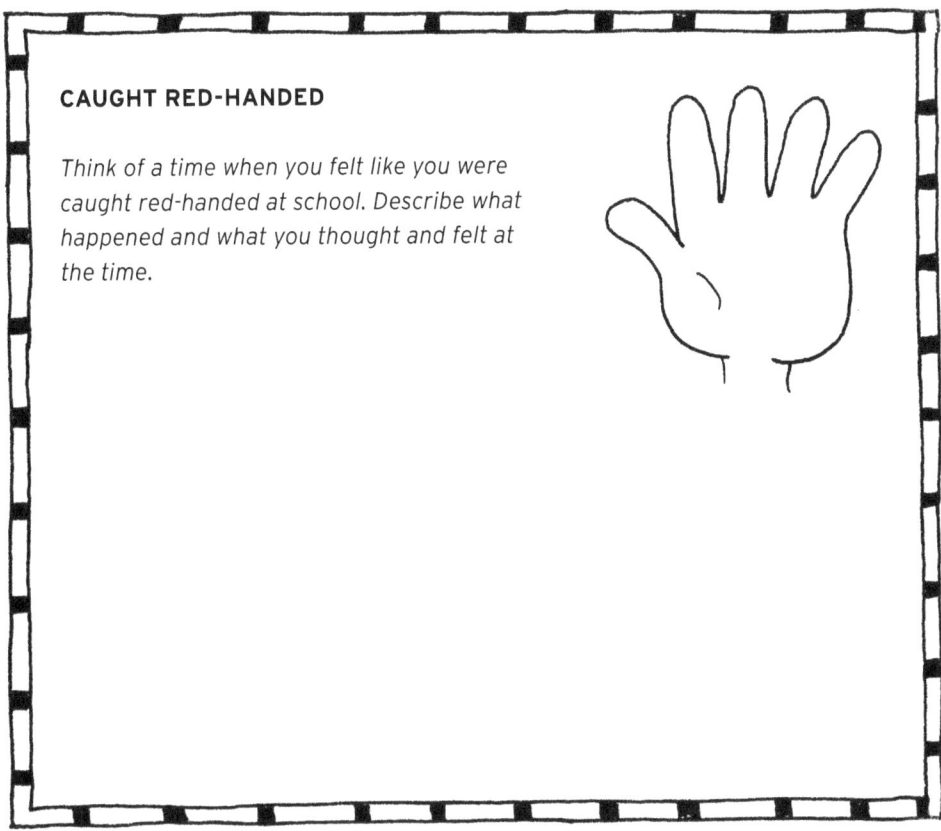

CAUGHT RED-HANDED

Think of a time when you felt like you were caught red-handed at school. Describe what happened and what you thought and felt at the time.

until now has somehow been substandard, or not enough. Say it long enough and it can just become the norm that others hear. Language can very easily apportion blame and affect levels of trust.

Yet all the while, we know that we function best, we learn best, we thrive when we feel safe.

So, when it comes to the idea of trust, let's move on to the big O...

Ofsted

For years, government inspection has been a huge area of pressure for schools and staff teams. It's not supposed to have been but speak to anyone in a school and they'll know that it has. Ofsted (2019) itself acknowledged that they have an impact on working practices. Felstead et al. (2023) noted that the pressure rises in a school environment and the workload becomes more intensive if an inspection is imminent. In the final report of the Beyond Ofsted Inquiry (2023) it states that post-inspection,

Only ten per cent of those with a Good or Outstanding rating saw it as a positive experience. When asked whether the school does anything to prepare specifically for future inspections in between inspections, only three per cent of respondents said the school does nothing special to prepare for Ofsted.

Often the overriding feeling that we have come away with in and around the process is: do they trust us? Do they trust us with what we're doing? What we're delivering? The progress our children are making? Do they believe us? Does all that we're doing count for anything in their eyes? Inspection has been the ultimate standard of measurement because so much rides on it . . . reputation, standing, funding. When it comes to Ofsted there has been this sense that as different emphases come and go, you always have to keep on your toes (Bousted [2022]), because you don't quite know what they're going to throw at you next. What they're measuring (and so what you're evidencing) now, might not be what they're measuring next, so keep up so you don't get caught out. That's how the narrative has been. Almost like a game of cat and mouse, of trying to work out what we think they want, or where they'll be hiding so we don't get pounced upon and caught. There's been more of a sense of surveillance than support, and the inquiry also noted the perception of how 'inspection is not just about surveillance, but the threat of surveillance' (Beyond Ofsted Inquiry [2023]). We use the word 'threat' when there's a sense of perceived or felt danger to our safety. From working in schools over the years I know it's been a felt thing.

Fortunately, Ofsted are now moving away from the one- or two-word post-inspection rating phrase which was something of a permanent feature of their reports. Outstanding, Good, Satisfactory, Inadequate, Requires Improvement, Special Measures have all been used in the past. It's a good thing that they're no longer the be all and end all, because when you feel like what is your life's work is summed up in one or two words it's a dangerous thing. Get something that's unsatisfactory and it totally fails to capture all the passion, effort and expertise, the heart, blood, sweat and tears, the people, the children and families, their names, their stories, the things that cannot be measured. All of it swallowed up in a black hole of nothingness. Even Good was sometimes not seen as quite good enough by outsiders, even though good is surely good enough, but if it's still fallen short of Outstanding then there's a question mark in some people's eyes. Outstanding has always had the most prestige, with its big shiny first place which boosted reputation, numbers coming in, bulging waiting lists and money. Anything less than Outstanding was seen as less than the best, although if you got that badge the effort to maintain it was immense. You shone and rode on the crest of the wave for a while, you held your head up high, but that soon wore off with the reality that next time round or if something just went a bit wrong you had further to fall.

The one- or two-word phrases were only part of the issue. The main issue was always the potential shame they could communicate. That was the crippling thing, the nasty taste left in your mouth thing. It has felt like a process that has lacked care and trust.

For years teachers have been saying the pressures around it are too much. Waters and McKee (2023) talked about the importance of listening to the profession saying enough is enough. Perhaps now a very real change is coming. With the growing focus on wellbeing and the recognition of a link between mental health and Ofsted, following the tragic death of a head teacher, the Beyond Ofsted Inquiry (2023) has brought about significant changes to the process. In their report they recognise that 'educators want to change how the system makes them feel; instead of fear, they wish to feel trusted, professional and supported.'

The emphasis is now on school performance reviews (much like schools have already had in place), with an annual self-evaluation of strengths and challenges and plans for improvement. These now have nationally agreed areas of focus with room for flexibility within the local context and community. The premise is that they prioritise staff and children's mental health and wellbeing, a broad and balanced curriculum, inclusive and supportive practices and a sense of belonging, so that everyone can flourish personally and academically. The review process includes working with an external school improvement partner for support and accountability, and the practice of collaborative working, peer review and mutual support through networking with local schools will continue. Coupled with this, the Education Inspection Framework (EIF) has moved away from the previous focus on outcomes-led approaches and now majors on the curriculum, and the inspection process now no longer considers internal assessment data, which was a huge part of teacher workload (DfE, 2023a).

With all this, we've got to be moving in the right direction, or at least a healthier direction when it comes to wellbeing. Hopefully the journey over time will convey more trust. There's still probably some work to do in undoing the legacy of past practices and policies or at least an undoing of their tone. It's been acknowledged that myths around inspection requirements still need to be busted. When it comes to professional judgement and trust, the real conversation is always around the demands upon us and the lack we experience around us, which can create anxiety and fear. In that climate if we're not careful, fear can drive what and how we do things, and fear doesn't always bring out the best in us.

So, there are all these not enoughs around us. Not enough time, resources or trust. This is the context within which we find ourselves. Might we sometimes wonder deep down that if we were valued enough, there might be enough of these things? If and when feelings of your own 'not enoughness' come, sit with them a while. Examine them. Where do they come from? Look at the evidence of how these come about, when you feel these things and what you think at the time. As we examine and evidence what we think and feel, it can start to undo our feelings of not enough. Because the truth is, you are enough.

Need a break? . . .

*****Go Grab a Cup of Tea*****

Examine and Evidence

CHECK YOUR DIALS

Imagine a car dashboard and the dials that indicate how much fuel you've got in different areas of your life and work. How are your levels? Where might you be low in fuel or even running on empty?

WAY BACK WHEN

Think of a negative memory from your own school days. Can you describe what happened and how you felt at the time? How might it have impacted you? How has it influenced how you teach or support children and young people?

SCENE OF THE CRIME

What evidence do you notice around you and within you that leaves a trace of something distasteful that has happened at work? What crime do you feel has been committed?

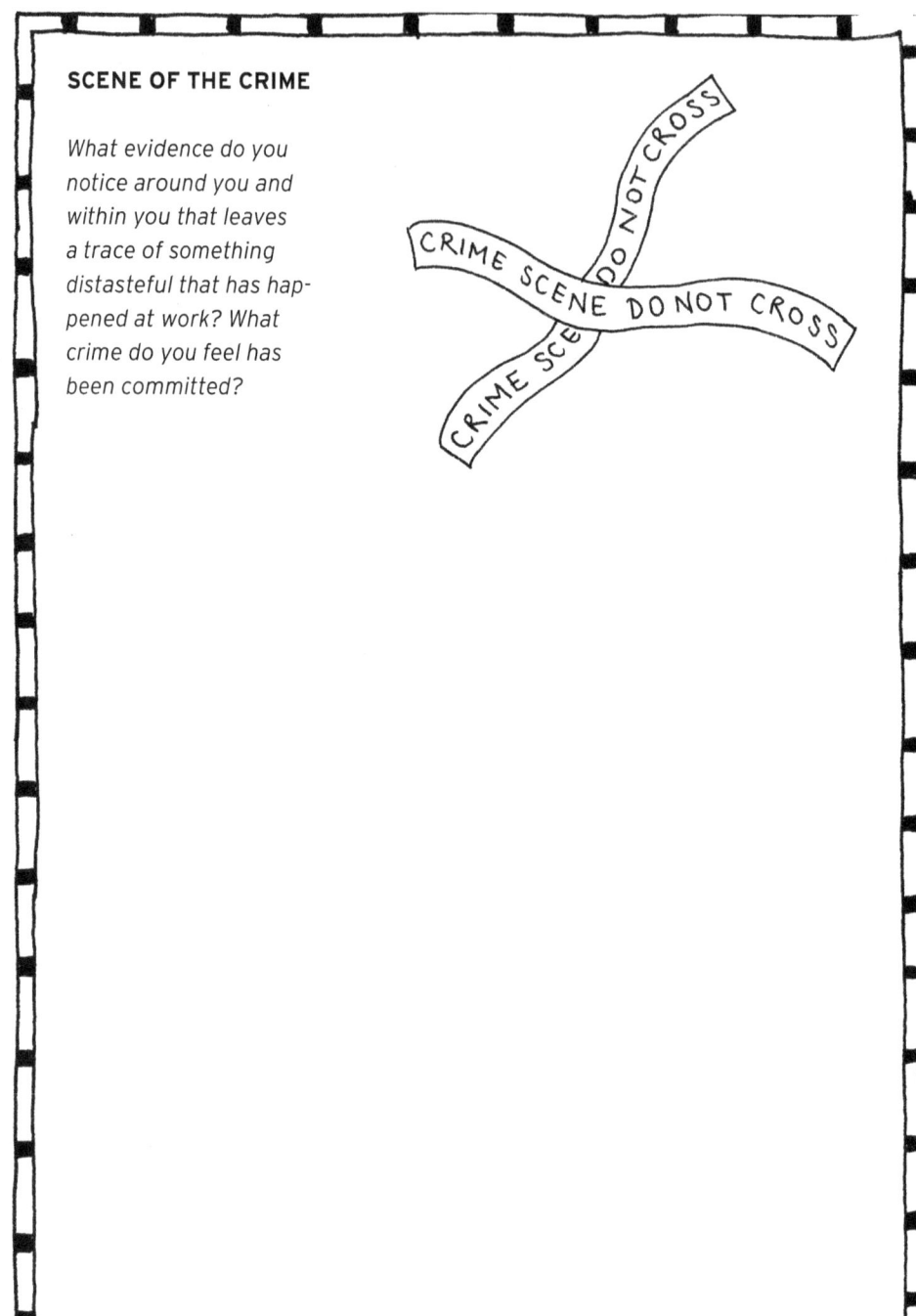

LEAN ON ME

What does it look like for you to lean on someone else when you need support? How does that feel for you? If someone else leans on you for support, what does that look like and how does it feel? Is there anything you would like to see change about these dynamics and what could that look like?

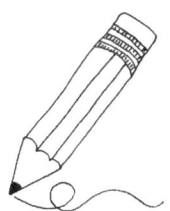

QUIET WHISPER

What might you just want to tell a trusted friend about when it comes to work this week? Think about the thoughts you've had and the emotions you've experienced. Who could you talk to? Why is it important that you do?

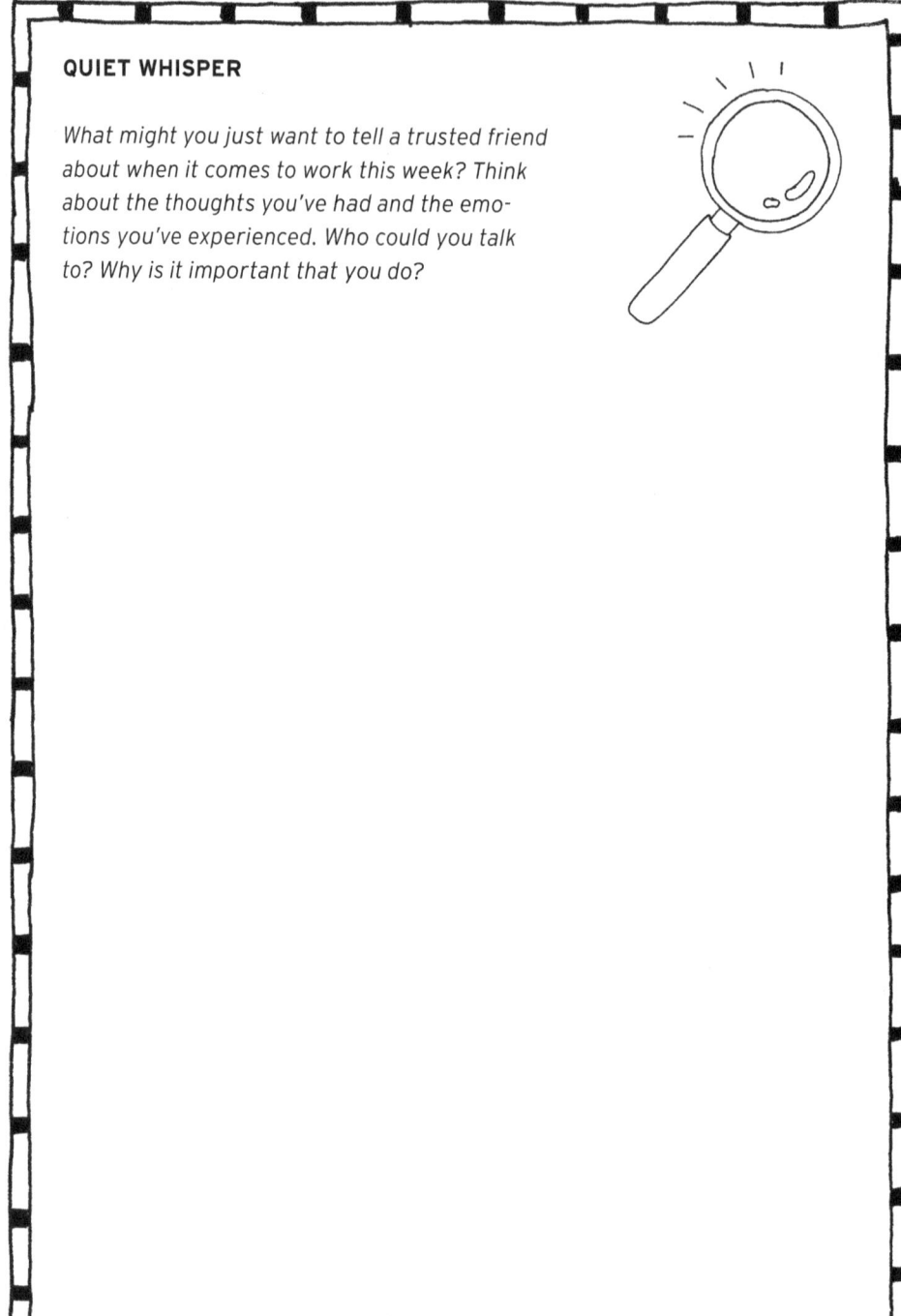

STRESS RELIEVER

What healthy rhythms can you build into your days and weeks that might help you with the challenges you regularly face?

IN MY HEAD

What are some of the unspoken things that sometimes go round and round in your head that you would love to be able to say out loud?

STUCK

Where do you feel stuck right now? Why might you be feeling that way? Who could you talk to about this, and what could that look like for you?

2 + 2 = 4

What are some of your default ways of thinking about yourself when it comes to your capabilities or 'deficiencies'? Where does your thinking automatically go?

If you think of areas where you feel you are lacking in your work and instead frame them as areas for development, how does this shift your thinking about yourself?

GRIT YOUR TEETH

When do you sometimes feel like gritting your teeth? What might you be feeling and thinking during these times? What might you really be wanting to say but feel that you can't?

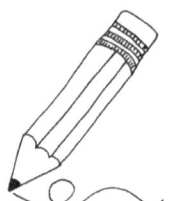

SNAIL

When do you sometimes feel like just hiding away at work? Why might that be? What are you anxious about or fearful of?

ECG

Think of a monitor and the zigzag line showing the activity of your heart. If you were to draw a line that spoke of your journey in teaching so far, with the ups and downs, what would that look like? Show the intensity of your experiences by the depth of the up or down line. What have you learned about yourself and others during those times?

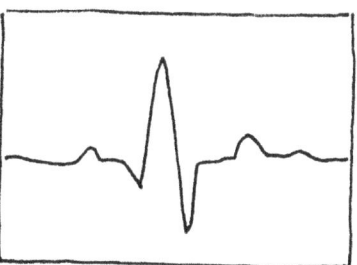

KINTSUGI

Kintsugi is the Japanese art of transforming broken vessels by incorporating gold into the cracks to recreate the whole. The finished items are often considered to be more beautiful as they are threaded with gold and tell the story of the vessel. With this image in mind, what might your vessel look like?

(IM)POSTER SYNDROME

Instead of feeling the exclusion of imposter syndrome, and feeling like an outsider, think about flipping the phrase on its head so the image becomes an 'I'm in' poster... Think about all the qualities you bring to the classroom and staff team, and imagine them as a poster all about you. One that declares this is rightfully your space. What would it reveal?

A LONG OLD ROAD

If you were to map out the road ahead, where would you be able to find some places to stop and refuel?

BRAIN DUMP

What are you thinking? What are you feeling?

YOU ARE ENOUGH

References

Beyond Ofsted Inquiry. (2023). *Final report of the inquiry* (pp. 23, 31, 58). NEU.

Bousted, M. (2022). *Support not surveillance: How to solve the teacher retention crisis*. John Catt.

Department for Education. (2023a, January). *Department for education's progress on our commitments in the education staff wellbeing charter*. https://assets.publishing.service.gov.uk/media/65a11ad53308d200131fbeeb/DfE_Education_Workforce_Wellbeing_Charter_2023.pdf

Department for Education. (2023b, March 2). *Policy paper: SEND and alternative provision improvement plan* (p. 16). https://www.gov.uk/government/publications/send-and-alternative-provision-improvement-plan

Department for Education. (2024a, June 20). *Special educational needs in England: January 2024*. https://www.gov.uk/government/statistics/special-educational-needs-in-england-january-2024

Department for Education. (2024b, September 27). *Research and analysis: Working lives of teachers and leaders: Wave 2 summary report*. https://www.gov.uk/government/publications/working-lives-of-teachers-and-leaders-wave-2/working-lives-of-teachers-and-leaders-wave-2-summary-report#leaving-teaching-in-the-state-school-sector

Department for Education and Department of Health and Social Care. (2022). *Consultation outcome: SEND review: Right support, right place, right time*. https://www.gov.uk/government/consultations/send-review-right-support-right-place-right-time

Education Policy Institute. (2022, June 14). *The teaching workforce after the pandemic*. https://epi.org.uk/publications-and-research/the-teaching-workforce-after-the-pandemic/

Felstead, A., Green, F., & Huxley, K. (2023). *Teachers' job quality before and after the pandemic: First findings*. https://wiserd.ac.uk/publication/briefing-teachers-job-quality-before-and-after-the-pandemic-first-findings/

Gavish, B., & Friedman, I. A. (2010). Novice teachers' experience of teaching: A dynamic aspect of burnout. *Social Psychology of Education: An International Journal, 13*(2), 141–167.

Kim, L., Owusu, K., & Asbury, K. (2023). The ups and downs in perceived societal appreciation of the teaching profession during COVID-19: A longitudinal trajectory analysis. *British Educational Journal, 50*(1), 93–111.

Long, R., & Danechi, S. (2022). *Teacher recruitment and retention in England (briefing paper 7222)*. House of Commons Library. https://researchbriefings.files.parliament.uk/documents/CBP-7222/CBP÷7222.pdf

Maslow, A. H. (1943). A theory of human motivation. *Psychological Review, 50*, 370–396. http://doi.org/10.1037/h0054346

NHS Providers and NHS Confederation. (2023). *Community network survey on waiting times in children and young people's services*. https://www.nhsconfed.org/system/files/2023-05/Community%20Network%20survey%20on%20waiting%20times%20in%20CYP%20services.pdf

Ofsted. (2019). *Teacher well-being at work in schools and further education providers*. https://www.gov.uk/government/publications/teacher-well-being-at-work-in-schools-and-further-education-providers

Perryman, J. (2022). *Teacher retention in an age of performative accountability. Target culture and the discourse of disappointment*. Routledge.

Waters, S., & McKee, M. (2023). Ofsted: A case of official negligence? *British Medical Journal, 381*, 1147. http://doi.org/10.1136/bmj

3
The Too Much We Face

Hold onto the good stuff of the job. Remember all the good we looked at in the first chapter? Don't lose sight of it (it's so easy to do, right, when we're faced with the hard?). But, enough of all this not enough. What about the too much?

Too Much Expectation

Closely linked to the 'not enoughs' we face is the 'too much' we face in schools. They're like the flip side of the coin. Too much to do in so little time. Too much to do with so little resources. Too much to do with what can sometimes feel like so little trust. A lot is expected of us. Even with some of the not enoughs we've still got to produce the goods. We've still got to get on with the job and make it all happen. People are counting on us. A lot of people. Not just the ones and twos. If you take a look, it's so much more than that. Do the maths. Children and young people, parents and families, and maybe it even stretches wider than that. But before we get onto everyone else, how about we start with us? What part might our own expectations of ourselves play as we go about our work?

Our Own Expectations

We bring expectations with us that stem from our own experiences of school and life. Whether they are grounded in positive or negative experiences these memories and ideas influence our thinking about the kind of person we want to be and how we want to show up in the classroom, how we want to interact with the children and families with whom we work.

Going into teaching, I knew I didn't want to be like my chemistry teacher. I'd found him arrogant and distant, and on numerous occasions he had belittled students in front of others. That didn't sit right with me then and it still doesn't now. My French teacher, on the other hand, went out of her way to try to help me understand and build my confidence. It goes without saying that I ditched chemistry as soon as I could and continued with French. Our own school experiences play a part in shaping us and our values. We have hopes and expectations of ourselves in our roles that are not just to do with job satisfaction and working towards personal goals. They're most likely first and foremost around what we'll sow into

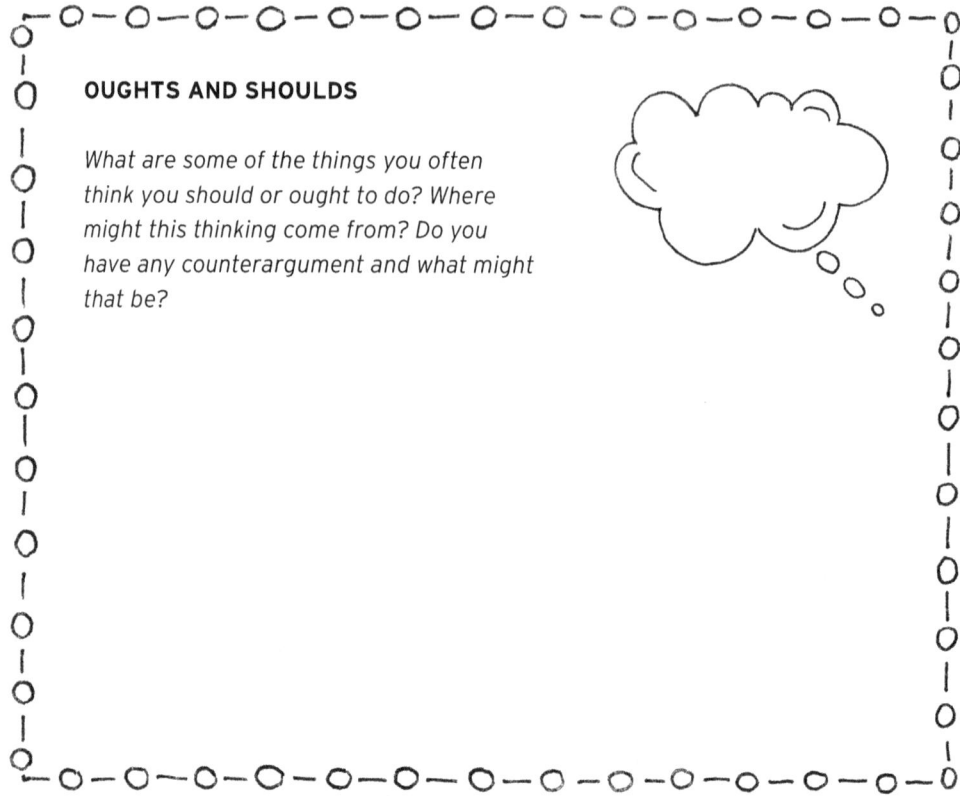

OUGHTS AND SHOULDS

What are some of the things you often think you should or ought to do? Where might this thinking come from? Do you have any counterargument and what might that be?

others, what we'll invest in them, the difference we'll make, the hope we'll inspire, the legacy we'll leave. For whatever reason, sometimes the expectations we place on ourselves are very high and holding these with the sometimes difficult aspects of the job can be tricky. Sometimes we just don't meet our own expectations. And with that, we can sometimes find ourselves asking whether we did enough, or whether we've been enough. Was I enough to make a difference?

Lots of us go into the job wanting to make a difference. When it comes to our expectations, sometimes settling for what seems like less is hard. But might our expectations sometimes be too high? Might they be too much? Unattainable, even? And what might be driving the expectations we place on ourselves that we could do well to examine? Even with a lot of years of teaching behind me, I still remember a comment from a teacher friend during my initial teacher training and teaching practice placements. 'You won't always be able to do your best,' she said. 'It's not sustainable.' It felt like an odd thing for her to say just as I was setting out in my career. Not the most inspiring tagline, if you like. But it was wise. We don't always do an amazing lesson, we won't always be on top form, we really do have good days and bad days and everything-in-between-days and that really is ok. For the sake of having any longevity in the profession and for the sake of our own wellbeing, we have to learn to be ok with that. But what if we're really not sure about that? What if even thinking that really unsettles us? And what if other people are not ok with us saying the expectations on us are too much? And who might those other people be?

Expectations of Children and Young People

Though they might not communicate it openly and might not even be aware of any tangible thoughts around it, children have expectations of adults in school. For the youngest, starting out on their school journey, maybe some of their expectations are borne out of their parents' reassurances. 'You'll have fun. You'll make friends. You'll learn how to read and write. There'll be so many things you can do, so many things you can play with. Someone will help you if you're sad or worried or don't know what to do.' We are those consistent 'someones,' the people who will help. We know that when it comes to attachment theory, where children have experienced consistent responsiveness, warmth and sensitivity from their caregivers they feel more secure to explore the world around them (Bailey et al., 2022). If you are an Early Years practitioner, you play a significant role in creating a sense of safety that helps children to regulate and adjust to their new environment. Even the very young will come with these unwritten expectations that they will be cared for (that we will keep them safe), that they will have fun (that we will facilitate this fun) and that they will learn (that we will teach them). As they continue through school, they'll have more and more opportunities to voice their opinions and ideas, and with them will come an expectation (or for some, maybe it's more of a hope) that they will be seen and heard, and that what they have to say is important. Some children don't know this is what they deep down want and prefer to merge into the background, so they think they are not seen or heard at all. Others will let you know loud and clear that they are here and that they want their needs met, and they want them met now. We value pupil voice, and we facilitate it in both informal and formal ways in our settings. We know it is important if children are to feel that they belong and know they are a vital part of our school communities. There's a sense of safety in being able to speak up and know that you will be heard.

Trusted relationships between adults and children in schools are key. As children become older, students may have increasingly sophisticated language and ideals around their expectations. Many will expect to have developed friendships with other peers, to be taught in classes where their needs will be met, where positive behaviour management is such that they feel safe and can learn in their classes and their learning won't be disrupted by others. Many will expect or at least hope to do well enough to leave school with the qualifications they want or need to go on to further studies or apprenticeships or employment. They will expect us as educators to help create cultures and environments in which they are seen and valued and heard in a variety of ways. Maybe they'll have opportunities to participate in and lead mentorship programmes for younger peers; maybe they'll organise events, lead extra-curricular activities and engage in work experience and other enrichment activities. We will give them opportunities to develop life skills and engage in deep debate and discussion about world issues and values, all to prepare them for adulthood. We will play a part in these expectations being met or otherwise. We will play a part in these expectations being Fully met, Partially met or Not met at all. Do you recognise the language around expectations? Have you seen those phrases on a monitoring or feedback sheet somewhere before?! Are they met? Do we meet them, in the eyes of the children?

But this might only be the case for some children. For others, perhaps they carry very different expectations as they walk through the door. Perhaps they or their families have experienced very different things. Perhaps they anticipate not being safe, not being able to learn, not being valued and not being happy. Perhaps they anticipate being very alone. Then we are facing very different expectations of us that over time we hope will change, as trust is slowly built. We know that this process is a long, hard journey on both parts. It's a process of us consistently showing up and being a safe space for these children every single day. They might not expect anything different from us, but they're sure deep down hoping for it.

Expectations of Parents, Carers and Families

Just as we have expectations of our roles based on our own experiences and values, parents and families also have expectations of us as professionals. By some, we may be seen as people who can deliver everything, who will perfectly teach their child everything their child needs to know at the right time, in the right way, without any hiccups along the way. Their child will always be happy, always be keen and always have friends . . . and these friends will be good and kind and just the friends the parents want them to be. Everything will be like this all the time, and at the end of their schooling their child will be perfectly skilled and ready to take on their next venture in life. We all know that classrooms are not quite as simple as that. But though unrealistic, perhaps this really is what some parents hope for. This is how they would love it to be. And who can blame them? None of us want difficult things to come our way.

Think of a parent where it's their first or only child, starting school in a Reception class. Think about their preparation for their first day: conversations about going to 'big school' with proud grandparents, the buying of school shoes, the new haircuts, the compulsory photo of them in their school uniform outside their front door, the walking to school and finding the right place to wait in the playground. There's a lot of hope held in us. The hope of what they're going to learn, of what we're going to nurture, the trust they place in us as they hand their child over at the door. It's a big deal. They literally entrust their child to us. They expect us to keep them safe and happy and return them that way at the end of the day. Each and every day. No cuts or scuffed knees or knocked head letters, no tears or anxieties about returning again for another day, and everything eaten happily from their carefully created packed lunch box. That's a lot of expectations, and we have to manage those expectations. We have to guide both parent and child through when those expectations are not met.

What about a parent of a child they kind of want 'fixing' in some way? They don't say that, in so many words, but maybe that's their expectation, their hope. Maybe they say, 'you'll have your hands full with that one,' or 'she's got a right temper on her.' Or maybe the parent has a child who they say just can't sit still, or finds it really hard to share their toys with anyone else; maybe it's a child who gets really distressed day after day when their parent says goodbye or one who's in their own little world; maybe they're parents of a child who are wondering why he doesn't seem like other children, even at this young age, or maybe she's just not like her sister. Think about the possible expectations these parents might have of us. That we might somehow be able to remedy some of these things or at least help them with them.

Think about the parent of a child whose birthday is at the end of August, and they've literally just turned four when they arrive at the school gate . . .

Think about the parent of a child who arrives on day one and they can already read and count to 20 . . .

Think about the parent of a child where neither the parent nor the child speaks any English . . .

Think about the parent who had a really bad school experience when they were a child . . .

Think about the parent who is in a high-flying profession and has the same kind of aspirations for their child . . .

Think about the parent of a child who has already had three children go through the school . . .

Think about the parent of a child who has recently fled their home country and arrived here as a refugee . . .

Think about the parent of a child who has a serious medical condition . . .

Think about the parent of a child who already has a diagnosed additional or special educational need or disability, or a parent of a child where they wonder if this might be the case . . .

All of these parents will come with their own expectations of us. They'll probably mostly be unspoken, but they'll be there. Some of these expectations we might deem manageable or appropriate, and others perhaps not. But they'll come with them . . . and these expectations will play a part in the dynamics between us as teachers, or support staff with the parent, and between us and each child. That's a lot of expectation to hold, carry or simply be aware of.

Expectation and Trust

What if we swap out the word expectation, for trust? Think about the *trust* parents put in us. Consider the trust a parent places on the adults in a class, where they literally hand their anxious child over to them at the start of every day, hoping that they'll be able to distract and relieve their child's distress quickly so that they can settle. Think of the trust invested in us by a parent of a child with high-level needs or intimate care needs or medical needs, which require meticulous following of specific care plans and close monitoring of the child's physical health throughout the day. That's a lot of trust. That's a lot of responsibility. What about the added complexities that can arise if support staff are parents themselves, parenting and yet also working as colleagues, walking the fine line of friendship with other parents as well as maintaining professional boundaries. Perhaps parental expectations might be even higher if you're entrusting your child to a friend?

For some parents, there is still a notion of the teacher knows best. After all, we're qualified professionals with the job of teaching their children. Socioeconomic factors tend to come into play, but we can unintentionally reinforce this perception by the way we go about engaging and communicating with parents (Crozier, 1999). In the world of SEND, we've moved away from things being 'done to' families, with closer partnership working with families and the co-production of plans to support pupils around shared outcomes. With all families, there's a balance to be had, but some parents will still always defer to what the teacher says. Trust is sometimes placed on us by very virtue of the position we hold, and it's sometimes earned over time. The danger can be that we are somehow put on a pedestal, through no choice of our own, but there we are, until such a time as the trust is fractured, either slowly depleted or abruptly deleted, and because of the height of expectation or trust, the fall is great.

How might this fall from grace happen? It doesn't have to be a big news-worthy headline. It might well not even be our fault. It might just be our job. It might just be a great big dollop of reality that we have to dish out carefully, but even so, we might feel the weight of it, the weight of the fall. Maybe we are the first person to say to a parent that their child was not very kind to someone today, or that they're finding something difficult or they're not meeting expected levels for their age. Notice how things are expected of us in the very language that is used around learning? Emerging, Expected, Exceeded. It can sometimes feel like it's not just the child who's being measured. How do others rate us as we go about our jobs? Maybe in that moment of saying a hard thing to a parent your credentials are questioned, you're not believed and trust starts to erode. With your fall from favour, maybe you feel a pull within you to have to prove your worth or maybe what you really want to do is tell them to stick their opinions where the sun doesn't shine, but you know what you probably have to do is start the ground-up work of rebuilding healthy working trust again. Maybe there's no fall from grace, but we anticipate one. We're aware that at any point one could come our way. Parent-talk in the playground or on social media is a powerful thing, and relationships with parents, even when strong, are a fragile thing that can never be taken for granted. Think about it too long and that can feel like a lot of hidden pressure to face.

DIRTY WASHING

If we feel that we're not meeting expectations, it can sometimes feel like all our dirty laundry is on show for all to see. What does that look or feel like for you?

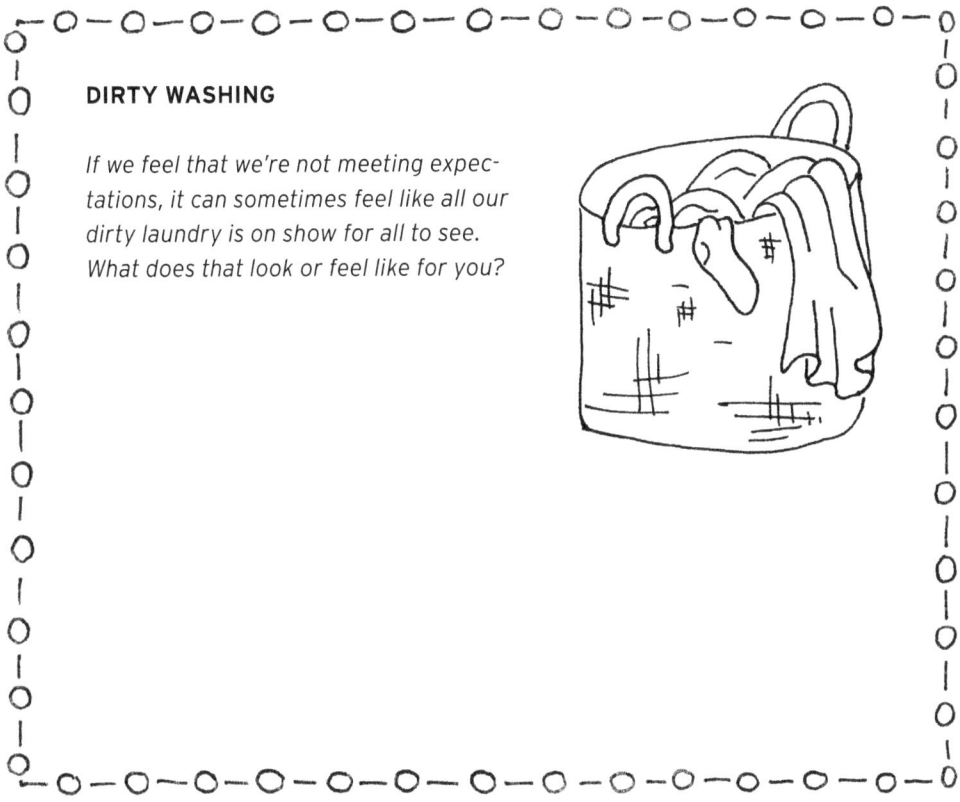

Pseudo Parents and Pseudo Family

What about if we take this whole idea of parental expectations just a little bit further? As parents entrust their children to us, is it conceivable that we might almost become like pseudo-parents or carers? Don't be alarmed. Hear me carefully. We are not their parents, and we have to know our roles and maintain professional boundaries, but just think of the emotional investment in us, in working with parents to try to meet the needs of their child ... their learning needs, social and emotional needs, physical needs etc. We don't have to do this for one child, we have to do it for 30 children or more. From Early Years right the way through, the basics are that we've got to feed them, make sure they're kept alive, make sure that they don't hurt anyone or get hurt themselves. Head teachers have to pay other people to do this consistently (us), and return every child safely at the end of the day. Every day. Everyone is trusted to do this. They're non-negotiables. Children are not just items we have to do things with, in order to achieve projected targets; they are extraordinary precious, living, breathing human beings. In schools it's all about people.

Schools are a hub of life and relationships are key. We're communities in our own right. Mini populations with all the wonderful diversity you can name, as well as all the challenges that can bring. Staff, colleagues, parents, carers, children and families all plonked together, finding their way. As an adult in a classroom, we have all the dynamics of 30 individual children in our class, and all their 'stuff' (hopes, dreams, fears, anxieties, disappointments, cares, needs and expectations) is in the mix. It could be said that we've also got all of the parents' stuff (hopes, dreams, fears, anxieties, disappointments, cares, needs and expectations in relation to their child) in the mix too, but just slightly further afield. A parent might love that their child is friends with little Johnny, but if they're not, they might well want us to do something about it. They might want us to follow up on their concern or step right in and change a seating plan, or monitor said child's behaviour. When it comes to helping children and young people with their social interactions, we have an important part to play. Gronlund (1959) suggests that we need to have real expertise in building relationships with children and helping them navigate their social relationships. Children learn from us explicitly and implicitly. Farmer et al. (2011) say that we are role models and guides as children begin to understand societal rules and learn to develop close relationships. Kindermann (2011) talks about the 'invisible hand,' of the teacher, and how even without any explicit teaching around it, we still influence children's social development and peer interactions. We are building relationships and an understanding of community every day, and that comes with a lot of spoken and unspoken expectations.

You may think I'm belabouring the point, but perhaps there's also an element that we become something of a pseudo family by the very way that things are structured in schools. Usually, in the Primary phase, children become *your* class. Your class has an identity of its own, and you, along with any adults and children in your room, shape that identity. You are referred to as Mr so and so's class. Or maybe your class has its own name, with all the other classes interconnected by a family of related names that speak of the community as a whole. Red class, blue class, yellow class ... Colours that together become a rainbow, trees that together become a woodland, storybook titles that together become a library. You get my drift. You're all interconnected. There's a sense of belonging, of community, of family. And in your class, you have shared experiences, shared challenges, shared joys. It looks slightly different in secondary schools, with form tutors and house systems, but in many ways, it's just a grown-up version of the same kind of thing. You *invest* in your class. It's not an emotionless transaction. You invest in each other. They're people, *your* people. You get to know them, you get in on their lives, they share with you their lows and their highs. You notice when one of them has a new haircut; you notice when someone is absent; you encourage them when they feel a bit lost; you all make a card for a child who's off school for an extended period of time; you celebrate someone becoming a new big sister and that celebration extends to congratulating the parents at the door when the new baby arrives. You feel a sense of communal loss when something difficult happens to a child or their family ... and all the while, trust grows. Let's not look at it all through rose-tinted spectacles though. Trust might not grow between all of you. It won't include every parent and child, but it is there, in that little community that you've nurtured, within the larger school community as a whole ... and with that sense of community comes expectations.

This trust, this relationship, this safe space is crucial for children's learning. Learning happens in the context of relationship, the relationship between the children and adults in the room (Roffey, 2010). You have to trust, to be able to step into the risk of learning something new (especially in the company of others), to venture past the not knowing, to put your hand up to answer a question (because what if you get it wrong?), to venture into the vulnerability of going beyond what you know. There's a vulnerability about learning. There's a vulnerability about failing. There's a vulnerability in practising. The child has to trust the adults (and other children) in the room about not being shamed in the process of learning. So, there's this deep connectedness that happens. There's a shared space that is created and experienced at an emotional level, whether we realise it or not, and that sense of connectedness lends itself to a sense of family, of responsibility and expectation. It can all feel pretty life-giving when things are going well, but if we're facing something tricky, might all those dynamics and expectations sometimes feel a bit weighty? A bit too much?

Trauma and Mental Health Needs

What about when we teach, support and nurture children who have experienced trauma? We all know the challenges of this. We know the facts and the implications for us in schools. Trauma and Adverse Childhood Experiences (ACEs) in the early years can have a sustained impact on children emotionally, mentally and physically, often with long-term effects (Hartman et al., 2025). The Timpson Review (2019) detailed links between children's vulnerabilities around their experiences of trauma and their increased likelihood of exclusion from school. We know that with great challenge often comes great reward, but the reality is that supporting children who have experienced trauma is highly challenging and can affect staff's wellbeing and mental health (Frearson, 2024). When it comes to supporting children with mental health needs in schools, Lowry et al. (2022) stated that only 40% of teachers in the UK felt equipped to do so, and with long waits to access mental health services, as school staff we are under pressure to meet children's needs in the here and now. We're under pressure to meet their needs for the child's own sake, as well as the wellbeing of everyone else in the class. We're under pressure from their parents or carers to respond well, and from other parents who expect that their own children's learning and experience of school will not be disrupted along the way. It is expected of us that we will do our very best to support these children just as we do any other.

Indeed, we have a responsibility to safeguard children and that includes seeking to understand the underlying causes of their behaviour, liaising with Mental Health Support teams for support and having adequate training around how mental health needs can affect behaviour (DfE, 2024). Earlier government guidance is more detailed about risk and protective factors and how childhood trauma can impact on their mental health, behaviour and education (DfE, 2018). It's serious business. It's also interesting to think of the language around nurture and safeguarding. We have a *duty of care* towards children. That's the expectation. It's a legal requirement of our roles and it speaks of duty and responsibility. Expectation and responsibility and care. Sometimes we fail to recognise how it feels for us as we teach and interact with children who face these challenges, and what it's like to be with these children every day. For many, their trauma might play out in the form of difficult or challenging behaviour which is tricky to manage in the classroom. Their shame might spill out all over the place and be full in your face with every interaction. Often, we feel the very real challenge in the moment, but there's an intense emotional cost to experiencing that on a regular basis. Children are in our classes and there is this thread of connection, of relationship. We feel compassion, but sometimes we also feel overwhelmed. Grist and Caudle (2021) have spoken of a rise in burnout when examining the relationships between early childhood practitioners, ACEs and job-related stressors. Klusmann et al. (2023) found an increase in compassion fatigue among teachers during the COVID-19 pandemic, due to a greater awareness of children's trauma and the effort of re-engaging children in learning post lockdowns. We face a lot of challenges in schools, and yet so much is still expected of us. It's ok to admit that sometimes it can all feel a bit too much.

Primary and Secondary Settings

Maybe a sense of connection is heightened in primary school settings, because they are usually much smaller communities than secondary schools, and because of differences in structure that inevitably come with larger environments. In Primary and Early Years settings there is closer proximity and contact with parents and families, and children are younger and more dependent. In the secondary phase there is significantly less face-to-face contact with parents and students are more independent. In secondary education you don't just have 30 children in a class; you have multiple classes. Aside from being a form tutor for a year group they're not solely *your* class. They're not wholly your responsibility. The children's learning journey is spread across different teachers. Their experience and their outcomes are shared. Even so, there are parental expectations at play. Perhaps some might say the stakes are even higher in secondary schools. Parents will hope that their child will leave school with at least adequate qualifications, and many will hope that their child will excel. Parents will have expectations around communication and the curriculum, teaching and learning, progress and results, safeguarding, wellbeing and behaviour, to name but a few ... and when lots of parents and families have similar expectations of a school it becomes an expectation of the community.

Expectations of Community and Society

If parents and grandparents have lived in the same area and have attended the same school for years, there may be generational expectations of a school either meeting or not meeting the needs of families. People live in connectedness with others. They share and communicate common positive or negative experiences. You only have to stand in a school playground for a few minutes to see this in action or join a social media group to see how connectedness can play out in good and sometimes less healthy ways. You feel the sense of community and expectation at Parents' Evenings, in school fairs and performances, in fundraising events, sports days and interschool competitions. You feel it in the camaraderie or the friction.

CARE

Think about situations and relationships where you have experienced care in your own life, either as the giver or receiver. What words do you equate with care? Is it possible to care too much?

A communal expectation of a school grows over time. Schools have good (or less than good) reputations for meeting the needs of children with SEND; they have good (or less than good) reputations around behaviour, results, citizenship, sporting accolades, routes to higher education, academia and employment. Ofsted reports, and school performance tables or league tables play a big part in consolidating or altering community expectations. Regardless of the current language being used around government inspections, if you've historically been a school that has excelled, then the pressure is on everyone for it to stay that way. It's expected that everything good about it is maintained and it is frowned upon if it becomes anything different. If things become less than what they were, what's felt is almost like a collective, communal disappointment. It's probably not too far of a stretch to say some might think the school has not just let itself down but let the community down. You can almost hear those words being said. If you have a less attractive reputation as a school, it can take years of solid hard work to rebuild bridges and trust and alter the perspective or prejudice in the community. Expectations and reputations are powerful players that have huge practical implications around the uptake of places, funding, staffing and provision. The cycle can go up in the right direction for you or down in the wrong one. It's hard when you're at the top or the bottom or anywhere in between, because there's so much at stake.

But community expectations don't just come from results and reports. A school's reputation grows through people's contact with its people. Through word of mouth, through PR, good communication and community engagement. It grows through the shopwindow of the school website, prospective parent visits and open days, performances and community events. Each plays a part, builds a picture and shapes an expectation, and the expectation grows. At times it gathers a momentum of its own and begins to impact more of the surrounding community, such as affecting house prices and the desirability of living in a particular area. So, as schools we are always being observed. Points of view are always being expressed, and judgements are always being made.

It turns out that people on the whole are quite good at playing judge. If things are good, then great. If something's wrong, then most likely someone has to pay. In schools it can sometimes feel like that. Whilst we agree with being held accountable, the air around us sometimes feels restless. The wider environment can feel at times like a litigious one, and that can feel unsettling. Complaints can be made to Ofsted or Governing Bodies at the drop of a hat, and some without following the steps of complaints procedures that are in place. Regardless of process or validity in your eyes, as soon as that email drops in your inbox you have to do something about it. Things can be escalated to higher levels that could simply be resolved at lower ones. When it comes to SEND, here in the UK thousands of pounds are being spent on SEND Tribunals brought by parents around provision, placement and unmet SEND. In the 2023/24 academic year there was an increase of 55% in the number of registered SEN appeals compared to the previous year (Ministry of Justice, 2024). Some complaints are around legal timescales not being met and provision not being in place, and the powers that be, rightly, need to be held accountable. But it can sometimes feel like there's an air of mistrust and fear, where things don't always feel that safe . . . and that can leave us feeling a bit vulnerable.

That sense of vulnerability only increases when we look at the scarcity of other local resources. With the paring back of Local Authority budgets over the years, gaps in community provision are all around. Gaps that might once have been small are now gaping holes with stretched services in all directions. This has led to education and schools trying to plug those gaps where we can, in order to meet the needs of our children and families. There is so much need represented in our school communities and there are so many 'not enoughs' all around. Waiting lists for other services are long, services are overrun and the need seems to have to be 'too much' before a child can access the provision they so desperately need. It goes without saying that early intervention is key, but when wider provision is lacking, we find ourselves with the responsibility of trying to meet these needs where we can. We're not social workers or mental health experts, but we run therapeutic programmes and interventions to support children around their social, emotional and mental health needs. We're not speech therapists, but we run bespoke language and communication interventions. We liaise with relevant agencies, we get more training and we upskill ourselves so that we can do the best that we can . . . and whilst we've been doing this for years at lower levels of need, it can feel like we're now having to do it for those with much higher levels of need too. Sometimes it can feel like there is too much responsibility placed on school staff, that the expectations are simply too high, as we try to make up for the shortfall in wider provision.

In the name of safeguarding and wellbeing, we give children breakfast, provide food bags and bags of essentials for struggling families. For some, we wash and give out children's clothing and school uniforms; we knock on doors to encourage a child to physically get into the school building. We run holiday clubs and provide wraparound care. If we can, we find funding to employ Speech and Language Therapists to support children with language delay; we seek the expertise of Play Therapists, Music Therapists, Mental Health Support Teams and therapeutic Counsellors to support children's mental health, and Family Support Workers to support engagement with families, and we signpost children and families to other expertise and provision wherever possible. We're not going to be able to meet all of the needs before us, because education alone can't. Some of these needs are intricately interwoven with other social factors such as poverty, families not in jobs or education, family breakdown, addiction, violence and poor mental health. It can sometimes feel like the need, pressure and expectations are so much. So, let's take a break, shift focus and take a look closer to home.

Expectations of Colleagues

When it comes to expectations that colleagues have of us, and that we quite possibly have of each other, perhaps they look something like this. First and foremost, we're in this together and we're on the same team. So, we'll work hard together and look after each other, to try to get this thing over the line. But is there sometimes still an undercurrent of a different narrative? Maybe if we're really honest it sometimes also looks a bit like this . . . Because so much is required of us and we're all under pressure, I'll have an expectation of you that you'll pull your weight, that you'll be up to the task, that you won't be flaky, that you'll be flexible and adaptable and won't let your nose be put out of joint when obstacles come our way (which inevitably they will). I'll have an expectation that you'll be competent, that you'll roll with the punches, that you'll be here and won't have much (if any) time off, that you'll be a team player, that you'll not slack and you'll give of your best, that we'll share the same values and that ultimately we'll have each other's backs. Did I really just say those things out loud? We might not say these things to each other, but we might sometimes think some of them. There's not much space for grace in these kinds of expectations, not much space for asking for help or needing support. Thankfully, we are shifting towards a greater awareness and understanding of wellbeing and mental health in schools, and that includes the wellbeing of staff. But sometimes it's only when some of these things fail to happen that we realise that we actually *expect* them from each other. If we're honest, we can almost feel offended or somehow let down by the 'inadequacies' of another (all the while hoping that that other isn't us), because the demands upon us all are so great.

Of course, these expectations are unrealistic, but if we dig below the surface they're sometimes there. If we're in a school that is under acute pressure, where maybe attainment and progress are below par, or attendance is low or behaviour is poor, these hidden expectations might be more prevalent. Maybe they're also lurking around excelling schools, where the pressure to stay at the top can have similar effects. All of us have days when we're not doing so well, when we're tired or flagging and this is precisely when a sense of team needs to kick in, when we need to experience compassion, feel trusted and looked after, but that doesn't always happen.

Imagine you're a someone who others perceive as weak. Or at least, that's what you think. You feel like maybe everyone else has really got it together and you haven't. You feel like people are just waiting for you to miss the mark again. Imagine what that does to you each day. Imagine when someone's waiting on your bit of paperwork . . . again.

Or imagine you're a newly qualified, Early Career Teacher. Imagine you and another teacher join the school at the same time and for both of you, it's your first teaching post. Imagine you are doing well. Other people like you; the children like you; parents like you. You're coping well with the needs in your class and children are making good progress. It's hard work (hey, you knew it was going to be), but your mentor is pleased, and things are feeling pretty good. Imagine that's not the case for the other teacher . . . Or imagine you are the other teacher. That's going to feel like a long old slog to get to the end of the year. You might well wonder if you're cut out for it at all. You might forget that you're only in your first year, and that we're all learning, experienced and new teachers alike. You might forget that this is a really demanding job, and that there isn't such thing as a Fast Pass to becoming experienced. You might not be able to hear all those things, because all sorts of other feelings keep getting in the way. The expectations of others, or what we think others think of us, can spur us on or weigh us down.

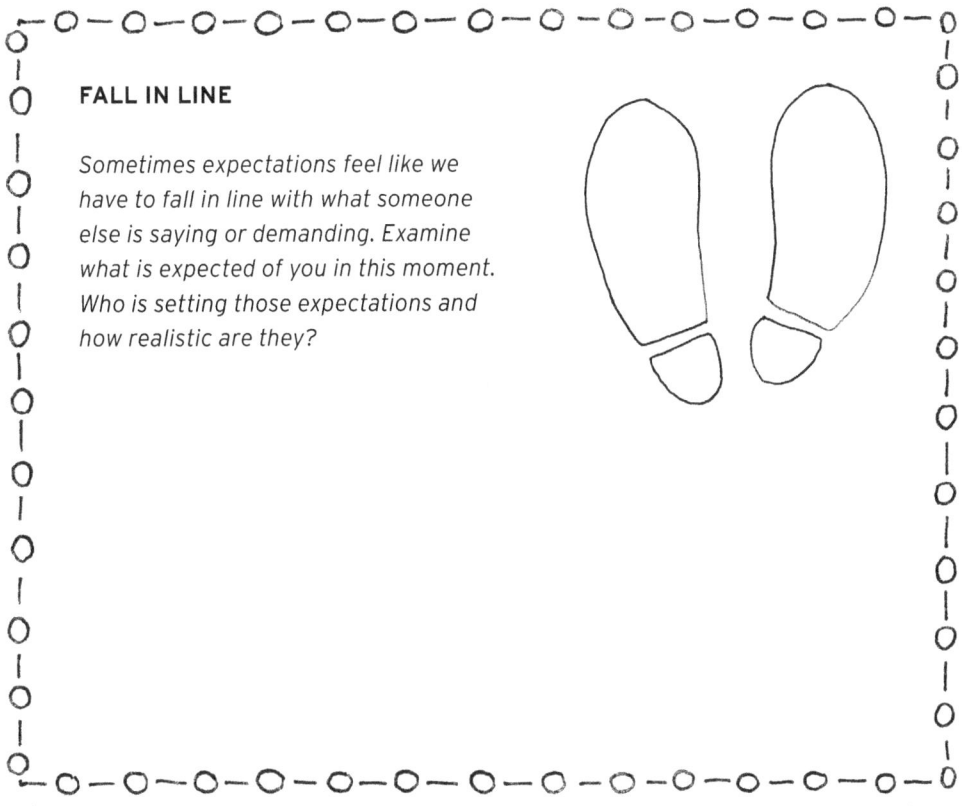

FALL IN LINE

Sometimes expectations feel like we have to fall in line with what someone else is saying or demanding. Examine what is expected of you in this moment. Who is setting those expectations and how realistic are they?

What about the relationship between teachers and support staff? The challenges we face are felt by us all, but when more and more demands are placed on me, I might then place them on you, and in the pressure of it all, I might be less thankful in that moment for what you do. I might rush a conversation with you. I might give hurried instructions or training. I might not give you time to say how you're really doing. I might expect more of you with the less that we have. As teachers, we have to justify how every adult is deployed, because people equal money and impact is paramount. We have to measure the effectiveness of all interventions. If you're a support assistant delivering an intervention, it can feel like you're being measured, delivering that intervention. It can feel like what is being measured is your expertise, your quality of interaction with the children, your ability to intervene and give feedback, your ability to critically observe, amongst other things. That's a lot of expectations in the mix, in your close working dynamic.

Expectations of Senior Leadership and Management

And then there are the expectations from management: Senior Leaders, Head teacher/s, the Governing Body, Local Authority or Academy Trust leads. There are expectations for us to meet targets not just for our own classes or subject areas but collectively, on action points in School Development/Improvement Plans and Local Authority or Trust action plans. More than that, we are in positions of trust. We're trusted with the teaching and nurturing of the children and young people in our classes, trusted with their safety and wellbeing. We are trusted to do all the things expected of us in our job descriptions and more. We are expected to become skilled and competent, to be willing to learn and take on any challenge. We are expected to grow in experience and resilience, to be flexible, to take initiative and be a team player. We are expected to interact well with others, to be able to problem-solve, to resolve conflict healthily. We are expected to be responsible members of the community, to always wear the school badge, so to speak. On duty and off duty, we represent the school. We wear the teaching badge, the badge of the profession. We wear the badge of Education.

We are expected to do and be so many things, some written into contracts and some unspoken, yet keenly felt. Anything can be written in a policy, but it's how it looks in practice that matters. Take professional development for example. It's good, right? We always want to be increasing our expertise and improving our practice, because that always leads to better outcomes, but might there sometimes be expectations at play that we really should have that sorted by now? What if we ask for support from senior leaders around helping to manage a child's behaviour in class? How is that *really* viewed by management? Is it viewed as a strength that we've said we want additional training or coaching, or is it perhaps seen as an inconvenience and an extra cost that is tricky to juggle in the budget? Are coaching and mentoring put in place early, before things get to crisis point, and with support and review structures in place? Are things like this seen as valued learning opportunities or have some people's minds already been made up about a person's capabilities? No one would ever say that, but might it be thought? Would asking for help almost be counted against you, if you were to apply for increased responsibility a little later down the line? Expectations from senior leaders can be explicit and also nuanced, and both have the power to build staff up or wear them down. The demands of our jobs are huge, and the pressures we face can be alleviated or compounded by those around us.

What about other expectations from leadership? For those of us who were in schools at the height of the COVID-19 pandemic, as with many other professions, we were asked to 'step up' to the challenges that came our way during that extraordinary time. For some, that looked like taking on or covering additional tasks or areas of responsibility. Post pandemic, and particularly in settings that are experiencing specific staff shortages, it can feel like this stepped-up level of working has become something of the norm. We're still doing everything we need to do, as well as being asked to 'just do this' as well. As part of our professional appraisal or cyclical Performance Management Reviews, we are often encouraged to work towards that next thing we want to achieve or that next skill we want to develop. There's always a direction towards more. More from us. More of us. But might what we're doing just now be enough? Might doing anything more be unsustainable? Too much?

You might think I'm overstating things. We don't feel all these things all the time. But it's important to see lots of these different expectations all lumped together. It helps us see the contexts within which we work and the things that can be at play. So just one more thing . . . Let's think a little about some of the expectations on us from Government.

Expectations of Government

The results are in. Except you're not talking with excited anticipation about some TV show public vote. This public vote is not for entertainment purposes. It's wholly serious and has lots riding on it. You're talking SATs or GCSEs (or make that whatever other kind of formal assessment you've been working towards since the beginning of the year). The results are in. And for the most part you're ok with them. They're pretty much what you'd thought they'd be. You are, after all, a skilled practitioner. But there are a few surprises in there. A couple of good surprises and a couple that are less so. And although you're generally pleased, it's the 'less so' results that niggle you, that make you wonder if you could have done more, that make you question if you did a good enough job . . . and you'll be held accountable for them all.

When it comes to results, everything is just so public. So out there for everyone to see. In spreadsheets, in tracking, in target setting, in league tables, in local standing and reputation, in parental support . . . And so much (maybe too much?) hinges on it. That's how the system works. That's how it goes. If you've been in education for a while it can feel like the pressure is always mounting, like the expectations are always growing, the standards are always going up, the goalposts are always being moved. New initiatives and guidelines are issued, and we have to meet them; documents are updated and we have to follow them.

Expectations from Government on schools and therefore school staff can feel weighty. Sometimes the expectations can seem random or out of touch. When it comes to the curriculum, you might wonder why little Johnny needs to know this specific fact or this particular concept by the time he's this specific age, especially when you know what he really needs to know right now is that he's safe. You might wonder how on earth you're supposed to close the gap between some of your learners, when try as you might, it's the kind of gap that's not easily closable, especially within the resources that you have. You might wonder how you're ever going to achieve that data that's expected of you with the class that you have and all the intricacies of their needs and how they interplay with each other in the room, when the people setting that expectation don't know these children, and don't know their life stories so far. It's right to have high expectations, to aim high for progress and achievement for all. Aim lower and you'll likely achieve lower, but the contexts within which we work have to be understood. So much is expected of us and surely this can have adverse effects on our wellbeing over time.

The stats bear witness to the challenges, and it can make for grim reading. Here in the UK, the Teacher Wellbeing Index of 2024 states

RUCKSACK

If you think of the hard things about being in school as rocks that weigh down your rucksack on your back, what would the name of each rock be? How weighed down are you at the moment? Are all the rocks yours, or do some belong to other people?

What about if the rucksack is not just a school bag, but your life at the moment...? What are you carrying right now?

78% of all staff are stressed, 50% of all staff consider their organisation's culture has a negative effect on staff's mental health and wellbeing, and 38% of all staff say their organisations do not support employees who have mental health and wellbeing problems well.

Recent National Foundation for Educational Research (NFER) findings state that between 2021-2022 and 2022-2023 there was a 44% increase in staff intending to leave the profession in England (McLean et al., 2024). A lot is expected of us . . . and when it all comes down to it, sometimes the expectations on us can feel a bit too much. When it gets that way, it's important we know that *we're* not too much, for feeling the too much-ness of it all.

It's understandable . . . with conditions around you always asking for more, you can sometimes feel that you're not really valued for all that you do. So, it's vital you hear this solid truth. You are highly valued. Not just for what you do but for who you are. Regardless of anything that may seek to tell you otherwise, you are of such great worth.

Why don't you think on that a bit before moving on to engage with some of the reflection activities that follow?

*****Take a break for five minutes and come back later*****

Examine and Evidence

HELP!

Where do you feel you need help right now? Who could you ask for help (in or out of school)? What would you say?

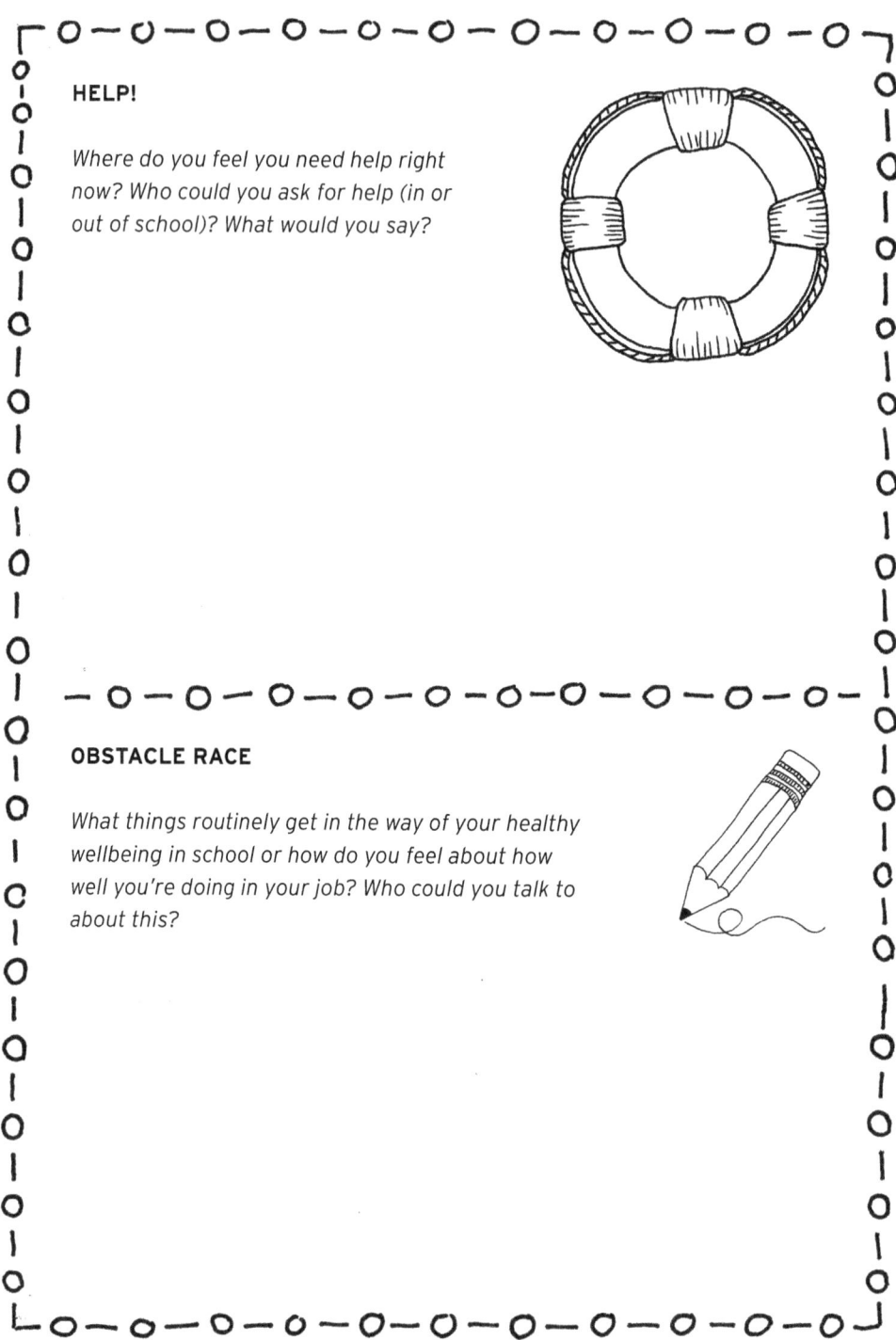

OBSTACLE RACE

What things routinely get in the way of your healthy wellbeing in school or how do you feel about how well you're doing in your job? Who could you talk to about this?

STILL THE NOISE

When things sometimes feel too much, it can all feel too noisy. How could you turn down the volume on some things? What do you need to prioritise and what can wait?

LADDER

What steps might you need to take to help improve your wellbeing in school? What could these look like?

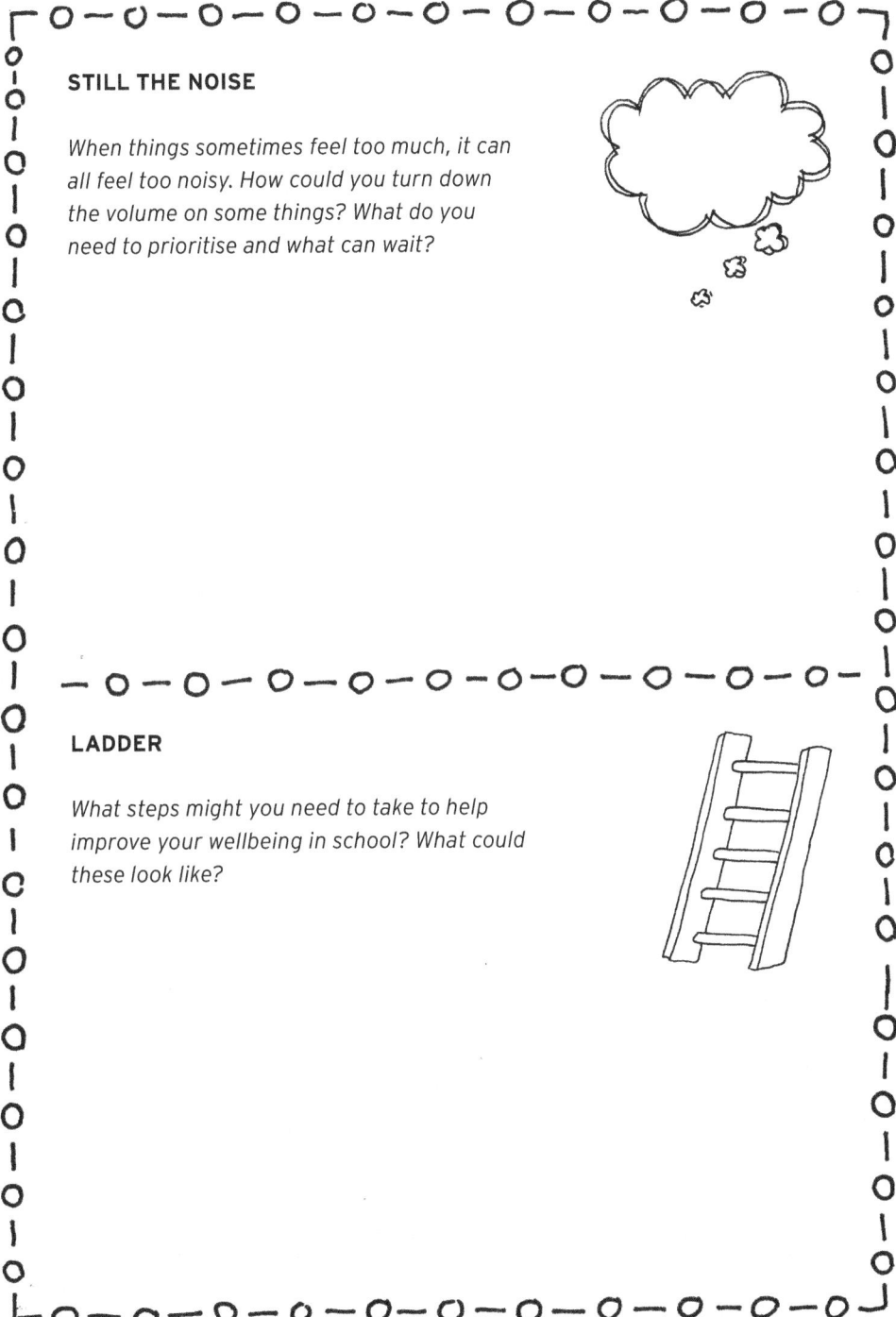

AND IT WAS JUST RIGHT

Think of the story of Goldilocks and the extremes of too much, too little and then just right. What measures could you put in place to help move you from one end of the extreme towards more of just right? Who could you talk to about this?

SAFETY NET

If you were to throw your safety net out wide, what kind of people or things would you have in it, and how might they help you?

THE FINISH LINE

What things will help you keep going to the end of term? What will help you get over the finish line? What could you put in place to help you along the way?

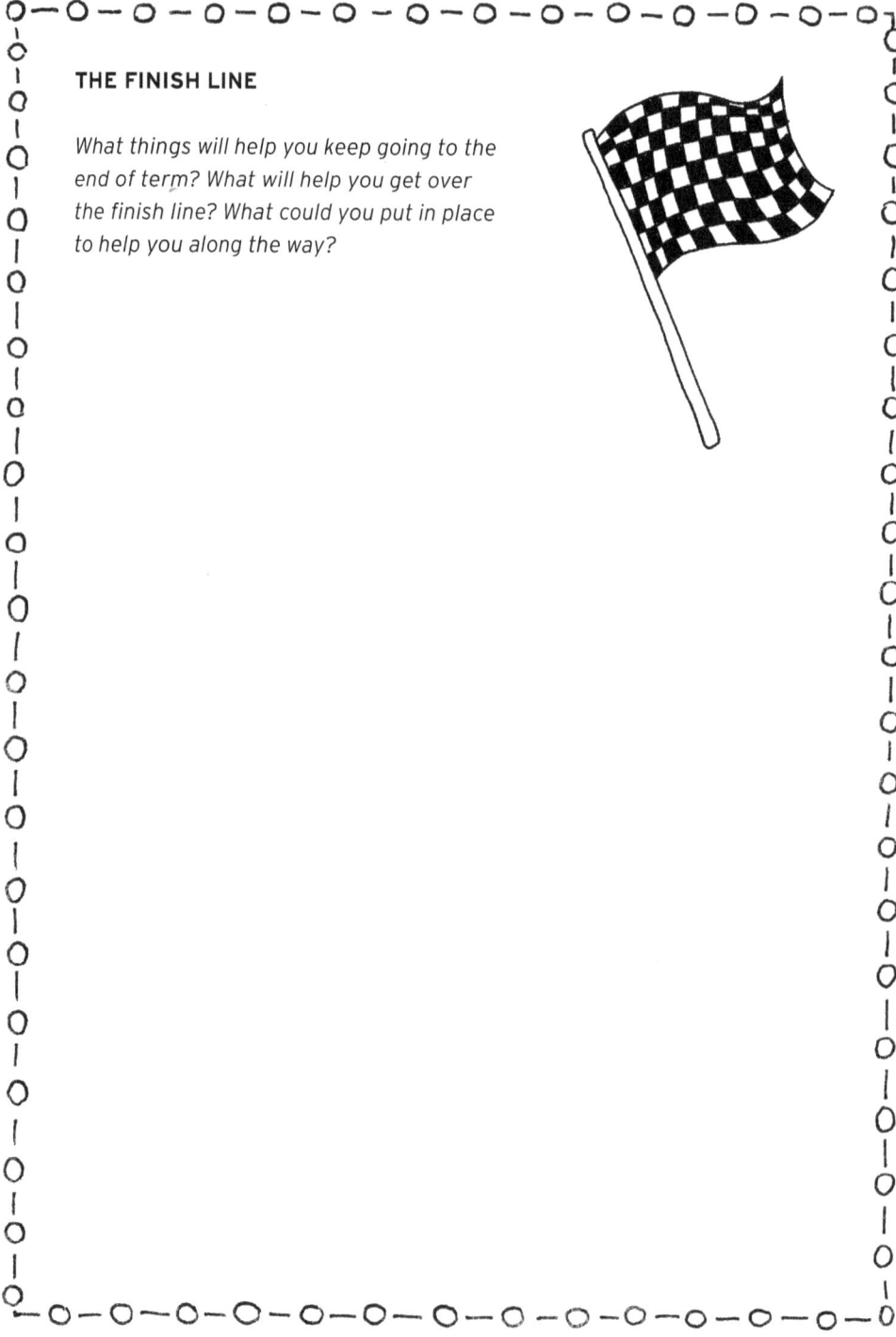

CUT TO THE CORE

Where might you be feeling offended when it comes to school right now? Write about the offence. Have you experienced this before? Is your reaction in any way disproportionate to the perceived offence, and what might this tell you about how you're doing right now?

WHAT'S THE HURRY?

With too much to fit in or do, we can sometimes feel hurried and out of breath. How hurried do you feel right now? How could working at a more measured pace help you?

TO-DO LIST

Reflect on your to-do list for today or this week. Can you highlight anything that doesn't have to be done this very moment? What of your list do you have to do, and what of your list might you just be wanting to do? And why might you have that expectation of yourself?

BREAKTHROUGH

When it comes to feeling like things are a bit too much, where do you want to see breakthrough? What would you like that to look like?

WHAT'S YOUR STORY?

Telling your story is a powerful way of bringing things out into the open. Who could you speak to if things are feeling like they're a little too much? What would you say?

SLOW

What could slowing down look like for you this week? Where might you be able to find one or two opportunities to slow?

WASHING LINE

Sometimes we want to hang all our things out in order, bright and clean on the line. How does ordering and prioritising things help you if things are beginning to feel a bit too much?

LIGHTEN UP

Who could you speak to, to lighten the load this week? What might you say?

BRAIN DUMP

What are you thinking? What are you feeling?

YOU ARE OF SUCH GREAT WORTH

References

Bailey, C. S., Ondrusek, A. R., Curby, T. W., & Denham, S. A. (2022). Teachers' consistency of emotional support moderates the association between young children's regulation capacities and their preschool adjustment. *Psychology in the Schools, 59*(6), 1051-1074. http://doi.org/10.1002/pits.22659

Crozier, G. (1999). Is it a case of 'We know when we're not wanted'? The parents' perspective on parent-teacher roles and relationships. *Educational Research, 41*(3), 315-328. http://doi.org/10.1080/0013188990410306

Department for Education. (2018, November). *Mental health and behaviour in schools.* https://www.gov.uk/government/publications/mental-health-and-behaviour-in-schools-2

Department for Education. (2019). *Timpson review of school exclusion.* https://assets.publishing.service.gov.uk/government/uploads/system/uploads/attachment_data/file/807862/Timpson_review.pdf

Department for Education. (2024, February). *Behaviour in schools: Advice for headteachers and school staff.* https://assets.publishing.service.gov.uk/media/65ce3721e1bdec001a3221fe/Behaviour_in_schools_-_advice_for_headteachers_and_school_staff_Feb_2024.pdf

Education Support. (2024). *Teacher wellbeing index 2024* (p. 8). Education Support.

Farmer, T. W., McAucliffe Lines, M., & Hamm, J. V. (2011). Revealing the invisible hand: The role of teachers in children's peer experiences. *Journal of Applied Developmental Psychology, 32*(5), 247-256.

Frearson, A., & Duncan, M. (2024, February 13). An interpretive phenomenological analysis of teachers' lived experiences of working with traumatised children in the classroom. *Journal of Child and Adolescent Trauma, 17*(2), 555-570. https://doi.org/10.1007/s40653-024-00614-9

Grist, C. L., & Caudle, L. A. (2021). An examination of the relationships between adverse childhood experiences, personality traits, and job-related burnout in early childhood educators. *Teaching and Teacher Education, 105.* ISSN 0742-051X.

Gronlund, N. E. (1959). *Sociometry in the classroom.* Harper & Brothers.

Hartman, L., Domaceti, B., & Ellis, A. (2025, May 22). *From our members: Death and adverse childhood experiences: A call to action.* International Society for Traumatic Stress Studies. https://istss.org/from-our-members-death-and-adverse-childhood-experiences-a-call-to-action-luca-hartman-ba-brianna-domaceti-ba-amy-ellis-phd/

Kindermann, T. A. (2011). Commentary: The invisible hand of the teacher. *Journal of Applied Developmental Psychology.* https://doi.org/10.1016/j.appdev.2011.04.005

Klusmann, U., Aldrup, K., Roloff-Bruchmann, J., Carstensen, B., Wartenberg, G., Hansen, J., & Hanewinkel, R. (2023). Teacher's emotional exhaustion during the COVID-19 pandemic: Levels, changes, and relations to pandemic-specific demands. *Teaching and Teacher Education, 121,* 103908. https://doi.org/10.1016/j.tate.2022.103908

Lowry C., Leonard-Kane, R., Gibbs, B., Muller, L. M., Peacock, A., & Jani, A. (2022). Teachers: The forgotten health workforce. *Journal of the Royal Society of Medicine, 115*(4), 133-137. https://doi.org/10.1177/01410768221085692

McLean, D., Worth, J., & Smith, A. (2024). *Teacher labour market in England: Annual report 2024.* NFER.

Ministry of Justice. (2024, December 12). *Official statistics tribunal statistics quarterly: July to September 2024.* https://www.gov.uk/government/statistics/tribunals-statistics-quarterly-july-to-september-2024/tribunal-statistics-quarterly-july-to-september-2024

Roffey, S. (2010). Content and context for learning relationships: A cohesive framework for individual and whole school development. *Educational and Child Psychology, 27*(1), 156-168. https://doi.org/10.53841/bpsecp.2010.27.1.156

4
Digging Deeper

Let's just dig a little deeper. With the not enoughs and the too much that we face all around, what if some of the structures and practices in education itself also impact us and our well-being without us even realising? We just work within the system as we know it. It's just how it is. But what if it takes a hidden toll?

When it comes to guidelines and policy and the way our education system works, there are messages, whether subtle or blatant (some of which might also be expectations), that shape the culture within which we work. We may feel them to lesser or greater degrees depending on the individual ethos and culture of each of our schools, but they'll be felt, nonetheless. The messages can trigger different responses in us and can be felt by many of us working in a school context, especially where we're experiencing conditions of lack. Let's look at some of them.

Keep Up

We work to the sound of the bell (metaphoric or real). It rings at the start of the day and off we go, and then at different intervals throughout, each bell signalling our hurried moving on to the next thing: assembly, the next lesson, break, lunch etc. We know that feeling of rushing from one thing to the next. But beyond the bell, there is this sense (and it can be a real 'felt' thing), that we have got to keep up. Keep up with delivering content, delivering the curriculum; we have to keep up with the pace, keep up with the deadlines, the demands, keep up with what's expected of us as professionals; we have to keep up with the progress, keep up with the attainment; we have to keep up with whatever new initiative comes our way, whatever new piece of research or issued guideline says we must or should do. Sometimes that keeping up can involve tweaks in policy and practice and sometimes it might require a complete overhaul. We have to keep up in this moment, this lesson, this day, this week, this term, this year . . . and then it starts all over again. The underlying message is we have to keep up because if we don't, we fall behind, and that means not only we fall behind, but others do too. The very nature of our jobs is done in the context of community; it's done in relationship, not in a vacuum. We are to teach others, to support others, and that means that what we do or don't do impacts others. It doesn't take much of a leap for us to think that if we don't keep up, we might well be letting people down . . .

And that can get you down.

Have you felt this pressure to keep up? Have you ever wondered that if you don't, what might that say about you? Might that lead to feelings of being somehow lesser than, insufficient or, dare we even think it, substandard? After all, we have Teachers Standards to meet (DfE, 2011). Perhaps you have a healthy work/life balance and you know what is your responsibility and what is not, and you know you alone can't save or fix others or the system, and that you leave your children at the door when you leave at the end of the school day, but what if that's sometimes just a way of coping with the pressure, and sometimes it's really hard to switch off, and sometimes under the surface, the weight of keeping up can still be felt?

You might say that you dance to a different tune, that what's important to you is not the keeping up, it's the individual child, it's the holistic view, that you have different values, you're not all about the drive of the system, and you hold your values at the forefront of everything you do. Yes, we cry! As inclusive practitioners, we know the importance of each child in front of us; we know that one size doesn't fit all; we advocate and speak up for those who find it difficult to keep up in the general mainstream throng. But even though we believe these things, we still work within a system which functions in a different way. Whether we like it or not, the message we can feel is to keep up. And sometimes that message doesn't just feel like a collaborative thing of doing this together. Sometimes when it's hard it can feel very personal. Very lonely. If you've felt these things, you're not on your own. So many of us feel the pressure of keeping up but we're just practised at keeping it under wraps . . . because to bring it out into the open can feel like a hard thing to do.

There Is No Place for Failure

Much like keeping up, we can also feel that there is no place for failure. There's no place for failure because there's too much riding on it. It's ironic that in an era where we work towards having a growth mindset (Dweck, 2017), rather than a fixed one, where we model making mistakes to children in the classroom, where we teach children to embrace making mistakes and recognise that feeling of vulnerability because it shows that our brains are learning and we're taking risks, it can still feel like it's not ok for us to fail as teachers. It's like we play at making mistakes in the roleplay corner, but it's not actually ok for us to work really hard at something and find it doesn't actually work out. It's not actually ok for us to miss the mark; it's not ok for the children to not make as much progress as expectations say they should, it's not ok for any attainment gap not to be closed, because just as with keeping up, there's too much at stake. If they fail, we fail. If we fail, they fail. So, we can't.

But we do.

Because we're people.

Curran (2024) says, 'we're just human. And deep down we know, better than we'd like to admit, that all humans are fallible, flawed, and exhaustible creatures'. But, he says, 'our culture asks us to keep playing perfect aces hand after hand after hand'.

At the same time, we know that failing can be something that brings about good things (Edmondson, 2023). Failing can be good when we learn from our experiences and then better things and better outcomes come of it. We don't like the feelings that come with failing, but we know that bouncing back from failure and moving forwards builds resilience . . . and building resilience is a good thing, because we all need to be resilient in life. Yet, whilst we value resilience and teach children about its importance and try to help them develop it, it feels like there is still something at odds with it all. We who teach resilience still find ourselves in an environment, in a system where it feels unacceptable to fall short . . . because of how that failure might impact others. The fear of falling short or letting people down as well as having the best interests of children at heart can be a dangerous combination. It can weigh us down or secretly drive us beyond our capacity. Do that for long enough and it's not good for our health or wellbeing, and to avoid showing weakness, we can be tempted to hide the strain, shrink back from saying how we're really doing and be reluctant to ask for help. All those things can feel like being found out, and no one likes that. This is real stuff we have to grapple with. We might think it's a lesser thing and we have too much else to be getting on with, but the lesser things can become bigger things if we don't pay attention to them. It's important to stop, look and listen, as the old safety message goes.

Working in education, another message we can believe and that can impact us on the sly is . . .

When It Comes Down to It, You're on Your Own

That's a strange thing to say, when clearly we are not. There are a whole lot of other people around us, working with us, working alongside us. Everyone playing their part. Everyone doing their bit. That's all true, but at the same time, if you look a bit closer, your bit, your role, is all down to you. It's all on you. The buck stops with you. If you keep up and don't fail, well done. Roll on another year of doing the exact same thing. But if you fail to keep up, then it's your fault. You are the teacher. You are to blame. You are the member of staff providing that support and delivering that intervention. If it somehow fails, does that reflect on you? Might you somehow be lacking? After all, you are wholly responsible for your performance and the 'performance' (progress, attainment, achievement, wellbeing, safety) of the children in your class. So, we perform. Might the very structure of having our own classes exacerbate the feeling of it all being down to us? We might not be able to change this, but might being aware of its possible impact help us with understanding any difficult feelings we might face? When you feel on your own with something hard, that's hard. Shame has this way of isolating. It whispers that you can't pull your weight, that you're not really part of the team, that you don't really belong. It blames and shames.

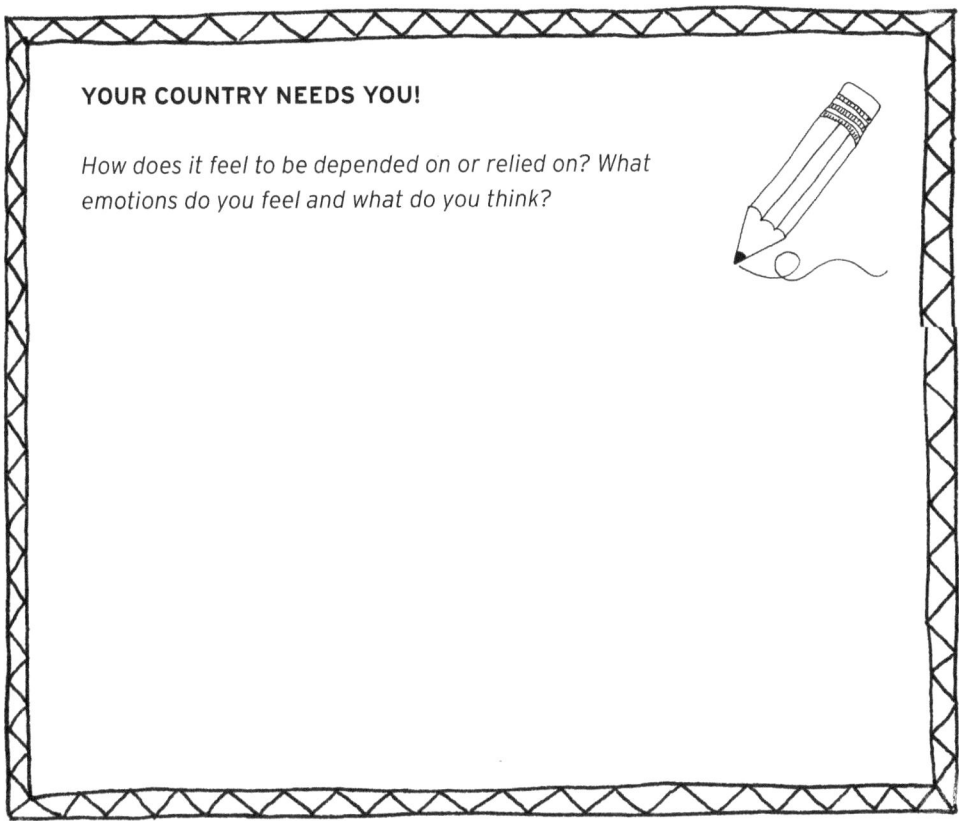

When it comes to safeguarding, we know that it is everyone's responsibility. It's not down to one person. We are all accountable and we all have eyes and ears and have a crucial part to play in keeping children safe. But there's also a but. Because when a child is in your classroom with you, that bit is down to you. We have all heard of when things go wrong, in lots of different occupations. We've heard of missed opportunities, investigations, inquiries and serious case reviews, and we feel sick every time. We can easily find ourselves asking the what ifs... What if that happened with a child I teach? What if I missed something? With safeguarding we can feel the pressure of things being down to us. We can feel the potentially accusing public finger-pointing of 'you're on your own, kid'.

And if it's all down to you, then you must...

Be Everything You Need

It's your responsibility after all. You might do collaborative planning, preparing and resourcing with your team, but you've got to bring the everything else-ing that you need. You've got to bring the pizazz, the energy, the commitment, the heart. You've got to bring everything into the room, into that space. And you're all too aware that everyone else is busy

BELONGING

Think of the others alongside you at work. How does this help remind you that it's not all just down to you? Where do you most feel a sense of belonging? What are some of the tangible things that help you see and know that?

trying to stay on top of what they need to do, so you've got to somehow get on with it and be all that you need in that moment, and all those moments that follow. Or if you've not got what you need, you've somehow got to *find* it from somewhere. But where to look?

The rumbling questions many of us have, deep down, are how can we be everything we need, when the needs are so great? How can we be everything we need when there is so much lack around us? When all the 'not enoughs' and the 'too much-ness' of it all are staring us in the face? When the new child who arrives midterm in our class has so many needs that we feel overwhelmed every day, but there's no give, there's no help and it really does feel like it's down to us, what can we do? Where can we go? In schools up and down the country we're often really really good at being a team, at stepping in and stepping up and supporting each other. But even so, there are times when we really do have to be everything we need, because there really is no one else around . . . and even if we just feel like we're on our own, if we feel we can't safely speak up about it, by default we end up having to be everything we need.

Often, the public message around funding is that we have enough. We have been funded, and we are equipped. Money has been given to education, so we must have everything we need. We now have enough. Except we all know that we don't. Might the political commentary around funding lend itself to the idea that if you don't feel like you have enough, or you don't have enough, then maybe that's somehow down to you? You're just not making good with what you have been given. If we don't have enough, we have to be everything we need and find what we need, and sometimes that means fighting for what we need or scrambling for what's left in the pot. But truth be told, we don't really like fighting. We intervene before there's even a hint of a fight in the playground. We'd much prefer to share and be kind, and for each of us to have what we need. In education, we don't call it fighting though, it's called competing. And it's supposed to be healthy . . . (unless you lose out).

Compete

On the one level it's all pretty harmless. With friendly rivalry between colleagues, we compete for house points and special awards, for the honour of the win. But there's a whole other level of competing going on too. Because of how things are measured and funded at national and local levels, we compete. It's built into the very structure of the system. In seeking to fill school places we compete for children and young people, because more filled spaces means more funding; we compete for ideas and budgets with colleagues, presenting our cases for priorities for action plans; we compete within different subject areas and departments in schools for more resources; we compete for our subject courses to run next year; we compete with our peers, with same-subject leads across different schools. We compete for reputation, for results, for progress. Surely we don't (but we do) compete between schools in our Academy Trusts, and across our Local Authorities. We compete in league tables, Ofsted inspections and reports. Head teachers are business leaders as well as educational leaders, and sometimes the two aspects clash. You really want to do this, but the budget doesn't allow. Or the business objectives of an Academy Trust have a particular focus that creates tension with an educational one. If money is a driver, this can clash with a deeply held belief around education and wellbeing. They can be opposing forces, and they compete. We don't always like to admit that we're competing, because it can all sound a bit ugly, but look carefully enough and we're probably aware of the desire or at least the need to win. The knives are out, the gloves are off, so to speak. Needs must, and all that.

When it comes to children, there's nothing wrong with competition you might say. We see this whole debate being played out in a primary school Sports Day. We have the old school races camp where there is a clear winner, with gold medal to boot, followed by second and third place runners-up who maybe get a certificate or at least a sticker. We also have the 'it's the taking part that's important' camp, where everyone is cheered, and positions are applauded from the point of view of effort and participation. Some say you can't all be winners, you have to experience losing; it's an important lesson in life. Life isn't fair. We've heard the arguments before and probably sit in one camp or other or somewhere in between.

But when it comes to competition within a nurturing system like education, in the practices that make it function, maybe competition has this way of pitching people against each other that might not always bring out the best in us. Competition lends itself to us trying to win, or at least not lose. It lends itself to us wanting to look good, or at least not look bad. It lends itself to us wanting to be right, or at least not wrong. If you look beneath the surface, it can isolate rather than create team. It can become a 'me versus you' thing without us even realising. If I am feeling under pressure to deliver, I won't want that to be seen, so I might inflate myself to try to make myself feel better. I might even inflate myself at your expense (discreetly, of course). If I'm trying really hard to meet that end-of-year expectation, and so is everyone else in my year group, what can surreptitiously happen is that rather than us being a team and working towards it together, the bit I play can become an individual thing, so rather than us achieving or not achieving this goal together, it becomes a 'you and me' dynamic. Often when we pitch ourselves against each other, shame and blame have crept into the mix.

Have you ever been in a school environment where everyone just knows who is or isn't in favour with the senior leadership or head teacher? Or where everyone just kind of knows, or thinks they know, who's doing a really good job and who's a bit on the weak side? That's an awkward and uncomfortable environment to work in. It doesn't feel safe for anyone, and it smacks of competition. You'll notice it in the undercurrent that can be felt in the staffroom or in unspoken vibes or quickly closed doors allowing certain people in and shutting others out. If you're on the winning side, you might feel quietly smug because the target's not on your back. But if you're not winning, then it's not so fun and it doesn't feel much like a team. Remember back in the day in PE lessons, that feeling of being the first or last (or somewhere in between) to be picked when team leaders were choosing their sporting team? There's shame right there. Were you chosen or were you part of the dregs, what was left over? Left out? That's what competition can do, and it happens on a big scale in our schools, because it's built into the way the education system works. You win at funding, you lose. You win at results, you lose. You win at reputation, you lose. So, we fight, we strain, we strive.

If there is this undercurrent of competing, then perhaps, too, there is an undercurrent of shame. If that all sounds a bit heavy, it can reveal itself in the most normal of ways. It can look like a member of staff leaning heavily on others to help them keep their own heads above water; it can look like not really working together to share ideas for fear someone will run off with your good one; it can look like wanting to be noticed and wanting to be seen to be doing a good job. All in a very cordial and British way of course, or at least most of the time. It can look like striving to get your reports in first or letting everyone know when you manage to get that 'notorious' parent on your side; it can look like a driven task-focused senior leader who makes things happen at the expense of others, scattering colleagues by the wayside. It can look like any number of things. If the education system itself breathes competition, it very easily breeds it, and a byproduct can be environments that are conducive to shame.

Every job has its targets to meet and competitive practices are intended to drive people to function at their best. But when shame is intrinsically present in our education system, that

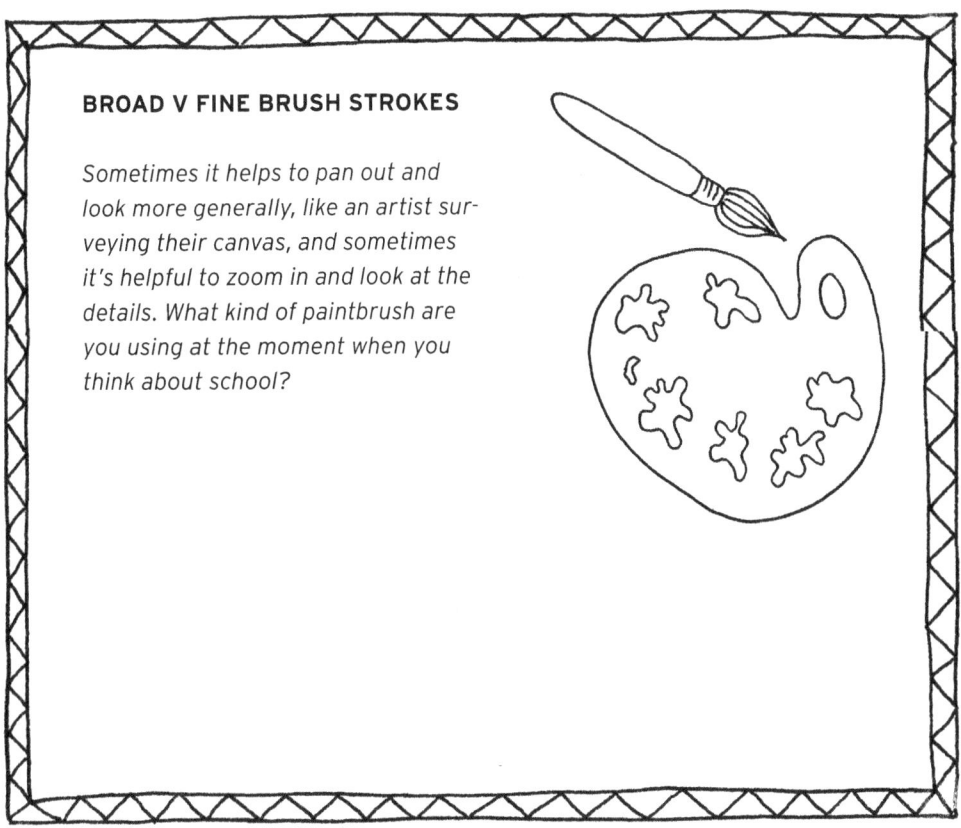

BROAD V FINE BRUSH STROKES

Sometimes it helps to pan out and look more generally, like an artist surveying their canvas, and sometimes it's helpful to zoom in and look at the details. What kind of paintbrush are you using at the moment when you think about school?

feels like it needs calling out. We've been calling it out for years now in the move towards more therapeutic ways of supporting children around behaviour; we've been calling it out in the valuing of individual effort, progress and resilience and the work towards inclusion. We're not about pitching children against each other when it comes to learning. We want every child to thrive and aim high and reach their potential, and that kind of growing happens when there is safety and trust. So, the same kind of environment is needed for adults too. If you look below the surface, competition has a way of undermining safety and trust in staff teams, not building people up . . . and when safety and trust are undermined, shame is often present. Feel the threat of losing, and what often goes with it hand in hand is a sense of having to prove yourself.

Prove Yourself

Evidence everything. So much of our time is taken up doing this. We have to evidence what we've planned and why, what we've taught and how we've taught it; we have to account for how we spend every moment of time in a school day, how we spend every penny and why; we have to evidence the whys and wherefores and progress towards our priorities and action plans; we have to record the content of conversations and discussions with colleagues and parents and children; we have to evidence the judgements we come to around children's learning levels. We have to prove ourselves. Might that deep down sometimes feel like we have to prove our worth? The powers that be say show me the evidence. Make a detailed case for what you say. It starts from the top. If, by way of the things we have to report on, what's communicated is 'these are things we have to prove,' might that trickle down into all the processes we put in place, and before we know it Academy Trust leads, senior leaders, parents and communities are using the same language too?

If you feel like you're having to prove yourself, what will often be lurking is the threat of feeling exposed and feeling shame. Under close examination we can feel like we have to defend ourselves. But we give children feedback to help them learn. We mark their work with them in a way to build them up and move them on. Why is it that, often, that nurturing side can feel like it's been missing when it comes to the scrutiny of *our* work? We work in a system where we are constantly marked and measured. With the current shift towards wellbeing, hopefully, accountability processes are now moving in a healthier direction, away from scrutiny with shame to scrutiny with support, a walking with or alongside, rather than a tripping up, a conversation rather than cold judgement. The tone of systems and practices is so important. The key to good accountability practices is when they're done in a context of safety and trust. Otherwise, they can easily become another weapon in the hands of shame.

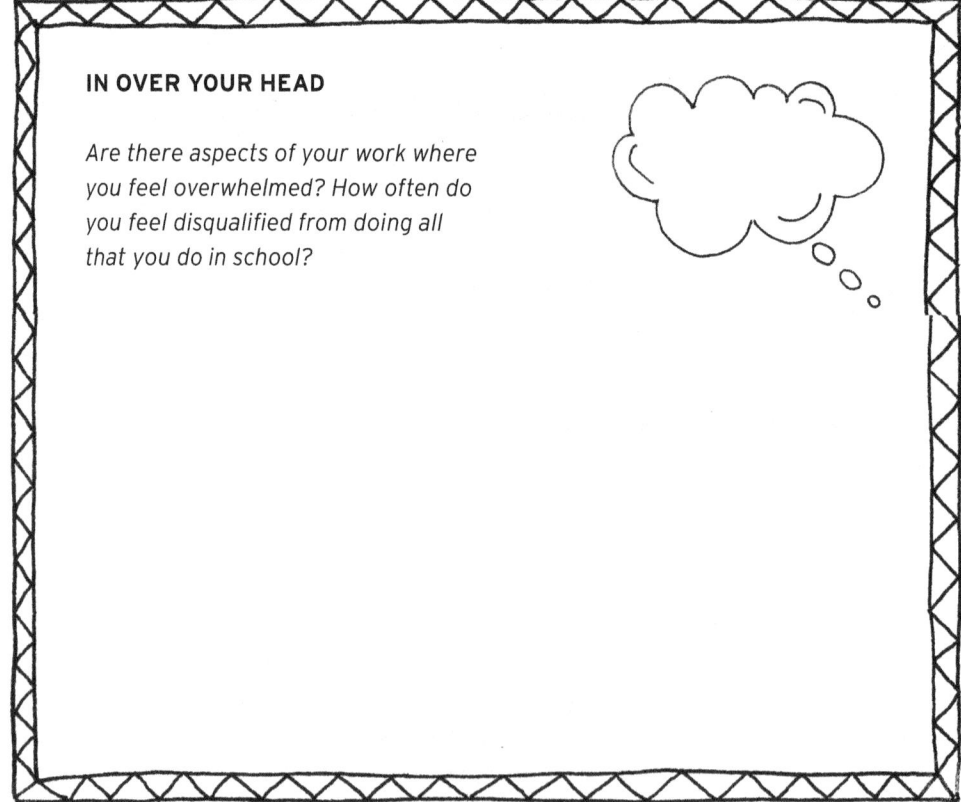

IN OVER YOUR HEAD

Are there aspects of your work where you feel overwhelmed? How often do you feel disqualified from doing all that you do in school?

You're Only Valued for What You Achieve, Not Who You Are

There is a danger with data driven accountability that you can feel unseen. That what you do becomes somehow incorporated into a percentage or reduced to a number or a carefully crafted phrase in a report. Where just your data is important . . . but people lose sight of you. Only some things will be measured, and those things that are measured might not be the things you deem most important; they're just what someone else thinks is the case. The message you can sometimes feel is that what's important is what you've achieved. Or rather, what your children have achieved. Forget about all the other things you input and bring value to in your school community, the relationships you establish, the connections you build, the words of encouragement you speak, the hope you bring, the lives you change. They might not be recorded in the league tables, but they're indelibly recorded in the lives of the people.

We say, this is what we've achieved! This, as well as all the other things. We have a far wider metric than others care to imagine. We have a more far-reaching field of vision. But sometimes these things can feel pushed aside or lost from view. It's always about what counts the most. The numbers? The people? We want it to always be about the people . . . and that includes us. We want our efforts to be seen, our voices to be heard. We want to be valued, even when it sometimes feels like the conditions around us whisper we're not . . . and so it goes on . . .

And This Is How It's Always Going To Be . . .

Regardless of policies, guidelines and ideas that come and go, you have this cohort of children now, and then there will be another and then another, and so it goes on. Regardless of what kinds of children you have, what needs they present, what kind of support and resources you have available, what expectations and pinch points you face or who else is on your team, each time you will do baseline assessments at the start of the year and will work from those towards aspiring targets, with a whole load of demands upon you. The school calendar is a cyclical one. So, this is how it's always going to be. There's a seasonality about it all. A beginning and an end. A rise and fall. A coming together and a parting. As we head towards the end of that final term and children prepare to move on to other classes, we gather together and remember and celebrate moments of triumph, and sometimes even then, with that last tired push over the line, we can have a rumbling question of what could have been, and did we really do enough?

When you feel end-of-term tired, it's easy to get to the end of yourself.

But before the summer term's even finished, you've met and are already starting to plan for the next cohort; you're pulling down old displays and putting up the start of new ones; you're clearing out cupboards and gathering new resources; you're camping between two rooms as you move your things around; you're prepping and thinking about how to meet the needs of the pupils who will be yours . . . and so it continues. Our project of teaching is never

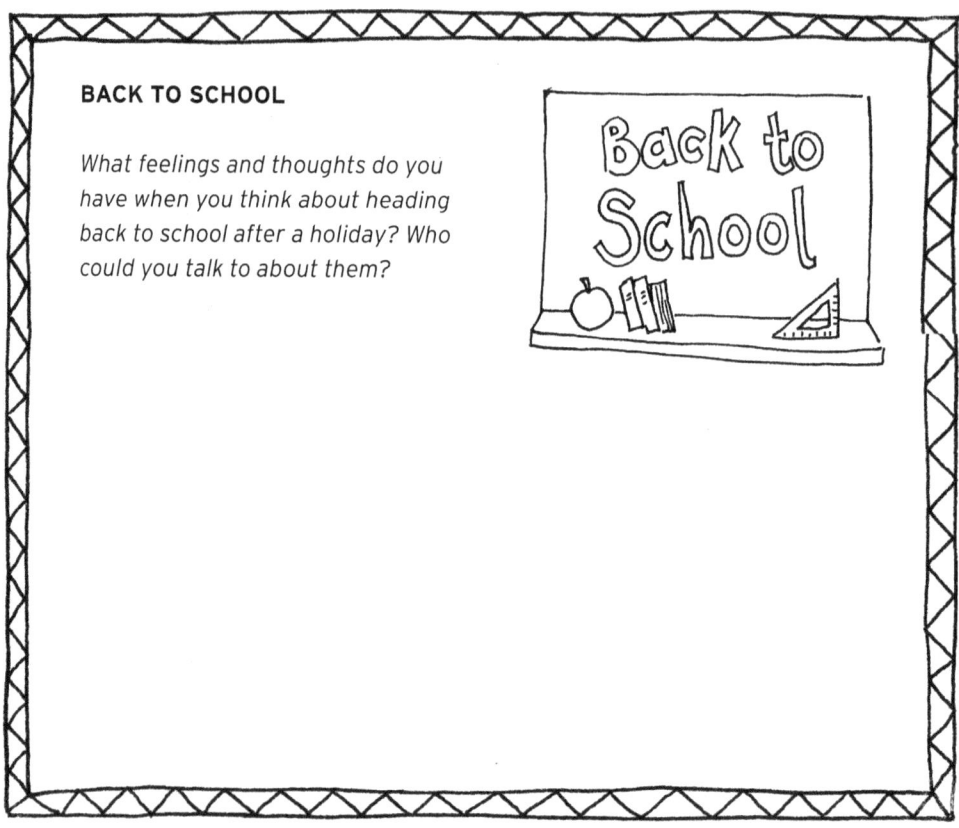

BACK TO SCHOOL

What feelings and thoughts do you have when you think about heading back to school after a holiday? Who could you talk to about them?

complete. We're forever starting again ... and that's the way it's always going to be. Usually, you don't get to see the long-term outcomes for the children you teach, but you do your bit and pass them on. Perhaps that's why it brings so much joy when a former pupil comes back to pay a surprise visit? They interrupt the cycle for a moment, and you get to hear a bit more of their journey, see some more of who they are becoming. You get to pause and know that you've been a part of their story ... and then they wave their goodbyes, and you marvel for a bit with a colleague as you reminisce over their time with you, and then you're off again, back on with the present.

Keep up, there's no place for failure, when it comes down to it you're on your own; be everything you need, compete, prove yourself; you're only valued for what you achieve not who you are ... All in all, that's a lot of subtle messaging we're walking alongside in the day-to-day of our jobs, and if that's the way it's always going to be, it's ok for that to sometimes feel a bit hard. It's ok if sometimes the pick-yourself-up-and-start-again-in-September feelings have something more of a plod about them rather than starting back with a spring in your step.

These messages are so inherent in our education system that they almost go unseen; they're camouflaged and hidden from view, but they're part of the very fabric of the system. The problem is that they have the capability of increasing feelings of not enough in the environments they create. Like mould that grows unnoticed, they can contaminate and put people at risk. Health and wellbeing can deteriorate over time, and you don't even know why. It can leave us wondering why we might sometimes be finding things hard, because we can't see what's going on underneath. And if you feel like you're the only one that feels that way, you can feel unseen. The way of our culture is that only bright and shiny people tend to be seen. If you're a bit on the dull side or in need of some work, you can get overlooked. But remember the names and faces of the children and families you've taught? You are valued. You are seen.

If we can find ways to safely speak up and share when we feel difficult feelings, that's got to be good for our wellbeing. It's got to be a better way of doing things. Sometimes we're not even sure what our feelings are but it feels like an ache inside.

That's a lot to think about. So maybe what's needed now is to . . .

*****Chat to a Friend*****

Safely Speak Up and Share

STARRY NIGHT

Imagine the sky on a clear night, full of stars. Little me in the grand scheme of things. How might this help give you some perspective of where you're at right now?

OUT OF YOUR DEPTH

Is there anywhere you feel out of your depth at the moment? In what way do you feel it the most? Can you think of a way to walk towards the shallow end a little? Could speaking to someone else be a way to do this? Who could you speak to?

NEST

A nest is a place of safety, provision, nurture and learning. Where or with whom can you find this sense of safety? What thoughts and feelings come to mind?

I AM A ROBOT

How much of what you do feels robotic? What thoughts and feelings come up for you when you consider this?

GO ON WITH THE SHOW

Think of a time when you felt like you had to do this. Did it end well or what might you have wanted to do differently? If so, what could that have looked like?

PUT DOWN

Think of a time when you've put someone else down, even if ever so discreetly, to make yourself feel a bit better about yourself? What triggered it? What was your inner narrative at the time?

PLEASE DO NOT SWEAR!

What does letting off steam look like for you? Do you do it in ways that are good for your wellbeing or ways that might be less healthy?

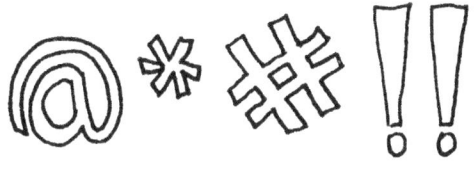

KEEP CALM AND CARRY ON

In what ways do you try to keep calm and carry on? What does that look like for you? Is there any balance you need to reset?

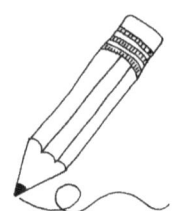

FEELING FRAGILE

What currently leaves you feeling fragile about school and the relationships within it? Who can you look to for support?

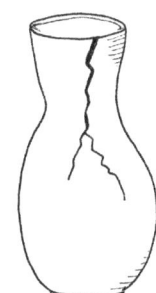

UNDER THE WEATHER

If you were to go to the doctors' for a checkup right now, what would you say about how you're doing? What advice do you think they might give?

COMFY OLD ARMCHAIR

Imagine curling up in a favourite old chair and feeling the safety of being there again. Allow your mind to wander. Write what you think and feel.

SUNDAY NIGHT FEELINGS

What would your Sunday night feelings be, if Sunday night was right now?

CANDLE

What brings light to the space around you when things feel a little dark?

GROUNDHOG DAY

Describe aspects of your job that you don't feel ever change. How does that leave you feeling and who could you talk to about it?

HOLD BACK THE RIVER

Think of a tidal wave approaching. What do you try to hold back to protect others from its impact? What do you notice about the toll that might be taking on you? Who could you speak to about this and what might you want to say?

BRAIN DUMP

What are you thinking? What are you feeling?

YOU ARE SEEN

References

Curran, T. (2024). *The perfection trap: The science of why we never feel enough* (pp. 16, 18). Scribner.
Department for Education. (2011). *Teachers' standards*. https://www.gov.uk/government/publications/teachers-standards#full-publication-update-history
Dweck, C. (2017). *Mindset: Changing the way you think to fulfil your potential* (6th ed.). Robinson.
Edmondson, A. (2023). *Right kind of wrong: The science of failing well*. Simon + Schuster LLC.

PART III
Doing Better With All the Stuff

5
Let's Talk About Shame

Introducing Shame

We talk a lot about resilience in teaching and thriving in the face of adversity. It all sounds very strong and superhero-like. But the truth is sometimes we don't feel very strong at all. Sometimes we just feel up against it. Adverse weather comes in on all fronts and we bear the brunt of it. We feel its full force. So, to weather the storm we wear the gear we need. We have a whole wardrobe of different outfits and life-saving equipment to draw on, so that we can select what we need and wear the right clothing for the elements. We get so practised at it that when we don our protective layers, some of what we wear fits us so close to the skin we don't even know we're wearing it. It's just part of who we are and how we function.

As teachers and support staff, we show remarkable resilience with everything we face every day. Just think about the pressures of safeguarding, managing pupil behaviour and monitoring children's wellbeing, let alone everything else. Our passion, commitment, creativity and heart, our sense of vocation all keep us in the game when we're faced with the reality of our day-to-day challenges. But over time, it can take its toll. We talk about stress and workload and all the obvious not enoughs and too muchness of our roles because these things are very real, but what we don't often talk about is how we can feel in the face of these things … and even if we're starting to get better at that, what we're sometimes totally oblivious to is the underhand work of shame in it all. What feelings do you become aware of when you hear the words Could Do Better? What thoughts come to mind? If you feel an ache, a wrench in your gut, an averting of your eyes, a sense that you want to shout off, shut off, shut down or shut up then it's possible that shame is around. Shame can creep up on us in all sorts of ways.

So what is shame?

Researcher and sociologist Brene Brown talks about the differences between shame and guilt. She says (2013b),

> I believe that guilt is adaptive and helpful – it's holding something we've done or failed to do up against our values and feeling psychological discomfort. I define shame as

the intensely painful feeling or experience of believing that we are flawed and therefore unworthy of love and belonging – something we've experienced, done, or failed to do makes us unworthy of connection.

Perhaps those words feel a bit big and heavy and that they surely have nothing to do with us as we read them, but what if they actually do? If I can't keep up or prove myself or be the everything I need to be, all the time in school, then I'm guilty as charged. I can't do all these things all the time, even when I might try my darnedest to. But when I think about these things what surfaces for me? Guilt or shame? It is often summarised, guilt is 'I did something bad,' whereas shame is 'I am bad.' There's a very real difference between the two. Reflecting on Brown's definition, if we think about the climate within which we work, we can sometimes feel like we're failing. It can feel like there are lots of things we have failed to do. We've failed to turn things round; we've failed to meet the needs of that child ... Maybe what we sense is that education has failed that child, that education has let that child slip through the cracks, that the system has failed them, but we can't help but think that we are somehow a part of that, and we have had a part to play, and we have fallen short. We are flawed (or is that floored?). What if, with the magnitude of what is asked of us every day, we feel that we have *failed to do* what is required of us ... and maybe we've not just failed to do it once, but we fail to do it time and time again? We cannot do all that is required of us, all that is expected of us all of the time, because it is not possible to, but if in our mind's eye our *we cannot do* equals *we fail to do*, this can trigger shame that we might well also feel in other areas of our lives. Shame is a deeply personal, felt thing. The narrative goes, I am not up to the job, I am not up to scratch, who am I to think I can do this? Who am I to think I can make a difference? If those words sound familiar, if they're what we sometimes think (and feel in our bodies), it's likely that shame is somewhere in the mix. Churchill and Musters state that 'shame triggers self-condemnation, self-criticism and the desire to hide' (2019). Left unchecked, it has a way of causing havoc within our communities. So, what if shame is hiding in plain sight in our workplaces? What if some of the hard things we face and feel in schools are insidiously connected with shame? What if they are deeply connected with how we view ourselves? What if it's not just what we do that sometimes feels like it's not enough, but it's more that we ourselves are not enough? Or that we ourselves are too much, to really be able to keep on offering ourselves to this thing, or really belong in this community?

Factors like our early childhood development, our experience of attachment and life experiences play a huge part in our resilience and the impact shame can have on us. Research suggests that some of us are more predisposed to the impact of shame than others. Some of us seem to fundamentally need the right conditions to thrive, whereas some seem more able to thrive wherever they are (Thomas Boyce, 2019). But shame is all around us. Regan (2023) refers to different factors that can affect the levels of shame that we feel. These can include age and gender, family background, work status, financial situations, being a parent or not, physical and mental health, stereotypes and unhelpful labelling, body image, religious beliefs, trauma and surviving trauma and compulsive behaviours. Shame can be triggered in all kinds of life experiences, and no two people are the same. It has a way of showing up in all kinds of places and it's sticky. If you feel it in one way in your life it doesn't take long for it to stick to you in others, and it has a habit of getting us stuck. We get stuck with inner narratives that are not helpful or hopeful, and we find it difficult to move past all the 'stuckness' towards healthier things. We're getting better at noticing it in the lives and experiences of the children we teach, and the families we support, but there's still some work to do in being aware of it in ourselves and the way we work with each other. Even with all the recent good work around wellbeing in schools, all the moving in the right direction, there's work to do in calling out the part that shame often has to play in our interactions and environments, if we are to do and be better.

The problem is this work is hard. When it comes to shame, we have a built-in survival response to it. Our brains are literally hardwired to run away, hide and cover it up. We will do anything to resist, to not feel it. So, if in this moment you notice a pushback, an inner resistance even as you read these words, I urge you to stick with me for a moment and invite you to tentatively go on this journey together. You may not even be able to put words to what you feel, but you feel something, nonetheless. In all this there's a balance to be had. Because the effects of shame can sometimes feel debilitating. Is there a way that we can call shame out into the open, examine it from some kind of safe-ish distance and begin to recognise its impact on us? Is there a way we can begin to acknowledge it in ourselves, in our settings, and then maybe find ways in which we can respond when it's around? It's important to see the games it plays, because at the end of the day, shame devalues. It robs us of any sense of worth. Any shame you feel is not the end of you. You are worth so much more than you may think. You are worth so much more than you may ever fully know. If we really understood how much we are worth, it would be like solid ground to walk on, fresh air to fill our lungs and songs of joy on our lips.

When it comes to teaching and working in schools, it can start at the very beginning. A few years in, and sometimes we can feel a disparity between what we hoped the job would be and what it sometimes is, and we can find ourselves holding the two in tension. The hope and the lack. If that sense of deficit shifts from being something we face to something that is inherently about us, shame might well have come riding in. The problem is me. I'm not enough. Maybe I'm the one who should just be doing better? That's the way the shame voice goes . . . and as we carry on in the job, the good stuff continues and so does the hard, and sometimes we have to learn, and keep on learning to reset the balance. Because heavy things have a way of weighing things down and loud things have a way of drowning other things out. Sometimes all we can hear is that we're not enough. Not now, not ever, no matter how hard we try, no matter how much we give, we won't ever be enough. The powers that be, the system itself, always asks for more, requires more, always whispers that we could do better, and many of us carry this around with us without even realising. Carry it around long enough and we can begin to feel other things, like there's not enough hope, not enough peace, not enough stability and maybe even that things don't feel that safe right now. We don't feel that safe right now. No matter how much people say to just bring your 'good enough,' sometimes it can still feel like that's not enough when everything around you is always asking for more.

Maybe we prefer to use the language of stress instead. We're more familiar with this vocabulary. So, for the moment let's leave the rumble of shame in the distance, like the hum of a fridge that you can kind of filter out but if you shut down all the noise and listen carefully is still there. With that hum in our ears, let's consider how we cope with stress . . .

A People Under Stress

Let's be honest. With everything we've considered up to now, a lot of the time we're under stress.

Most of us are probably aware of the illustration of people being like containers. As we face different things, as we experience different stressors, as we contain different things, our containers fill up, a bit more here and a bit more there. Over time, if there is no outlet, levels increase to a point when our container is full, our capacity is reached and stuff spills out. Maybe we find ways to let out some of the pressure as it builds, and then we carry on. We might have different capacities as different people; we might have different capacities in different seasons of life, and sometimes we might only become aware of our capacity when adversity comes our way, and we realise we are full and cannot take that much more.

Consider how full your container is right now. Consider what you're holding or containing. You might be holding some of the difficult things the children in your class are facing. You might be holding the anticipated stress of a conversation you need to have with a colleague. You might be holding stuff for others in your staff teams, like the weight of a parent/teacher dynamic, or the gravity of a child's medical needs. By the very fact that our roles are nurturing and protective of children and young people, this makes for a ripe environment for stress, regardless of any additional specific stressors we may face . . . and however full your container is with school stuff, there's also all the out-of-school things that we hold too. There's no separating the two. There's no other container for the out-of-school stuff. It all gets lumped together in one big bucket, all sloshing around in the mix. So, what are your stress levels right now? What's on your plate? What have you got your hands full with? What are you up to your eyes in?

How about looking at it a different way . . . What are your overriding feelings on a Sunday evening, just anticipating your going back to work in the morning? What do you feel when you think about it? What do you notice in your body, and what words come to mind? Perhaps there's a real mix. Maybe you're looking forward to delivering that particular lesson this week, or working on that particular project or unpacking that specific concept. Or maybe you're looking forward to seeing that child building on the confidence they're beginning to gain. But maybe you're also dreading a child potentially being dysregulated again, or you're hoping against hope that you won't have to be treading on eggshells with that parent or that colleague. Some of the sources of stress will be obvious to us, whereas others may be more hidden. It can do us well to sit with our Sunday night feelings long enough to take a look at them and ask ourselves why we might be feeling some of the things we do. In so doing, we may be able to identify more of the stressors we face.

CONTAINERS

How full is your container right now? How much is it holding? If it's full, that sometimes looks like us trying to hold everything together. What might that look like for you?

Often, we notice the stress we're under. Perhaps we notice it in our minds and our bodies, or in our families and friendships. Perhaps we notice it in the snap of our tongue, our welling up at something so small or our reaching for another glass. Perhaps we're in such a cycle with it all that it just seems to perpetuate the stress all the more. Stress is a greedy monster that likes to be fed. Maybe stress has been part of the job for so long that it's even something of a badge of honour, and we wear it with some kind of distorted pride. Were it to leave our side, what would that look like, and what would we be left with? Who would we be and would we be enough? And in that moment, perhaps we feel the full force of shame with its accusing finger, so we shut down the conversation and carry on with the stressing.

When we experience stress, our bodies go into a higher state of alert. When the conditions we crave and need as human beings, such as to be seen, safe, soothed and secure, are under threat, our automatic fight, flight and freeze responses kick in to try to protect us from perceived or actual threat. Shame has a way of activating our stress responses and because we feel unsafe, we find ourselves trying to alleviate the things we feel in all sorts of ways. When we come up against shame, we typically respond in three ways. We move towards, move away or move against others (Brown, 2013a). We use all kinds of subtle and not-so-subtle coping mechanisms that we often couch in perfectly acceptable ways and these behaviours just become part of the culture in which we work. Using Brown's language as headers, here are some of the things we do.

Move Away

We withdraw; we hide; we distance ourselves from others, and at work, that might look like distancing ourselves from our colleagues. Maybe we literally physically withdraw and stay in our classrooms most lunchtimes under the guise of doing some marking or prepping something for later. Of course there are always jobs to do and these things still need to be done, but if we take a closer look, maybe we're sometimes not just getting some headspace or a bit of quiet or getting ahead of the game, maybe we just can't face being with everyone in the staff room when everyone else seems to be doing ok but we don't feel like we are. Perhaps we find ourselves disengaging from conversation with others. Maybe we don't have any real interest in the lives of our colleagues; maybe we find it hard to consider that any of them could be genuine friends; maybe we just can't bring ourselves to join in with spontaneous or planned fun. Maybe we make it into the staff room but keep ourselves to ourselves, sitting on the periphery. Maybe we become more rigid and set in our ways, with an 'I just work my hours' mantra, where there's no give or take and less and less flexibility around what we do. Maybe we create hard and fast rules for us that we won't budge on, regardless of the circumstances. Maybe out of principle, we would never come in for a day in the holidays to get our classroom ready even if that would actually really help us, or others.

Maybe we just get our heads down and do what we need to do on our own, and in so doing miss out on the help, support and camaraderie that can come from doing things with others as a team. In our moving away, maybe we feel more and more disconnect with people, and that then becomes more and more disconnect from the cause, and we begin to lose sight of why we came into the job, and why we care. Maybe we become less and less motivated and put things off to the last minute or procrastinate to such an extent that we put ourselves under more pressure as we get closer to a deadline. Maybe we have a growing reluctance to go on or genuinely engage in training, and maybe that contributes to a sense of feeling or becoming de-skilled. Maybe we begin to under-function and do just enough to get by. As we become more emotionally isolated from others, maybe our anxiety rises and over time we see it affecting our mood, our energy levels, capacity and functioning. When our response to shame is to move away, as we become (and feel) more and more isolated, it only amplifies the silence around us and propels our feelings of shame all the more. Moving away can feel lonely.

Move Towards

When it comes to battling with shame, another mode of defence is the secret or sometimes not-so-secret art of people-pleasing. We work, and we work hard. We jump through hoops to meet targets, to meet expectations, to please people. Maybe we're always the first to arrive and the last to leave. Maybe we do ever-so-meticulous planning; maybe our action plan targets are always keenly and consistently met. Maybe our results are exceptional; maybe our lessons are always inspiring, compelling and super shiny. Maybe our reports are always completed well within the deadline of when they need to be written, or maybe they're the ones that are held up as exemplars for others; maybe our classroom displays are always immaculate and a source of dynamic learning for the children. We're loved by parents. We're the teacher they're always so pleased to get when children find out who they're going to have next year, and we feel the love. And so, the cycle continues. We keep pleasing others. We are buoyed by the affirmation we receive, and we work harder.

Maybe we rarely take a day off, even if we're ill. Maybe we go above and beyond to make things happen, maybe we always go the extra mile; maybe we say yes to anything and everything, even if we don't really have the time or energy. But in doing all of this, maybe that means work tends to take over and we don't have sufficient boundaries to keep it in place when we get home, which might mean staying up late into the night again to finish that planning or cutting short that weekend family gathering because we've just got to get that thing done. Maybe we work part-time, but our three-day paid week looks more like five full days of work with all the preparation and extras. Maybe we don't make a big song and dance about it, but we do all the extras in secret. Maybe we over-function, driven by perfectionism, by the desire to get things right and look good, without even realising. We want to do our best; we care about the children; maybe we even care too much. But we are good at what we do. We work hard, and then we work harder. All the time. Dedicated and efficient.

Sometimes it's hard to spot shame at play when things are just so good. Too good.

And for a while we have boundless energy and enthusiasm, until one day we don't.

What if one day we just can't keep it all up anymore? What if everything has somehow gotten out of balance, so off-kilter? What if we find we have reached our capacity, and we have nothing more to give? If for our own sanity we had to stop working so incredibly hard, might we wonder if we are credible anymore? What might not striving for perfection do to us inside, and could we even contemplate such a thing?

If our sense of self and our sense of worth is wrapped up in what we do, we can quickly find ourselves overworking, with limited boundaries, where life is consumed by the demands of the job. If work takes over our hearts and minds and time and space, it can feel like this *is* actually all we do and there is nothing outside of it in our lives. Our identity becomes so inextricably linked to our roles that maybe it's difficult to even know who we are outside of the job. That might sound extreme, but it happens. And if you live and breathe the job, then when things are difficult, or if things go wrong or get messy, then *everything* is a mess, and it impacts you deeply. What about if everything you have invested in is one day brought into question or trashed, taken out of proportion or lost in a moment in an inspection report, or at least that's how it feels? What happens when your life investment is hung out to dry, and all your hopes and dreams with it? Maybe you've vowed you're never going to let that happen to you. You're never going to be consumed by the job. Even so, the pressure and the demands on us can still very easily push us in that overworking direction, especially if shame drives us to please or appease those around us.

Move Against

Sometimes in a bid to keep shame at bay, instead of moving towards others, we move against. It's like we go on the offensive or take a fighting stance without even knowing. Maybe we compete or undermine, criticise or point the finger or come across all passive aggressive with others. A telltale sign is that we find ourselves doing or saying things that can create shame in others, whilst trying to combat our own feelings of shame. Maybe we don't say anything out loud, but we *think* it; maybe what we say has a sarcastic edge to it. Maybe our move against is against the system. We don't give new guidance or initiatives a chance; we don't give new people a chance. Maybe we huff and puff and make it clear we're not happy; we'll toe the line this time, but someone owes us. Maybe we focus on the brokenness of the climate we work in, to avoid looking at any inner shame we might feel. We blame, to shield ourselves from what we feel. If we can be cross about something else, we can have a united front with others and then don't have to look at or feel so much of the shame that is hammering at our door. Trying to build ourselves up by knocking others down is a fragile way to build a community. It doesn't grow trust or security. It doesn't feel safe. It feels like cliques and them and us. It doesn't feel like together.

We will do everything we can to avoid feeling shame, because it renders us feeling totally emotionally exposed. Encountering shame, feeling shame is not just a cerebral thing, it's something we literally feel in our bodies, and so bringing hidden things out into the light can feel shameful, and shame filled. We don't like it. It feels uncomfortable ... and we feel bare. Maybe even now you notice you're feeling a bit uncomfortable or unsettled. Shame is a powerful thing. It takes courage to bring it out into the open.

The Emperor's New Clothes

Do you remember the tale of 'The Emperor's New Clothes' by Hans Christian Andersen (1943)? A couple of con artists come into town claiming to be weavers of the finest cloth. In fact, they are spinning a yarn and there is no cloth. The story goes that the cloth is so exquisite that only people who are skilled or fit for their posts can see it. People who can't see the cloth are those who are unfit for their jobs. So, the tale speaks of advisers and courtiers to the emperor, feigning their delight at the beautiful clothes that have been made for him, when in fact there are no clothes at all. The townspeople continue with the pretence to the point that the emperor parades through the streets supposedly dressed in his new finery, when in fact he is clothed in nothing but his underwear. It is only when a child calls out what's going on that the truth is exposed.

Could we draw parallels between this tale with shame and the hard stuff of working in schools? What if we are sometimes the ones who seek to dress ourselves up and put on ever more elaborate costumes, covering up our shame and telling ourselves we've got this and we're ok, and it all looks good? Everyone else always goes along with it and says the same thing too, so we all kind of almost believe it. But then one day something happens, and the truth is out. We're not really ok and we don't really feel fit for our posts, and we find

CHESSBOARD

In what situations do you typically find yourself moving towards, away or against others? Think of a situation where you have done one of these things. Write about what led up to it, what you thought and felt in that moment, and what you did in response to those feelings. If you wish you had shown up differently, what might that have looked like?

ourselves standing butt naked in the street, with everyone looking and standing aghast. Perhaps up until recently everyone's been pretending schools are ok; the whole system's been saying it. Any notion of anything being untoward has been swept under the carpet by those lining the route. But now it's being called out. Wellbeing is on the agenda, it's in the public eye, and maybe something of the shame we can carry is now too out in the open. What's been before has been a bit of a fraud. The clothes we were all wearing were see-through all along, but no one had felt able to say. Maybe now the truth is out and there's no turning back.

The problem with shame is that we get into the habit of clothing ourselves with all sorts of things, to distract us and distract others from what's really going on underneath. Hey, I love that new scarf! Or those shoes are amazing! We comment on the exterior when perhaps on the inside things feel very different. It's like when someone asks you how you are, and you automatically say 'fine,' when actually you're anything but . . . Yet you somehow manage to carry it off, or at least you think you do, but really something deep within you wants to say how you really feel. Shame is a powerful thing, and it impacts our wellbeing, and affects how we show up with others. In the face of shame, we can make any or all of the three moves. We can move away, towards or against. What tends to be your go-to move? And how does that play out for you? What might this all look like for us in school?

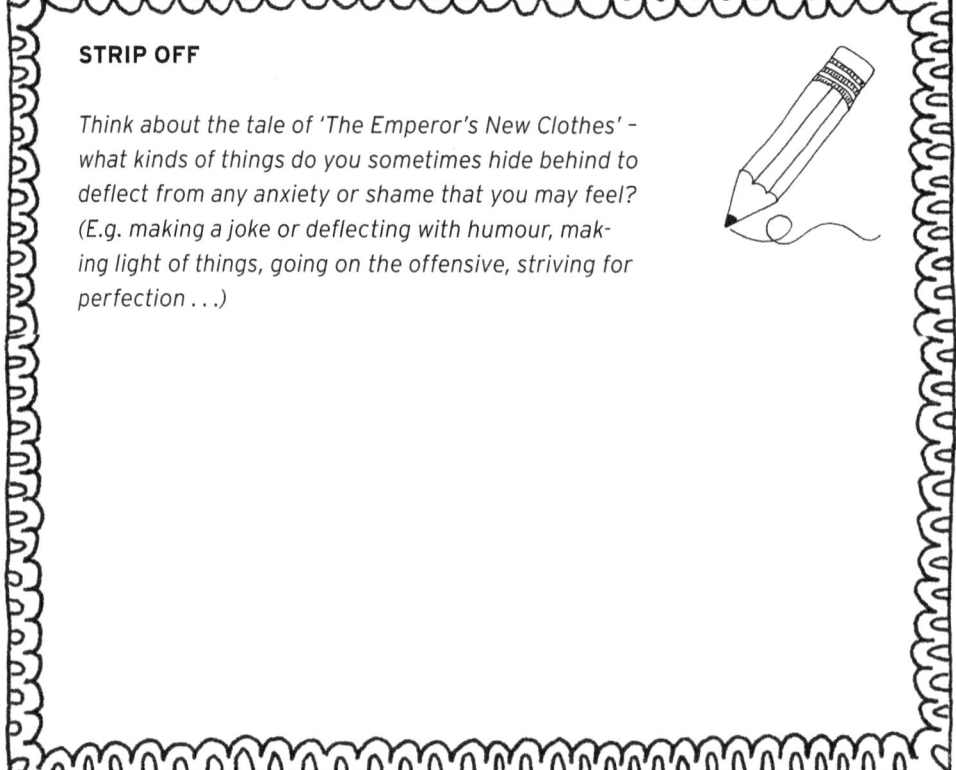

STRIP OFF

Think about the tale of 'The Emperor's New Clothes' – what kinds of things do you sometimes hide behind to deflect from any anxiety or shame that you may feel? (E.g. making a joke or deflecting with humour, making light of things, going on the offensive, striving for perfection . . .)

Day-to-day Examples

Do you notice any feelings of shame rising in you in your workplace? Do you notice how you respond when you feel under threat? Do you see what defence mechanisms come into play for you, and do you notice what triggers them? These are all important questions to ask ourselves if we're going to look at the place of shame in our places of work. But where do we even start? It doesn't have to be with the big things. In fact, it's often in the little things that we become aware of shame being at play. It's when we suddenly realise that our reaction is disproportionate to the 'crime,' that we've maybe somehow been offended by something that others might not even notice.

Imagine these scenarios. A timetable change has failed to be communicated to you. Maybe the room you'd booked out for an intervention is now being used by someone else. You walk in with a group of children, and you have to turn round and walk straight back out again and try to find somewhere else to work. Maybe you find somewhere else quickly and the inconvenience is soon forgotten. It was just an oversight, a communication blip. But maybe this is not the first time it's happened, and there's a lingering unpleasant taste in your mouth which you can't seem to get rid of, and it kind of feels like you were forgotten or overlooked, or swept aside and you don't matter. Maybe you rock up to the hall with your class for an assembly but no one else is there. Everyone else seemed to get the memo except you. Or maybe someone said they'd get that document to you by Monday, but they still haven't, and now what you have to do is going to be delayed, and that's going to put pressure on a whole load of other people. Maybe if it was anyone else it would be ok, but this person's not getting round to it yet - feels like it's got a bit of a sting to it - and what you're left with is thinking that you don't matter. So, the sting stings, and instead of putting something on it to calm it down, you let it get angry.

How about another scenario? What about when you know you're going to be observed by members of the senior leadership team or governors, or colleagues from another school within your Trust? How do you feel in the run-up to that? What kinds of things go through your head? You want what you've planned to go well, you want the children to behave and learn. You want them to say the right things to the people who question them about their learning. There's a sense of pressure for most of us when someone is watching. We want to impress or at least be competent, because it says something about us. It says something about whether we have the right to be here doing this job. It says something about whether we fit here. If you've ever felt imposter syndrome, you'll know you question how you got to be doing the things that you do. You disqualify yourself from the position you're in or the role that you have, and the fear is that you'll one day be found out. When shame comes to play, it's not so much 'what will they think of my teaching?' but 'what will they think of me?' So, you work harder to excel, you work harder to please, to stay in people's good books.

What about moderation? Peers sharing best practice, peers supporting each other and making decisions together, peers holding each other accountable and making professional judgements. Surely that should feel like safe practice? But it only really feels safe if you feel safe with the people you do it with, if you trust and respect each other. Moderation feels like more of a difficult thing if you're sitting alongside a colleague you've had disagreements with in the past, or with someone with whom you just don't get on or with someone who you fear will just drown you out. So maybe you don't speak up as much as you might in other situations. Maybe you hold back from sharing your opinion, for fear you'll be knocked down or knocked out. All sorts of dynamics can go on in conversations and discussions, and where there might be disagreement, shame might well rear its head.

What about if you're finding a child's behaviour challenging? What if the child's anxiety is increasing and they are becoming dysregulated? That process might happen in an instant or it might happen over a period of time, but all the while it's likely that as their anxiety is rising, so is yours. Inside you're hoping beyond hope that one of the strategies you're using to try to de-escalate the child and the situation will actually work. What if while this is all happening a colleague comes along and offers to help? How do you view that offer? Are you relieved and see it as you both working as a team? Or might you feel a touch of embarrassment, and wonder if they think that somehow you weren't quite up to the job, but they were? You are flawed and they are not. Boom! And before you know it, shame has thrown its sucker punch and we're somehow left reeling inside. All alone. Can you see how subtly shame can get in on the action? Can you see how it can just piggyback on any other shame we might feel?

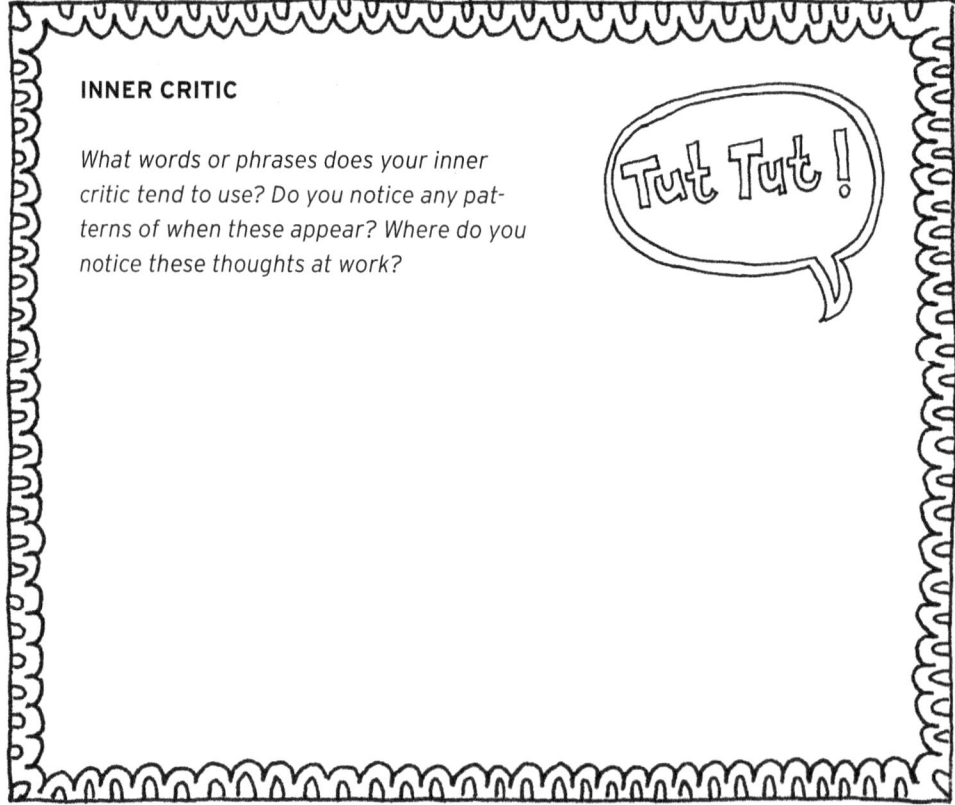

Let's Talk About Shame   143

And if your class are the ones that are not making as much progress across the cohort, or are letting the side down with their behaviour, do you notice the difficult feelings you might feel? Do you notice what you might be thinking around it all?

So how are you doing right now? How long have you been in the game? Are you soldiering on? Are you tired? Sick? Stuck? Are you checking out or on the verge? Or maybe you're inspired, passionate and leading the way. Wherever you're at, if we're going to take staff wellbeing seriously, we have to be aware of shame and its impact on us and those around us. It feels vulnerable to acknowledge shame. It feels dangerous to look it in the eye. It's a daring thing to call it out when we've been more accustomed to covering it up or hiding it away. Brown (2013a) says, 'Vulnerability sounds like truth and feels like courage. Truth and courage aren't always comfortable, but they're never weakness.' So, if we're to consider shame and vulnerability, we're not going to be in for a comfortable ride. But if we venture bravely on the journey, it's one that does well for our wellbeing. Because it's one that helps us know that we're not alone.

The Cycle of Shame

We've said before that shame is sticky. It sticks around and sticks to us and its fingerprints and mucky marks can be found all over the place. Your shame can very quickly become my shame without me even knowing. A parent's shame can weigh us down; a child's shame can be projected onto us so that we feel totally de-skilled in a moment. Shame has a way of being passed on and coming round again and again. How about these for some examples?

Kell (2018) mentions how we can pass on passion or stress to the children we teach. So, a people under pressure can pass it on. Let's think about exams for a moment, or tests. Baseline tests are fine. We're just measuring each child's starting point. But anything after that, well that includes us. That includes our input, our expertise, our effort. That somehow measures us . . . and will we be enough? Will we be up to scratch? Subconsciously, we can pass on the pressure of this to the children we teach, in the form of shame. If they don't do enough, achieve enough, it reflects on us. We try not to pass this on, of course, especially when children are younger. Maybe we're very careful with our language and we call optional end of Year 2 SAT assessments 'quizzes' or activities, to try to avoid creating a climate of pressure, but we still do practice papers and want each child to do their best on the day. When it comes to Year 6 children there'll no doubt be more practising in the run-up to their end-of-year assessments. Maybe these results count for more, and the pressure feels greater in an environment that already feels stretched. When numerous stress factors are pressing in on us, and when shame is on the prowl, we can pass it on. If we're not careful, in the heat of the moment we can deploy 'shame full' tactics if we ourselves feel at risk of shame.

'Shame Full' Messaging

Just think about the messages we looked at earlier that we can feel in the education system. Keep up, there is no place for failure; when it comes down to it, you're on your own; be everything you need; compete; prove yourself; you're only valued for what you achieve, not who you are; this is how it's always going to be. Older pupils studying for their exams before they leave school might well feel the weight of these very same messages. However nurturing we may be, however holistic our curriculum, however good our pastoral care systems, young people working towards their public exams will experience the pressure of having to keep up with the content and pace of their subject lessons. They will be told repeatedly that they need to keep up with revision if they are to attain the targets they have been set or attain what they are capable of. The pressure is well and truly on. In an attempt to motivate pupils who are late to the game, it's easy for us to communicate a sense of urgency that can overload those students that are already working hard. We feel the pressure. Results reflect on us and our professional expertise, as well as our personal review targets and career-development opportunities. Results reflect on schools and reputation and uptake and funding. Try as we might to assure young people that their exams are just a stepping stone for what they will go onto next, and that there are always other opportunities, and that they are worth far more than what they achieve, individual voices saying these things are very easily lost in the general anxiety that surrounds exam season. You just need to walk into a secondary school and sit in with some Year 11's to literally feel the tension in the air. Many of us will know from our own experience that people overcome failure; people survive the disappointment of lower grades and are worth more than a graded number or letter. We might try to communicate these things, but all the messages of our performance-driven education system say otherwise. Young people can have all the support from good staff teams and peer mentorship programmes, but for a student at the end of the day it is only them that's going to be sitting that paper. On exam day they are actually on their own, and they will have to be everything they need. Like it or not, they'll be competing against thousands of others across the country and so they will have to prove themselves, and unless there is a radical overhaul of the education system, this is how it's always going to be. The shame-based messages that we can feel as staff can be felt by our students too, however much we try to protect them.

What about when we throw parental expectations into the mix? We see some parents getting tutors for their children at a young age, if they fear their child is struggling with their learning. If parents have very high aspirations and expectations of their children's achievements, they can inadvertently or very obviously put excessive pressure on their children to gain good qualifications. Perhaps all those shame-based messages are very real things for the parent themselves, and so their children's results become an extension of their own self-esteem. What about parents who leave school without any qualifications, or those who live in areas with high poverty and deprivation factors? How might their experiences impact on their children's experience of education, and where might shame be at play? If generations of families fail in the education system, might this perpetuate a sense of institutional shame within whole communities? If children, young people and entire families become marginalised over generations, that's a long hard road of walking with, supporting and empowering fragmented people and communities, of forging connections where there have been years of disconnect.

Shame and Pupil Behaviour

What if we move away from results and expectations and look instead at pupil behaviour? Shame engages smear tactics. It speaks of being smeared with something, and we tend to use the word 'smear' when the product that's being used is not very nice. Historically (and shamefully), shame has shaped a lot of the way adults manage children's difficult behaviour. Think of the use of peer pressure: stand in the corner, face the wall or the dunce's hat. With trauma perceptive practice and relational therapeutic approaches more recently reshaping thinking and policy, echoes of less helpful practices still remain, but perhaps in less overt forms. Current practices in some schools still include behaviour management systems that carry undertones of shame without people realising. For example, putting a child's name on the board as a warning, moving steps down the rewards ladder or having rewards removed publicly. The problem with these systems is that power and shame are at play, instead of fostering prosocial behaviour and boundaries that are nurtured through relationships. Crudely put, when you're under pressure, or when you feel at risk of shame yourself, sometimes it can still be a case of 'your behaviour has made me feel small, so I'll look big in my response to you, so you feel small' . . . and so, the cycle of shame continues.

Think about what we acknowledge and communicate as achievements in our schools. What does something as simple as 'have a sticker' communicate, where we are the ones saying that a child has earned one (and others have not, by their sticker's absence)? How might shame be at play here? What if we were to say everyone gets a sticker and 'you put it by the piece of work you most love or think is your best this week,' and then we talk about it? How could that work? How much more meaningful could that be? If we're not careful the whole giving a sticker thing can just perpetuate a cycle of looking for affirmation from someone else, rather than nurturing intrinsic engagement and motivation. We can subtly continue and mirror messages like 'you're only valued for what you achieve, not who you are' without even knowing we're doing it. So, it's worth considering the systems we have in schools and asking if shame might be present in their very design, or at least in how they're used, particularly when we feel under pressure, or our own shame is triggered.

Shame and Inclusion

What about the wider work of inclusion and shame? With pressures for results and pressures on budgets, some schools can be reluctant to welcome children with high-level needs. Perhaps you notice an internal hesitancy, or uncomfortable feelings in yourself about not wanting 'that child' in your class or cohort, because of how their needs may impact your data or classroom management, workload or stress. These thoughts might not be outspoken; they might just be a sense of unease that can feel ugly to even admit, and you wonder how this could have even crept into your thinking. It grates against an inclusive ethos, and it feels a bit like prejudice, and shame loves to get involved when prejudice is around. There is a real tension around inclusion in many schools. There is the wonder of it and the hard work of it. Words like diversity, justice, equity and fairness come to the fore, but when it comes to inclusion, there can still sometimes be some 'them and us' undercurrents around, where things spill over into school interactions and dynamics. Parents who are desperate to seek the best for their child, and who are tired of grappling for what their child needs, parents who start wondering what could have been or should have been but now is not, parents wanting to protect their child from a broken system that suggests their child doesn't quite fit (maybe they're not quite enough or are a bit too much . . . can you hear the overtones of shame here?), parents who are at breaking point or under pressure can look like they're fighting against you. Even if you're on the 'same side' as a parent of a child with SEND, schools can sometimes feel like a battleground when it comes to inclusion. Shame can be at play and stress can be high.

When it comes to working with children with social, emotional and mental health needs, and particularly those who have experienced trauma, there can be a whole lot of shame around. The key thing that we provide in the space between us is relational: the safe base that we nurture, the safe environment that we create, which little by little we hope will become the place from which they can venture to trust. There is good work being done in many schools to raise staff awareness of the impact of trauma and ACEs (Adverse Childhood Experiences). Trauma perceptive or informed practice is helping staff have a greater understanding of shame and its cyclical impact on children and families, and work is being done with parents to raise their awareness of the impact of trauma on their own emotional wellbeing. But maybe there is something of a gap with this kind of work also being done consistently with staff, where we could consider our own experiences and the possible impact of shame or anxiety in the way we relate to those around us? It's a matter of wellbeing.

Sometimes shame paralyses us. We can't think past it. We can't go past it or even imagine past it. It completely blocks our view. It can keep us from believing that things will ever look any different. This happens to children we work with, and adults we work with, as well as ourselves. Everything we do is relational practice, and sometimes we have to practise being relational. How do you recover if something during your day has completely undone you? How do you go back into the classroom and be what is needed? Teaching and learning happen in the context of relationships. Connection is part of the dynamic, and what we know is that at every point, shame seeks to sever connection, whether that be shame in our students or in us. When pupil behaviour impacts on us, if we feel already under pressure, the possibility of our own shame shaping our interactions with pupils increases all the more. If you're on the end of a child being dysregulated and that is expressed in a controlling, verbal or physical way that includes potential physical harm, how do you feel in the thick of it all, especially if the interaction has echoes of other experiences you've had? Whilst schools work hard to support their staff during these challenges, there is sometimes little time to process feelings and thoughts around these kinds of interactions because of the pressure to return to teach and support the rest of the class. Without processing, shame can sit in that space and accumulate, one such interaction then getting layered on top of another. It's worth looking at the kind of language we use when we're describing the moment of a child's challenging behaviour. Are we factual about what happened before, during and after the moment, or do we use emotive language? How do we then feel about the child and their family? Do we have empathy or compassion? What kind of judgements might we make? How do we communicate with the child's family, and how do we communicate about that family to other colleagues? How do we keep staff morale up for that family? How do we create a culture of hope for the child and family? And if that feels hard, how does that leave us all feeling?

And what about the fact that as professionals, we often feel a sense that due to a lack of resources we can't or are not doing enough to meet the needs of a child who has experienced trauma? We feel that the system is broken. At times we are plugging the gaps at a cost to ourselves because there's a deep-down sense for us all that we could be doing better in this thing called education, and it's not ok that try as we might, some children still slip through the cracks. We can feel that we haven't done enough, because the system hasn't done enough for these children we teach. It's not ok for children to not have what they need, it's not ok that there is a lack of specialist provision; it's not ok that they can't cope, that they can't access the curriculum, that there are not enough alternative pathways; it's not ok that some children are at risk of repeated exclusions and with that the loss of so many opportunities; it's not ok that their self-esteem becomes shot, and all the while the gap widens. We can't do all that we want to do, all that we'd hoped to do, because we can't fix the problems we face, the conditions we're in. We know that early intervention is key but there's not enough to go round and we can feel that we fail them when our hearts have always been set on the opposite. We can feel these things, and it's likely we can feel a sense of personal shame around that, and when this happens, where do we go with these difficult feelings? When everything around you says do more, be more, how do you just be ... and know, and feel that that is enough? All of these things call for a greater awareness of our own shame in and around these relationships.

The Wider Work of Shame

What about outside of work and the way shame can spill over into our homes and families? When you're exhausted, sometimes it can feel like you give everything of yourself to your job. Your mind, your energy, your heart, your time and resources, and then you have nothing, or very little left for anything, anyone else. Partner, spouse, children, family or friends. And maybe you feel guilty, or maybe you feel shame. I'm not a good enough mum, I'm not a good enough partner, son, friend. Insert whatever's appropriate. And so, the cycle continues...

If we're really going to think about resilience, wellbeing and self-care, we have to think about the part that shame can play, because it affects how we think about ourselves. A small amount of shame can help us empathise with others, but more than that and it can be destructive. If we can begin to speak up about the difficult things we sometimes think and feel in and around our job, we can know that we're not on our own with it all. Once we know it's there, how can we live and work and thrive, or at least bump along with shame?

IT'S ALL ABOUT PERSPECTIVE

Think of three positive attributes you have as a teacher. Ask a colleague to say three positive things about who you are. Ask a friend. Ask a trusted family member – write them all down. What do you notice?

Because the way we think about ourselves and how we view ourselves really does matter. It's vital to being and staying in the job (Eyre, 2017).

Shame has this way of cutting us off from each other and devaluing us. It has this way of making us feel alone. So, we need to find ways we can speak up about it and bring it out into the open. The truth is, you have value, and you are not alone.

*****And Breathe . . .*****

(Take a moment to focus on your breathing. Notice your chest rise and fall. Take three long, slow, deep breaths in and out.)

Safely Speak Up and Share

PATCHWORK QUILT

Think of a patchwork quilt and all its different fabrics, each one telling of a moment in time. Hand chosen and carefully placed, the overall pattern tells a story of rich life experiences, the rough with the smooth. When it comes to school, what would your quilt look like? Can you see the richness of your whole experience thus far?

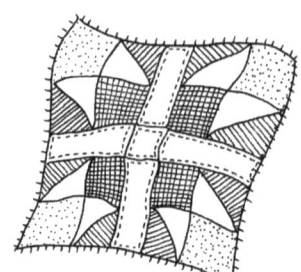

MY COMPLIMENTS

How well are you able to receive compliments from others? What's your typical response when someone compliments you? How well do they sit with you and why might that be?

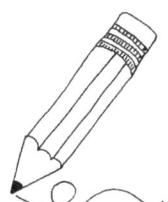

BALANCE SCALES

When you think about the good stuff and the hard stuff of working in school, what's the balance like? Which side is heavier at the moment and why? Is there anything that you know will tip the scales one way or the other? Who could you talk to about this?

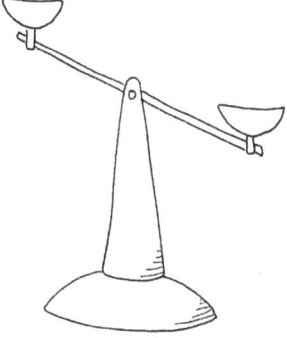

TENNIS MATCH

Imagine a long rally with the ball going back and forth over the net. On one side of the net is your shame voice, and on the other is truth. What kinds of things does your shame voice say? What truth could you bat it back with?

YOU SAID, I FELT ... YOU SAID, I THOUGHT ...

Think of a conversation you've had recently where you realise that you were triggered in some way. What did the person say, what did you feel and what did you think in that moment?

YOU DIDN'T SAY, I FELT ... YOU DIDN'T SAY, I THOUGHT ...

Think of a conversation you've had recently where you realise that you were triggered in some way. What didn't the person say, what was missed out, what would have helped but was left unsaid? And what did you feel and what did you think in that moment?

GO GENTLY

What are your go-to ways to take care of yourself? How easy do you find it to be kind to yourself?

WHEN THE BUCK STOPS WITH YOU

Where are you getting your support from? How seen, safe and supported do you feel? Who could you reach out to for more support? What might more support look like for you?

HOLD ON

How do you try to hold onto your values in the face of everything that pushes against them? How do you try to balance being task focused and people focused? What anchors you?

FRIENDS

Name some of the people in your life with whom you feel you can be totally yourself, warts and all. Describe a time when they were there for you. What did that look like and feel like for you?

CAST YOUR MIND BACK

Can you recall a time where you have felt shame at work? Write about what happened. Make a plan to talk to someone you trust about it.

PERMISSION TO SPEAK

Think of a time when you might have felt silenced or unable to speak up at work. What did you want to say, and why was it difficult for you to voice your thoughts? Who could you talk to about this in a way that might support you to speak up in the future?

ALARM BELLS

When you get defensive about something, what does that look like for you (e.g. do you explain yourself, justify your actions, raise your voice, interrupt, deny etc.)? What do you notice happening in your body at the time? Why might you be reacting in this way, and what might be behind it?

HOLDING UP A MIRROR

If you were to ask a trusted friend how they experience you, what do you think they might say?

DÉJÀ VU

Where you're at right now with your wellbeing... Have you been here before? And how does that leave you feeling? Is there anything about it that you would like to be different? Who could you talk to about this?

BRAIN DUMP

What are you thinking? What are you feeling?

YOU ARE NOT ALONE

References

Brown, B. (2013a). *Daring greatly: How the courage to be vulnerable transforms the way we live, love, parent and lead* (p. 37). Portfolio Penguin.

Brown, B. (2013b). *Shame vs guilt*. https://brenebrown.com/articles/2013/01/15/shame-v-guilt/

Christian Andersen, H. (1943). *The complete Andersen: The emperor's new clothes*. Hans Christian Andersen's "Keiserens nye Klæder" (J. Hersholt, Trans.).

Churchill, H., & Musters, C. (2019). *Insight into shame* (p. 20). Waverley Abbey Trust.

Eyre, C. (2017). *The elephant in the staffroom: How to reduce stress and improve teacher wellbeing*. Routledge.

Kell, E. (2018). *How to survive in teaching without imploding, exploding or walking away*. Bloomsbury Educational.

Regan, P., & Hoeksma, L. (2023). *Brighter days: 12 Steps to strengthening your wellbeing* (p. 60). SPCK.

Thomas Boyce, W. (2019). *The orchid and the dandelion: Why some children struggle and how all can thrive*. Allen Lane.

6
Enough Is Enough

When it comes to working in schools, we know that there's a whole lot of good stuff, and a whole lot of hard stuff. So, what do we do with all that stuff? How do we navigate it all? How do we cope with the highs and lows, and the ups and downs in all their nitty-gritty reality? How do we find a way to journey personally and together, to get some balance, and to reset when things feel unsteady?

When it comes to poor staff wellbeing, enough is enough. This has been the rally cry of recent years. At long last people are talking about the need for genuine and meaningful change in the conditions of teaching and working in schools, if teaching and supporting children are to be seen not only as valued, worthy professions, but also desirable ones, beyond the basic notions of job security, school holidays, the convenience of childcare and inspiring young minds. Change must come to not only keep people in their jobs but to bring them into the building in the first place. Change must come so that staff teams can not only survive, but thrive, even in the face of adversity.

With wellbeing coming high on the agenda over the past few years, there is a lot of good work happening. Commitments from Government and Ofsted mean that attention now has to be paid to wellbeing. It has become a collective priority. So, we have wellbeing leads and mental health support teams, we have commitments and charters and aims and objectives all seeking to support the children and adults in our settings. People are talking about wellbeing and emotional and mental health more than ever before, and helpful practices are being put in place. But even with all these things being developed and embedded in schools, there is still some way to go, and some schools lag behind others in their investment to the cause and their practice. Even whilst writing these words, I know of teacher friends who are working in environments that seem far from healthy. You can tick all the boxes you like about what you've been doing around fostering wellbeing in your setting, but if the staff don't feel it in the air, if it doesn't mean anything on the ground, it doesn't stand for much at all. With all the other challenges and things that are required of us, sometimes focusing on wellbeing can feel like something of an anomaly, especially when some of the inherent messaging, language and expectations around education don't always feel like they're on the same page. Catch me on a bad day, and it can sometimes feel like it grates . . . all this talk of wellbeing. But we really do need to be doing well with it all.

In our schools we need to work not only on the external processes and practices that create supportive cultures around our wellbeing but also consider the internal stuff that goes on in our heads and hearts. There is both external and internal work to do. Because even with all the talk and practices around wellbeing in your setting, you can still sometimes find yourself thinking that you're not enough, when you feel like you're just holding on or just getting through. But what if we could somehow begin to believe that we are enough? Maybe part of the problem is we're not sure that others really see the whole picture. We're not sure that others really grasp the good, the bad and the ugly side of the job. And that can leave us thinking that we're not really seen; that we're not really heard. If we feel unnoticed, sometimes we can feel a bit alone with it all. Sometimes we find ourselves all lost at sea . . . So, when those feelings come, what do we do with them? How do we process them and live and work alongside them? How do we get perspective? How do we get less stuck with it all? What if we could believe that what we bring is enough, regardless of everything that might seem to say otherwise? What if we could reflect on all these things in ways that, instead of weighing us down, equip us to grapple with it all? What if we could practise using tools that grow our self-awareness in ways that build us up, inspire confidence, develop our expertise and enable us to feel more empowered? If we're going to really make headway with staff wellbeing in schools, we have to look at ourselves just as much as the environments around us. We have to bravely look shame in the eye and work towards minimising its effects. We have to work towards environments where we feel more seen, safe and secure. If we can intentionally set upon this path, maybe we could not only do better but be better with our wellbeing. We could be more well. So how can we go about doing this?

Self-awareness

When it comes to giving feedback to those in our classes, 'Even Better If' have been familiar words in education in recent years. We can work towards creating external environments that are conducive to our wellbeing, but it's even better if we also look at growing in self-awareness. Maybe this is something of a missing piece to the puzzle . . . to engage in the internal work. When it comes to the wider education system, we may have less power to change some of the bigger external factors, but we are able to choose to engage with the inner workings of how we show up in different spaces and places, and to notice the work of shame. We are able to develop our awareness of how we think and feel and lean into the work of intentionally pushing back our feelings of not enough-ness, but this will take courage. The root of the word courage is 'cor,' coming from the Latin, meaning 'heart' (think of the present-day French word *'coeur'*). Its origins convey the idea of speaking your mind by telling all your heart (Brown, 2007). Just think of some of the phrases we use nowadays that have the same feel to them: 'putting your heart out there,' 'wearing your heart on your sleeve,' 'he's all heart,' being 'wholehearted.' When we encourage we en-courage others; the sense behind it is that we give courage (or heart) to others. Courage can feel uncomfortable and hard to do. Brown equates it to vulnerability. In her now famous TED Talk she says it is 'to tell the story of who you are with your whole heart' (Brown, 2010), and that's scary. Because that kind of vulnerability means choosing to let trusted others see me, and that includes being open about things I would rather others don't see and speaking up about things I would probably much rather avoid. But this is the crux of our wellbeing. Wellbeing doesn't tend to go well when we're avoiding looking at our whole selves. It doesn't tend to go well when we don't somehow speak up about our whole selves or look at our whole heart. Looking at our feelings of not enough-ness requires challenging an internal status quo that we painstakingly maintain, without even realising we're doing it.

So, where to begin? We first need to notice, and then think about what we've noticed, before we can do anything about it. In fact, the noticing and thinking, in itself, is doing something about it. Hopefully that's what we've begun to do already as we've been going through this book. Noticing and thinking. Noticing what's going on in us and around us, noticing what's at play, noticing what's important to us and the internal push and pull we sometimes feel in the face of different things, noticing when our inner anxiety is rising, or when we feel offended or put out, noticing the internal narratives we're thinking and noticing when we feel triggered, noticing the whiff of shame when it's hanging around. Perhaps some of the reflective exercises you've done so far have helped you begin to examine your thinking more closely. Perhaps some thoughts have come as a surprise to you, or even as something of a discovery as you've spent time mulling them over. If you were asked to describe yourself and say what kind of person you are, no doubt you could come up with a whole list of attributes, characteristics, skills and quirks. If a close friend of yours was asked to describe you they'd likely come up with lots of the things you listed, but they might also come up with others that you didn't. Some of those things might be things of which you weren't aware, or things you kind of glossed over, either intentionally or without even knowing.

Johari Window

In 1955, psychologists Luft and Ingham devised the Johari Window (Luft & Ingham, 1955). The tool can be used to help us identify what we know about ourselves and what we don't, as well as what others know or don't know about us. It helps us to see how much of ourselves we show to or share with others and how we show up in our relationships. It's a useful tool to sit with, if we're wanting to grow in self-awareness. It's often depicted as a grid, with four square windows, two above and two below. The four quadrants are as follows: The *Open* window is where I place what I know about myself and what others know about me – it's my Known or Public Self (e.g. maybe that I'm a good listener); the *Façade* or Hidden Self window is what I know about myself, but others don't know about me, it's my secret self that I choose not to share with others (e.g. that sometimes I can hide behind being a good listener so that I don't have to share vulnerably about myself). The *Blind Spot* or Blind Self window is what is known to others but not to me (e.g. maybe that I can sometimes come across as distant if I feel angry about something that feels very awkward or hard for me to voice, and at the time I don't even know that I'm feeling angry about it), and the *Unknown* or Unknown Self window is all the stuff that I don't know about myself and neither do others. Using this tool helps grow my self-awareness. I notice the myself I present to others and the myself I prefer others don't see, and that leads me to wonder why I don't want others to see (or do want others to see) certain aspects of me. The more I grow in self-awareness, the more I see how I interact with those around me, and the more I see how I tend to show up in different spaces and places.

As we become increasingly aware of who we are and how we tick, and how we automatically react in different situations, we can lean into being more intentional about how we want to show up with others. The more I grow in self-awareness the more I can choose to lean into aspects where I want to see change over time. I can't change what I don't know, but I can seek to change the things I do. Things that were at play subconsciously before, I can now consciously choose to work on (e.g. when I feel offended or angry I am trying to speak up about it with trusted people, rather than just giving people the silent treatment). As I become more self-aware, and as I engage with tools that help me do this, I can consciously seek to become more competent in areas where I have previously been incompetent. Why might I want to do this self-examination? And what on earth has it got to do with me being a teacher? The bottom line is because it makes me more aware of who I am and how I am when I am with others. It reveals how I work in a team and how I work on my own; it reveals how I show up when I feel anxious or when I am in a tough conversation; it reveals how I show up when I feel offended or out of my depth; it reveals how I show up when I feel that I am not enough or when things feel too much for me; it reveals how I show up when I feel shame. The more aware I become, the more intentional I can be about how I choose to show up in the face of different things, all of which potentially impact on my own wellbeing and the wellbeing of those around me. Growing in self-awareness must surely be a key part of fostering healthy interpersonal relationships and cultivating healthy work environments. It's got to be good for our wellbeing and the wellbeing of others, but we tend to shy away from it because it feels awkward, or maybe we wonder if it's all just a bit too 'personal.' But we're people at the end of the day. We're all persons. So, our interactions with each other (with children, families, colleagues) are personal. We interact. The prefix 'inter' speaks of relationship between two or more things. What happens and what we do happens between us, among us or in the middle of us. It all speaks of connection. Schools are personal communities. So, it seems a good idea to make sense of our persons, and to understand more of how we do that relating to each other, because it really does affect our wellbeing. We can use tools like the Johari window, as well as other simple practices that can equip us to become more self-aware.

Noticing Our Emotions

Let's not forget our feelings in all this. Feelings are often good indicators of something going on for us and in us, whether we're aware of that something going on or not. Paying attention to our feelings is important. It's ironic that as practitioners we are very used to supporting children and young people and helping them develop their self-awareness and self-regulation skills when it comes to emotions, but at the same time we can fail to do the same work ourselves. Consider some of the things you use in school with children and young people to help them develop their emotional vocabulary. As adults we are likely to have a wide range of language to describe our emotions in all their varying intensity. Think of feelings wheels like those of Willcox (1982) and ways in which you help children develop their own physiological awareness in different emotional states. Think of the ways that you support students to move from one state of emotional arousal to another. We use these all the time to support children but how often do we think about using these kinds of tools for ourselves?

Think about these scenarios . . . A student comments on your body image and it's something you already feel vulnerable about; another speaks over the top of you and shuts you down in front of their friends; people are kind to your face, but you know they speak behind your back . . . We feel all sorts of feelings in the face of these things and when we pay attention to what we feel, we realise we feel somewhat exposed, somewhat dismantled by shame. What emotions have you felt just this week whilst you've been in school and what has triggered those feelings? What led to those feelings? What came before? What environment were you in and what stressors were at play? What did you do with those feelings in the moment? How long did they stay with you and are they still niggling away at you, ready to spill over again in the blink of an eye? Why did that comment from that senior leader really bug you? Why did you stew over that email from that parent? Why did you feel so unravelled by that incident with that child? When we take time to look at our emotions and ask what is behind them, it can reveal a whole lot of things about how we think about ourselves that impact on our wellbeing. Maybe you didn't just feel angry about that comment, maybe what you thought was that that person was somehow disappointed in you, and what you felt in that moment was shame and that's what really cut you to the core. Maybe you felt so mad, but what you realise now is that you felt overwhelmed in the face of what you were being asked to do. Maybe you felt offended that someone might even think that of you. Maybe you just felt alone with it all, with everything feeling like it was just resting on you.

As adults we're often better at hiding or disguising our emotions than children. Sometimes we push them down for fear that if they surface things might get a bit ugly. Sometimes we play them down, saying I'm tired, when maybe if we dig a bit deeper, we're God-darned scared. The language we use around emotions is important, and the depths to which we honestly examine them are too. All the time we don't look at them and let them go undercover, we're often impacted by them without even realising, and if we misdiagnose what's really going on for us and in us, the kind of help we seek doesn't always hit the spot. What I need if I'm tired might look different to what I need if I'm lonely. Feelings have a tendency to sit in the driver's seat if we let them, and sometimes that can get us into trouble. On the other hand, feelings that are hidden away don't tend to go anywhere unless we get them out into the open. When the feelings we have are uncomfortable, we often have an autopilot response where we do whatever we've always done to make those feelings go away. Maybe that looks like blaming others rather than looking at the part we had to play in an interaction. 'If they would just . . . then I wouldn't feel so mad.' Or maybe what we've always been used to doing is taking on someone else's anxiety when we can feel it in the room. We can learn a lot about ourselves and what's going on around us if we notice our emotions,

ALL THE FEELINGS

What overriding emotions would you say often describe you? What might others say about you if they were asked the same question?

especially if those emotions are tied up with shame. When we feel shame, we can easily function from a place of woundedness, because shame hurts. Often, we don't know that's what we're doing, because our defences go up, so we just do what we always do in the face of it. If we could do better at recognising all these things, it will make for healthier relationships and working environments for us all.

In schools we're often so busy going from one thing to the next that by the time we get to the end of the day there are so many things we need to process. Many of us do some kind of decompressing on the journey home, just because we need to, in order to function, but maybe sometimes our days require a little more than that. Self-reflection might not be something else you want to add to your to-do list when you get home, along with all the planning or marking or everything else-ing you have to do, but perhaps it could be a helpful exercise to build it in as some kind of regular rhythm. Maybe just choosing an exercise from this book and giving yourself five minutes with it every now and then could be a helpful way to start. Without looking at some of this stuff we can feel powerless that any of it might change. But by engaging with these reflective tools, we become more self-aware and more equipped to do community together. Another area to consider is distinguishing between our feelings and our thoughts.

Thinking, Feeling and Meaning Making

Language is important. Sometimes we talk about how we *feel* about something but what we say is really what we *think* about it. Here's an example. 'I feel like he just doesn't care.' When saying this, what I'm *thinking* is that he doesn't care; what I'm *feeling* might be disappointment, sadness, outrage etc. We can easily interchange the language, but it's helpful by way of becoming more self-aware, to separate the two. Thinking and feeling. Using 'I' statements can help with this. 'He gets on my nerves' can become 'when he does this . . . (be specific), I feel this . . . (these emotions) and I think this . . . (these thoughts go through my mind).' 'She made me feel so embarrassed' can become 'When she said that I thought this . . . (these thoughts), and I felt this . . . (these emotions).' 'Always' and 'never' are also important words to look out for in our responses with each other. As soon as we frame any of our responses with a 'she never . . .' or a 'he always . . .' it's like we almost write the whole thing off and absolve ourselves of any sense of responsibility for our part in the interaction. 'I always feel like that' brandishes all our experiences as one and makes it difficult for us to see any moments where that might not be the case. When we use absolutes in our language there's no space for anything to ever be different in our minds. As we think more carefully about the words we use to describe our thoughts and feelings, this is a useful tool to help us become more aware of what is going on for us in our interactions with others.

As we go about our everyday life, we make meanings around all our experiences. Two of us could see the very same person walking towards us down the corridor in the same way at the very same time, and we could have very different responses to that same moment. The meanings we make will be framed by who we are and our experiences to date. 'When she came towards me, I thought this.' Or 'when she said that I thought this . . .' and our thinking might have very little to do with what that other person said at all; there's just a whole backstory around that situation or interaction that reminds us of other interactions and situations we've been in before, whether good or bad, or anything in between. We make assumptions without even realising and we feel things in light of the meanings we make.

Maybe the hidden expectations we explored in Chapter 4, the messages we see inherent in our education system, are also meanings we make. Maybe they are meanings we make that have a ring of shame about them, because of the climate in which we work, and because of the part our shame voice plays. As we go on this journey, can we find ways to engage in practices without feeling like we're being judged or that we're not trusted? Where we feel like we don't have to prove ourselves and that we're not on our own? The more we become aware of the meanings we make in our interactions with others, the more we can begin to respond intentionally or differently rather than being shaped by our automatic responses. As we become more aware of our thoughts and feelings and the meanings we make every day, it has the potential to make for healthier interactions and working practices in our schools. As we build more trust with each other, where less is hidden, nuanced or avoided, we can begin to have agreed expectations of how we do things together in the space that we share. The journey might feel uncomfortable and awkward at times, the conversations

MEANING MAKING

Think of an interaction you've had this week. What was said, what did you think, what meanings did you make in the moment and how did you respond in light of those things?

might not always feel easy, but environments that are doing this kind of work are pressing into matters of genuine wellbeing.

So, what else can we practise?

Identifying Our Stressors

It's become second nature to us as practitioners to support children and young people around their mental health and wellbeing. When it comes to supporting children around their emotional regulation and behaviour, we can often identify signs of stress in a child before they've even stepped through the door. If a child is dysregulated or somewhere on that trajectory we do the work of co-regulating with them. This can involve lots of different things but is likely to include helping the child to recognise their emotions and to tune into the signals from their bodies that let them know something is up. In all this work we do a lot of thinking around identifying their stressors. These can be complex and sometimes hidden, so we get to know the child and work with them and those who know them well, to help unpick what's going on for them. Stressors can assault them from all sides, impacting their minds and bodies and thus their behaviour. Just think of a child who is hypersensitive to noise or light when you've got a flickering buzzing strip light in your classroom, and you'll know that their level of stress is high, and their body is uncomfortable and in a state of near distress before you even begin to do anything else. This example shows biological stressors at play in the environment. As well as these stressors there can be emotional, cognitive, social and prosocial stressors. Self-regulation is about how we manage the stress we are under. Shanker (2016) notes that stress is all those things that mean we have to expend energy in order to maintain some kind of equilibrium, to keep the balance. We have to do a lot of this in and around the children with which we work. Shanker's work involves recognising when a child is overstressed, which means reading the signs and reframing the behaviour ('oh, so this is what's going on here' – which in turn changes me and my approach); identifying and reducing the stressors; helping the child know when they need to do this for themselves, and supporting them to be able to use strategies to self-regulate. How strange that we can expend so much of our energy engaging in these processes and doing this work for the children and young people in our care and yet have few resources to do the same for ourselves when it comes to considering our own wellbeing? How strange that we put in so much effort to help our children and young people try to find and keep some sort of balance, and refrain from doing this for ourselves? Throughout the course of this book, rather than feeling more overwhelmed by the challenges we face, my hope is we become more equipped in the face of them. Teaching is a wonderful work but also a hard one. You're not on your own if you sometimes (or oftentimes) feel stressed and think it's hard. It is! But all this work of self-awareness can see us better equipped.

So, what if we can begin to apply some of the same regulatory processes we use with children in our own lives? With the basic premise that an overflow of stress leads to distress, if we can begin to examine what our current stressors are, this can help us reframe our own experience. We can begin to see how all sorts of things are impacting on us, and in so doing we can expose any feelings and thinking around the sense that things are our fault, or that we are at fault, or not enough. Examining what we are facing can reframe the shame we can feel. Think about the kinds of factors or stressors that are impacting you at the moment. You are likely to have personal factors that perhaps no one else even knows about that are affecting your levels of stress. Maybe these are to do with your own health or relationships, or to do with situations with family or friends. There may be stressors particular to your class or cohort of children. Perhaps your school has specific stressors that are impacting on you all. If you have an imminent inspection that you have been expecting at some point over the last year, that is likely to be bringing a level of stress to the staff team. If you have a sudden influx of children that requires very specific provision, if you have a cohort of children or young people with high-level needs of SEND, if you have a building that is falling apart around you and you are all decamped into the school hall, if a member of your staff team is very ill, all these things are likely to be contributing to higher levels of stress amongst you and your colleagues. There may well be cultural stressors that are currently heavily impacting your community. You will feel something of this as you navigate relationships with children and families. Perhaps there are national stressors that you feel at ground level every day, such as the not enough of funding and resources that we've already explored. Whatever context you are in, whatever country you are in, you will have stressors that are impacting on you, and what's important is that you identify them. It helps you make sense of what's going on around you and in you.

When we become more aware of our stressors, we can begin to engage in self-regulatory strategies that we know work for us. We could develop what we might call a distress response plan. It might go something like this . . . 'When I notice this, I will . . .' or 'when I anticipate this I will . . .' It might include asking questions such as 'who are my people?' (aka 'who can I trust with this?') 'what can I do?' 'where can I go?' 'what has triggered this in the first place?' Engaging in this kind of exercise might be a way in which we can work towards finding informal and formal systems within school which support our own self-regulation and recovery process when we are experiencing stress. There are so many self-regulation programmes and interventions we use in schools for children. We have plans like this in place for children all the time, but sometimes in the thick of it all, we don't get round to doing something similar for ourselves. No doubt many of us already use strategies to alleviate our stress whether we realise it or not, but more focused thinking and identification of our stressors can help us develop a more focused response. It can help to shift any misplaced sense of blame as we reframe our thinking and so help to counteract the effects of shame.

What if the anticipation of shame is a stressor for you in school? You recognise you're anxious, maybe, but at a closer look, perhaps what's going on more specifically is that you anticipate not being able to answer a question fully in your upcoming discussion with a governor, and you have this nagging sense that you'll somehow be 'found out,' or that they'll think you're not up to the job. What if you know a parent is likely to raise something that you know will feel awkward, when you see them at a meeting? Working with children, young people and families and feeling a sense of exposure can be excruciating, and sometimes

> **I'M SO STRESSED!**
>
> *What are some of the stressors that are impacting you right now? Can you identify those that are within your control and those that are outside of it?*

that feeling is shame. It can be helpful to take note of when we experience shame at work, of when we notice that nagging internal voice in any given day. Think of it like your inner critic. It may come in all sorts of guises for us, but some whispers you may recognise more than others. The voice that you're not enough, you don't belong, you're alone or that you're unseen or you have no voice. Or maybe it takes the form of 'who are you kidding? You're not qualified; it's only a matter of time before you mess it up.' Often once you start noticing this kind of inner narrative, you notice it all over the place, and although at first that can feel a bit overwhelming, there's a power that comes with uncovering it. The uncovering muffles it, and once out in the open we can get to work to try to silence the power of its words. Our shame voices can crop up all over the place, indeed, wherever we interact with others; schools make for ripe places for shame to grow because of the culture of deficit and expectation around us and the interconnected close working we have with each other . . . and shame especially speaks loudly in environments where it feels like things could be being done better, when things feel like they're not quite working as well as they could . . . or should.

When we see things that weigh children and young people down, things that inhibit their creativity, life and passion, we want to change these things. We want to protect them or stand against the stuff that grinds them down, the stuff that muffles their voices, that constricts or shuts them down. We want to build their self-belief and resilience to cope with the stress they face (Meek et al., 2020). At the end of the day, we want each one of them to grow into life-giving, hope-filled people, who do best what they love most, who find their place, who give to and receive from others. That's what we want for each child we nurture, for them to be well . . . We want for their wholeness, we want for their wellbeing, and the same goes for all of us doing that nurturing. We want to still be able to hold onto our creativity and passion, we want to stand up for things that are good and right rather than feel silenced into just getting through. We want hope to remain alive, even when we face challenges. We want staff teams to be well, to be less broken and more whole. Not just because it's a good thing to work towards, or the latest on-trend theme or initiative from on high, but because we genuinely want what's best for each other. We want what's good for us. Education is about the people, the little ones and the big ones. Human beings and relationships should always be at the fore. Sometimes it can feel like that can get a bit lost along the way. Sammons (2019) insists that compassion and relationships need to be at the heart of it all. If we really care about the people involved, then we need to take note and do something about it when people are under stress. When it comes to shame, it's helpful to become more aware of when it's hanging around. There's power in the noticing. Shame is somewhat disarmed when it is brought out of the shadows and into the light.

Boundaries

Another tool that equips us is having and knowing our boundaries. It's easy to think of scenarios in school when these can be challenged. Imagine someone brings forward a deadline for a piece of work you need to submit, and you recognise immediately a sense of added pressure. Maybe you feel angry or resentful that this is now going to impact on your time in a way that it wouldn't have before. There are whole school considerations around this kind of situation. Senior leaders can communicate clear expectations around when regular information needs to be collected and be committed to sticking to timeframes, rather than changing them. But there are also things we can consider about how we show up if something like this does happen. For example, is there a way in which you could say no? Notice any feelings that arise in you as you even think about that as a possible option. Where are those feelings coming from? Why might they be in play? What could 'saying no' look like? What could it sound like? Literally, what words could you use? 'I'm sorry, but I just can't get that to you for tomorrow. I can do it by . . .' Is there a way in which you could have a calm conversation with the other person about the additional pressure and anxiety you feel as a result of their request? That is likely to feel awkward and vulnerable, but it could create an opportunity not just for your own growth but also the other person's growth, where they begin to see the impact of their actions on others. This could make for better working practices and greater respect all round. These kinds of conversations are brave precisely because they are important. Boundaries enable us to have an awareness of 'this is mine and this is yours'; 'this is where I end, and you begin.' 'What's yours (particularly when it comes to stress) does not necessarily mean it's mine.' Boundaries at their best are not just a 'talk to the hand,' which puts distance between people. They're things that, when in place and

> **BOUNDARIES**
>
> *Can you identify boundaries you have in place around your work? How effective are they? How healthy are they? Might any need adjusting and what could that look like?*

communicated well, still allow for a sense of connection (when that is a safe thing to happen), even if we think differently. They can become a safe bridge rather than cutting people off. They become a means for us to be curious and ask questions of the other person, whilst acknowledging the anxiety in the space between.

Boundaries include understanding that we have limitations. We don't have bionic superpowers, even though we may sometimes feel like we need them, with all that we have to do. We are human beings, and it really is ok for us to have a capacity. Becoming more aware of our limitations as well as our strengths is helpful . . . and realising that our capacity can change depending on different situations and seasons in life is also important to grasp. What I might have been able to cope with regarding my workload is likely to look different from when I was a young adult to when I am navigating the needs of a growing family too. As teachers we often have this way of keeping pushing through. With the end of term in sight, we just keep going, regardless of the impact on our health. Many of us will have experienced that just getting-to-the-end-of-term feeling, and then the first thing that happens when we stop is our bodies crash, and we become ill before we can even begin to recuperate. We can learn to be more aware of our limitations and strengths. There are lots of tools out there to help us. You could look at something more formal like personality profiling questionnaires, or you could just simply take some time to think about what you're good at, and where you'd like to work on things. You could ask a friend what they think. What does considering that you have limitations throw up for you? Pay attention to what you feel as you ask the question and pause to think why that might be. Perhaps you've had this belief that you've always had to be strong, or 'together.' There can be outward signs that indicate when we struggle to admit our limitations. Have you ever noticed that you minimise your personal limits to others? Or that you're guarded about your weaknesses? Are you reluctant to ask others for feedback, or to ask for help or say that you don't know? Sometimes we can deflect from our own weaknesses by focusing on what we perceive to be the flaws of others. For others of us, perhaps our weaknesses or limitations are the first things we see. However it is for us, it's important that we have an awareness of our strengths and limitations, and how we show up in light of them.

Having an awareness of our limitations also helps us to know what's within our control and what's not. When we feel like we have little or no control over something it can negatively impact our mental health and sense of wellbeing. Examining our circle of control (Covey, 2020) can be helpful. It can help to shift our perspective away from the things that make us feel anxious, to the things we can control and our responses to those demands. It helps us to identify our circle of concern (something we are concerned about and need to adapt to, but is outside of our control or influence – e.g. there is no money in the budget), our circle of influence (things we can't control but can influence – e.g. having specialist knowledge that we can share, or knowing who to turn to ask for help) and the circle of control (things that we can control). Having greater clarity around these things can help not only with joint or individual problem-solving, but also just with how we view and respond to the challenges we face.

Self-compassion

Practising self-compassion is another expression of a boundary. It's an acknowledgement that you are worthy of being valued and protected. Perhaps we could just call it safeguarding. Things that we put in place to keep us safe. If you're aware that you experience shame, often your inner narrative can speak the very opposite of compassion. Its words can be a brutal barrage. So, what might practising self-compassion look like for you? You might literally have to practise it, like a skill. Think of putting in training to do it and becoming more accomplished at it over time. Perhaps it might just be to speak kindly to yourself or kindly of yourself to others. Maybe that sounds simple, but it can be a real challenge if most of what you've heard, thought or felt deep down has been that you're not worthy of kindness. Building in rest is another expression of self-compassion. It involves valuing yourself enough to do this. The same goes for building in time for things that are life-giving to you or things that replenish you, things that are beneficial for your mental health as well as your physical health, your minds, bodies and souls, if you will. We have to consider how we use our time and how we guard our time. We might think we don't have time to do this, to work out what that could look like for us from week to week, but it's crucial that we do. Sayer (2020) speaks of the importance of being able to talk openly about mental health and wellbeing, and within that, being able to set clear boundaries around our own time. We've said already that work is just one aspect of our lives. We are not defined by it. It's interesting that when we first meet new people, introductions are often around what we do. 'Hi, I'm so and so, what do you do?' It's ingrained into us. Wouldn't it be amazing (and possibly feel awkward) if friends introduced us to others with something of who we are rather than what we do?! 'Hi! This is Matt – he's one of the kindest people I know.' Our identity and our worth are not defined by what we do, even if what we do is good. The truth is, we each have inherent value, whether we've experienced that in our lives to date or not. Practising self-compassion is a way we can remind ourselves of that.

What if the good enough that you bring is actually good enough? And what if you actually believed that, and could work out of that place? Out of that sense of value? What kind of a difference would that potentially make? What if the resonating voice you heard was one of value instead of something else? Of affirmation instead of possible rejection? Of being worthy of genuine support when things are hard? Of belonging and the right to be somewhere doing what you do rather than feeling like some kind of fraud? How would that sense of value enable the work of your hands to flourish rather than maintain or grip on tight for fear of letting go? You have value. You matter, and what you do matters.

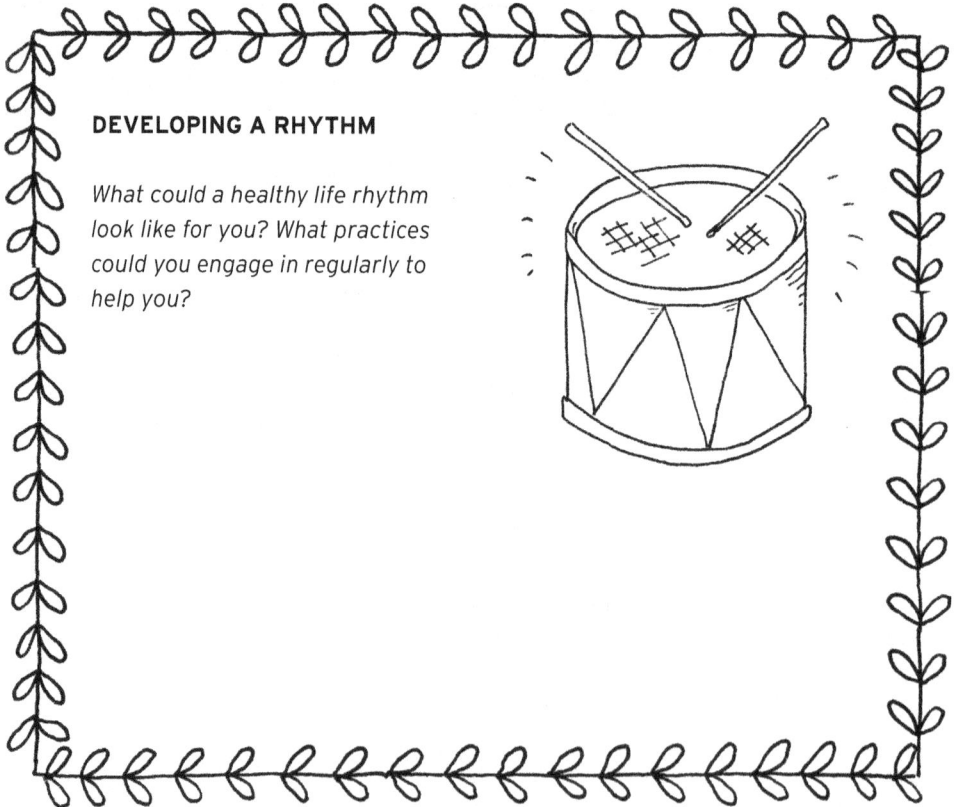

DEVELOPING A RHYTHM

What could a healthy life rhythm look like for you? What practices could you engage in regularly to help you?

Growing in self-awareness equips us with the self-belief and inner grit to recognise the pressures and vulnerability we feel, but also to acknowledge (and deeply know) that we are trained, we have passion and experience, and that we are also still learning. We are all a work in progress. We feel our vulnerability, but we still put our hands to the task. As we use all these kinds of tools to reflect and grow in self-awareness, we become more equipped to not just go through situations, circumstances and challenges, but to grow through them. We grow on the inside as we do the work of intentionally choosing to do this work, and we grow on the outside in the way that we then interact with others and build connection and community. As we go through and grow through these processes there's a sense in which we reset or recalibrate, so that we're good to keep going.

Reflecting and Reset-ing

On journeying through the book so far, we've been remembering and reimagining the good stuff about teaching in the opening chapter, examining and looking at evidence when it comes to the hard stuff of the not enoughs and too muchness of it all, thinking about how we might be able to safely speak up and share when it comes to recognising the place of shame, and then as part of this chapter looking at ways that we can be equipped and empowered when it comes to growing in self-awareness. In the final chapter we'll come on to engaging in the task of trying one thing that will help us work towards improving personal wellbeing in our settings in the face of shame. It's an ongoing process of noticing, thinking and then acting, of RESET-ing.

>**R**emembering and Reimagining
>**E**xamining and Evidencing
>**S**afely Speaking Up and Sharing
>**E**quipping and Empowering
>**T**ask and Trying one Thing

My hope is that this book will be an ongoing resource for you, and something you can pick up as and when you need it. My hope is that you'll be able to revisit some of the reflective 'remembering and reimagining' activities when you've lost your way a bit and need to remember the good stuff about who you are and what you do. If you feel overlooked, my hope is that you can look back and look over something that was good, and that you can also look for and look to other things. Remember all the children who have looked to you, those who have come looking for you at lunchtime, who have sought you out because you provided something they needed in that moment; remember all those you have looked after. See how powerful is that act of remembering? My hope is that you'll be able to choose an 'examine and evidence' activity and recognise something of the enormity of the challenges you face on a day-to-day basis when things feel a bit overwhelming, and in so doing, realise again that it's not just you and you're not on your own, but that you're up against a hell of a lot of things; that the 'safely speak up and share' reflections will help you begin to do that very thing with people you trust, around the thoughts and feelings that arise when you honestly look at your own wellbeing; that as you engage in the 'equipping and empowering' activities you will feel and become more skilled at growing in self-awareness, and that this will positively impact your wellbeing and finally that as you engage in the 'task activities of trying one thing' you'll have something in mind to do, to continue on your wellbeing journey. Maybe you might choose to revisit the RESET process regularly, or at the end of each term, or engage with the remembering and reimagining sections towards the end of the longer summer holidays, as a way of preparing for the start of the next academic year.

Each of the reflections become, by very nature, personal. They cause you to examine yourself, your thoughts and feelings, your hopes and desires, your wellbeing. To pay more than just lip service to them, you'll likely need to be somewhere you feel safe before you can be really honest with your thoughts and honest on the page. And you'll need to give them time, to mull them over and sit with them a little. You might want to engage with them in the privacy of your own home. Maybe you'll look at some reflection themes or questions and think that you can't look at that particular one yet. That's fine. Just move on to another one. They're for you to ponder on and come back to another time.

With no expectation to share anything of your reflections, perhaps you could bravely engage in the practices as a staff team, setting aside regular termly time to focus on a chosen reflective activity. A shared commitment to engaging in the process could communicate something powerful to the whole staff team and school community about the value of wellbeing in your setting. Perhaps the content and reflections could become part of your whole school cyclical wellbeing check-ins or questionnaires or used as resources by Mental Health Support Teams in your school. Maybe it might feel safer to engage with some of the activities in contexts where you could anonymously share with other like-minded professionals at a similar stage to you or with a similar area of responsibility. Perhaps this could be like an Early Career Teachers' forum, a SENDCO network, a middle management or senior leaders' forum, a Learning Support Assistants' forum or a Head teachers' forum via an online platform. Perhaps you could use the reflective practices as conversation starters in training sessions or supervision or other supportive contexts. Reflective practices are not navel-gazing static practices. They can support us to become more proactive and less reactive people, to be equipped and empowered. They can be intentional life-giving practices that form us and shape us as we consider who we are and who we want to be. You are worth putting in the time to do this. You have value. You really do matter.

Before you reflect some more, first . . .

*****Step Outside for a Breath of Fresh Air*****

(Go for a walk – notice what you see, hear, smell and feel around you)

Equip and Empower

UNDER THE MICROSCOPE

What has become clearer to you about the things that you face at work and the impact they might be having on you?

NOT ME!

How well do you take responsibility for your emotions? Can you think of an example to illustrate this?

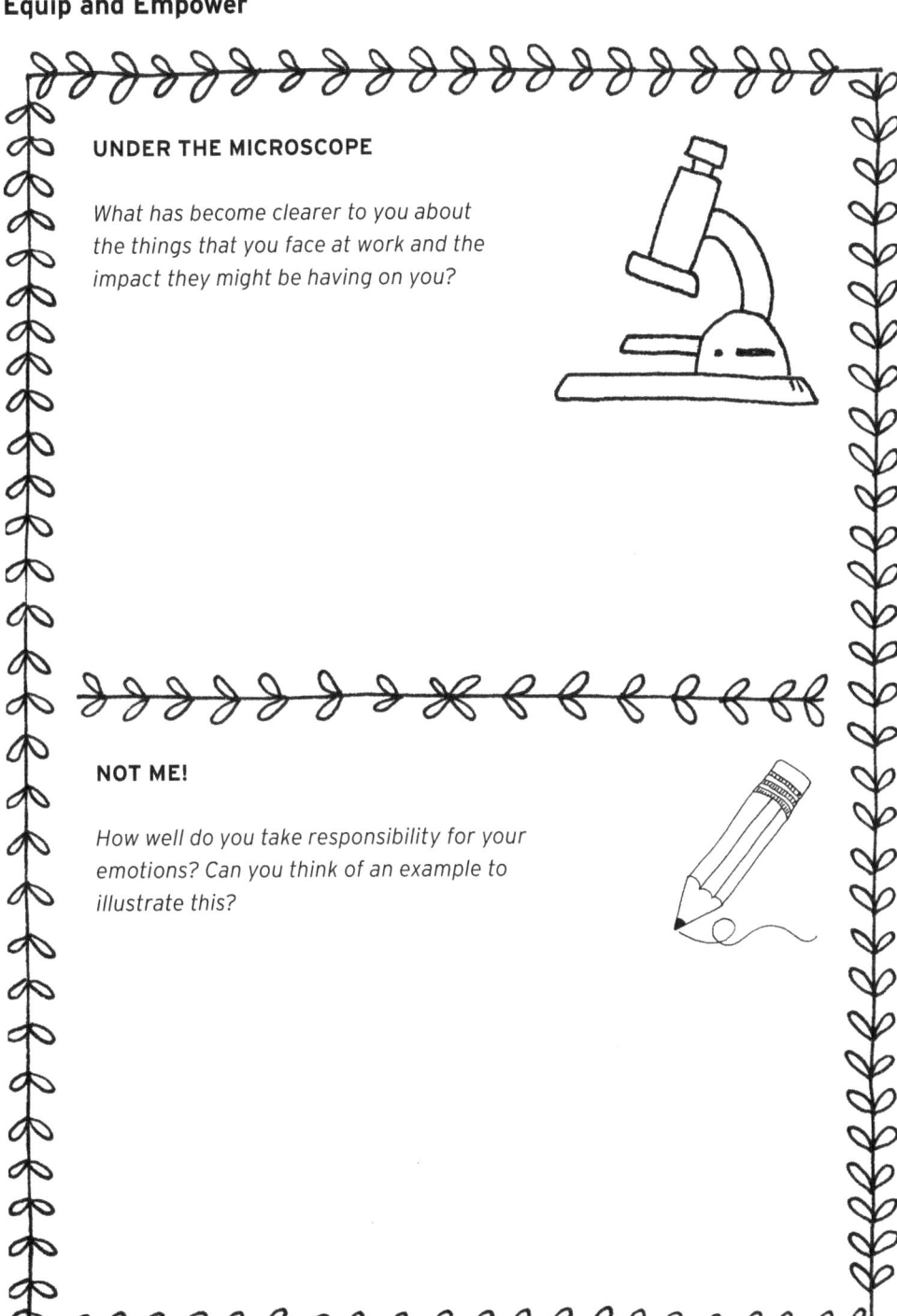

STOP!

How aware are you of when your emotions start to get the better of you? Are you able to pause before things get out of control? What can that look like for you?

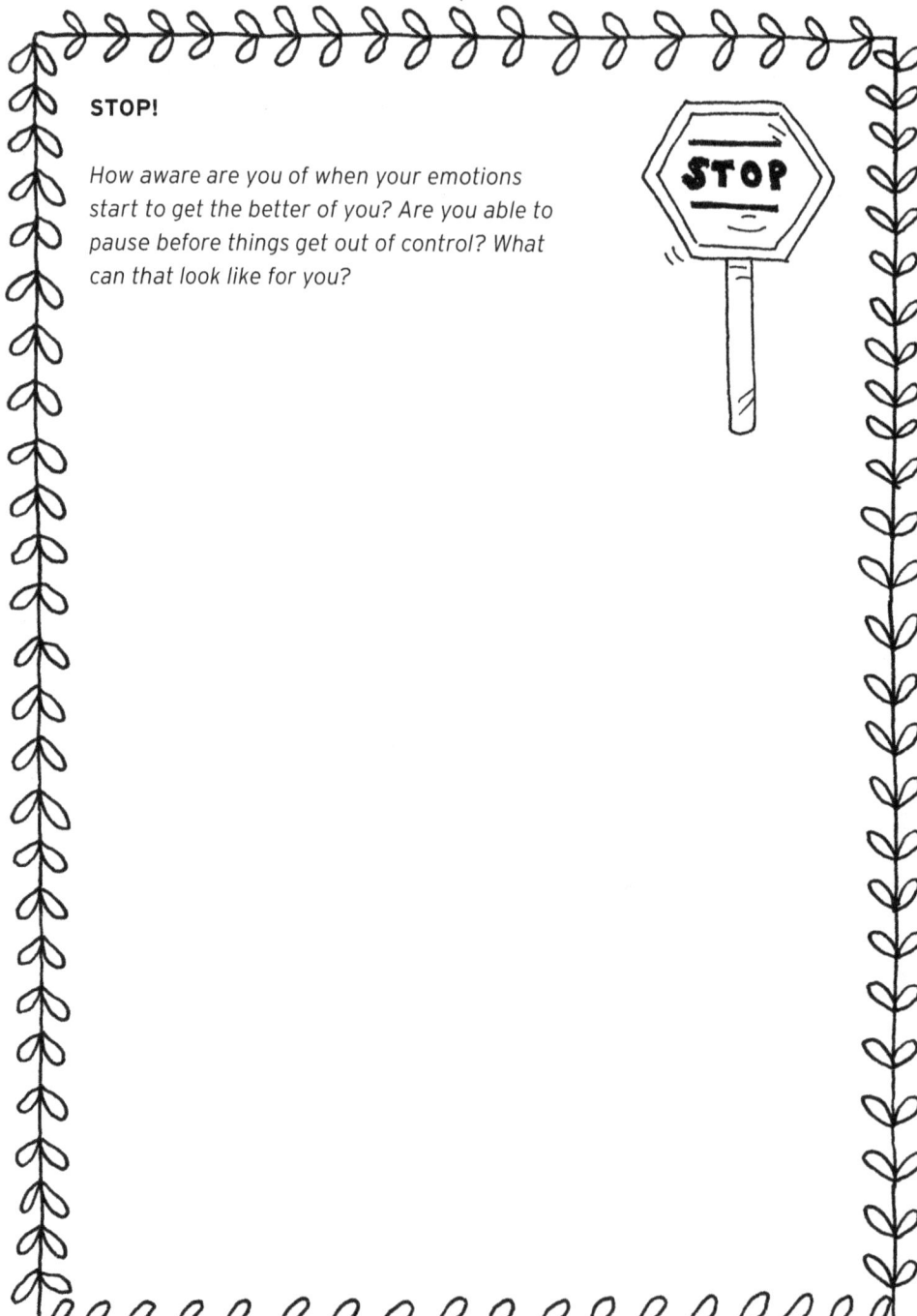

THINKING AND FEELING

Think about a conversation you've had recently where you felt awkward or anxious. As you recount it, can you identify what you were thinking and feeling before, during and after?

LIGHT BULB

What has been a light bulb moment for you on this journey so far? What impact has it had on you and how might it impact how you go about things going forwards?

AT THE CROSSROADS

Crossroads can signify a change in direction or a clarifying of the way ahead. What might this look like for you?

AT THE END OF MYSELF

Are there any things you may be carrying at the moment that are not yours to carry? What do they look like and why might you have picked them up? What's one practical thing you could do to put one of these down?

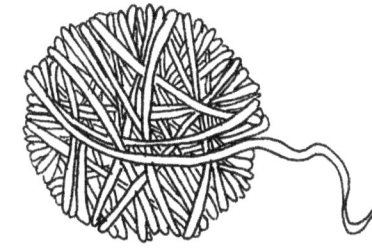

RISE AND FALL

Where do you notice anxiety rising in you? Notice what's going on in your body. What are you anxious about? And why might that be?

JUST SAY NO

*What could that look like for you?
What words could you use?*

A BIT OF LIGHT RELIEF

What do you tend to do to try to relieve your stress? How helpful or effective are those things? Are there other things you could try?

REACHED MY LIMIT

Think about your strengths and limitations as a person. Be brave and make a list. How able are you to express your limitations in front of others? Is there an aspect of your character or gifting where you would like to see some change?

LIGHT AT THE END OF THE TUNNEL

What, for you, might be a light at the end of the tunnel? When you're in the tunnel how easy is it for you to notice fellow travellers? How could you begin a conversation with others about this?

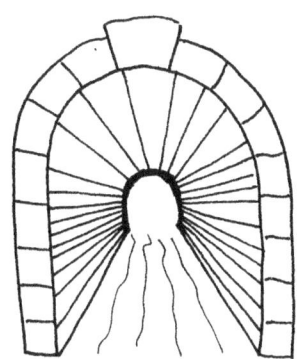

REST

Where could you carve out some intentional time to rest this week? What might that look like for you?

ROLLERCOASTER

What are some of the ups and downs that you're currently noticing about your work? Where might you feel like you're going too fast or plummeting out of control?

MARY POPPINS BAG

Imagine your work bag has limitless people resources within it. What kinds of things do you want to have to hand?

BRAIN DUMP

What are you thinking? What are you feeling?

YOU MATTER

References

Brown, B. (2007). *I thought it was just me: Women reclaiming power and courage in a culture of shame*. Gotham Books.

Brown, B. (2010, June). *The power of vulnerability* [Video]. TED Conferences. https://www.ted.com/talks/brene_brown_the_power_of_vulnerability

Covey, S. R. (2020). *The 7 habits of highly effective people* (Revised and Updated: 30th Anniversary ed.). Simon and Schuster UK.

Luft, J., & Ingham, H. (1955). *The Johari window: A graphic model of interpersonal awareness. Proceedings of the western training laboratory in group development*. University of California.

Meek, L., Phillips, J., & Jordan, S. (2020). *Mental health and wellbeing in primary education: A practical guide and resource*. Luminate.

Sammons, A. (2019). *The compassionate teacher: Why compassion should be at the heart of our schools*. John Catt Educational Ltd.

Sayer, A. (2020). *Supporting staff mental health in your school*. Jessica Kingsley.

Shanker, S. (2016). *Help your child deal with stress – and thrive: The transformative power of self-reg*. Yellow Kite.

Willcox, G. (1982). The feeling wheel a tool for expanding awareness of emotions and increasing spontaneity and intimacy. *Transactional Analysis Journal, 12*(4), 274–276.

7

Brave Leadership and the Way Ahead

All along, the process has been to notice and then think about what we have been noticing. This is the ongoing journey, the steady plodding of one foot in front of the other, which then impacts our collective practice and informs our internal dialogues and relationships. Noticing, thinking and then acting. It is the ongoing doing of it all. So, equipped with some tools, what to do now, and what to do next? What is the task and what do we try? We must first quickly venture back to the beginning and look at what we want in the first place.

Vision and Values

In schools we often talk about the kind of community we want to build. We think long and hard about how we create a space where children and young people feel safe, seen (which also means heard) and respected. We want them to know that they have value and that they belong, and that they contribute to the richness of the community of which they are a part. We spend time thinking about our vision and values . . . where we're going and who we are. We think about what they look like, and how we help communicate them and make them happen in the day to day. It's the old analogy of if you cut a stick of seaside rock it should have the same words running right the way through it. Anyone should be able to see and hear and taste and feel the vision and values as they walk around the place.

We come at it all with the children and young people in mind. We also know that if there is a mismatch between what we say and what we do, it throws things off . . . and children and parents can smell it a mile away. But sometimes there can be an odd smell around the place and we get so used to it that we don't even smell it anymore. Nose blind, they call it. Sometimes the mismatch happens in how we, the adults, interact with each other. There's just a feel about the place. Robertson (2020) refers to culture being what we do around here, and climate being how it feels to work here. So, what's the culture and climate of where you work? How does it feel? How does it feel for you and for your colleagues?

When it comes to thinking about where you work, you probably know of some schools you wouldn't want to touch with a barge pole, not because of the children but perhaps because of the leadership, culture and ethos of the place. You might even find yourself in such a school right now. How is it that some schools can seem to get it so wrong, and others seem to get it a bit more right when it comes to looking after the wellbeing of their staff? If you're an Early Careers Teacher, amongst your peers you'll know those who feel they might have landed on their feet with their first school, whereas others might have found themselves in far more pressured and negative environments with seemingly unrealistic, or unsustainable expectations around workload. If you're leading in a school, you're one of the people who shape what happens around you and you've got an important part to play. Robertson (2020) talks about a positive climate in schools being characterised by staff teams who are encouraged to take risks and where there are high levels of trust, along with appropriate accountability, where there is mutual respect as well as high standards of conduct, where the views of staff are not only sought after but listened to and considered, where there is genuine recognition of effort and high standards, where there is a sense of appreciation and the understanding of people over paperwork, and where there is a sense of team and collective pride. All of these things impact on staff wellbeing. What jumped out at you from that list? What do those things look like in your setting? How do you know? Where might your setting need to do some work?

These are big things to consider and work towards. They're not solved by fix-it-in-a-day training workshops. They're the ongoing hard work of fleshing things out and putting hands and feet to the task, to embed them in our school communities. We need to keep coming back to our values. We need to forge them and know them and believe in them and fight for them every which way. That's the impassioned plea, but we also need to be able to see them in action. They need to be tangible things we can measure, things we can describe and teach. They need to be part of training and accountability. In her research over the years Brown (2018) states that very few organisations translate their values into observable behaviours. When people know what this value looks like on the ground, when they can see it and hear it and touch it, it becomes a safe base on which to build. When they know what it looks like on the ground they can also see when it is absent or needs developing.

Take the first five years of being in the job. Think of what you learn. Morrison McGill (2015) speaks about skills that we develop in those first years. From building resilience by simply surviving your first year, through to refining your practice, and then building on that by being innovative and taking risks, to being more collaborative in working with others, and then being aspirational and moving into areas of leadership. It's worth bearing in mind that sometimes a progression like that might feel a little neat and tidy, especially if you're in a context where you feel like you're learning resilience for a good many years before you can even begin to move on to anything else. But all the while you're in a school, you're engaged with its values. At one level, you'll almost absorb them like osmosis from just being in the same space as others, but at another, they'll be far more explicit, and present in planning and policy.

If the values upon which we build our school communities are about valuing the people who are a part of it, then we're getting things the right way round. Relationships come first. It does us well to prioritise relationships (i.e. the people) and put relationships before results (Waters, 2021). Evans (2021) talks about the importance of relationships within the entire

FOLLOW MY LEADER

What of your own values do you see reproduced by others in your setting?

school community in promoting personal, academic and professional flourishing. Roberts (2020) reflects on Positive and Character Education, where character and wellbeing are at the heart of education and whole school approaches. She states that where the focus is on building relationships and trust, the people who are a part of the community, whether that be students, families or staff are more able to flourish.

That all makes very good sense. But let's be honest, relationships are messy. People are messy. We all do things and show up in ways we sometimes wish we hadn't. We don't always bring our best selves. Life does its messy thing with us, and things get in the way of us relating in healthy ways. We can feel fearful and let that fear drive our actions in less than helpful ways; we can avoid difficult conversations; we can fail to trust each other when it really matters, to name but a few. So, whilst we're behind the idea, how can we actually do this work? What does it look like in practice? Brown (2018) identifies four skill set areas that can not only be taught but also observed and measured. She calls them rumbling with vulnerability, living into our values, braving trust and learning to rise. These call for internal and external work, especially if we're going to try to navigate the terrain when it comes to shame. When it comes to brave leadership, we all have a part to play. If we work in a school, we lead. We lead by example. If we lead in no other capacity at all in our teams, we still lead the children and young people that we teach and support. So, if we're going to be brave leaders, if we're going to fight against the war that shames wages upon our wellbeing, we can go about the task on three fronts. They are three things that help to repair the ruptures that shame brings. Firstly, we need to build a community where shame can not only be acknowledged but where we seek to combat it whenever it breaks its cover.

Build Community

So, what do you want to build?

I held a tiny newborn the other day and I could have stayed there for ages. Smiling, looking, just struck by their perfect little features and the wonder of who they were, while they slept, safe in my arms. There's something deep inside us that can rest when we know we are smiled upon, when we feel seen and safe. It settles something within us.

Brown (2018) says,

> If we want people to show up, to bring their whole selves . . . so that we can innovate, solve problems, and serve people – we have to be vigilant about creating a culture in which people feel safe, seen, heard, and respected.

Is your school community one in which people (both adults and children) feel safe, seen, heard and respected? Do the adults in your school teams feel and know the very things you want the children and students to feel and know? You may have a range of thoughts and feelings opening up inside you as you consider these questions. Do I feel safe, seen, heard and respected? Do I foster an environment that enables those I lead and work with to feel

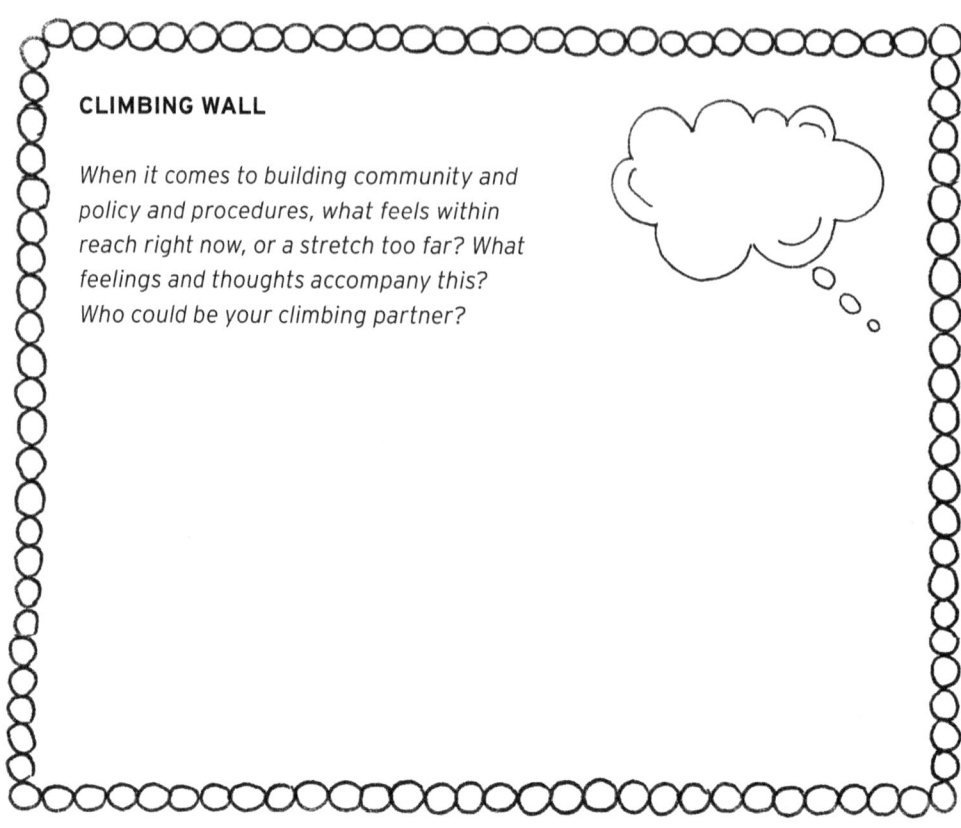

CLIMBING WALL

When it comes to building community and policy and procedures, what feels within reach right now, or a stretch too far? What feelings and thoughts accompany this? Who could be your climbing partner?

these things? When do I or others not feel these things and why might that be? What might need to change and how could we go about doing that?

When it comes to the children in our schools, we know the importance of pupil voice and pupils feeling heard. We know that to be effective and meaningful, they have to be genuinely in the mix and embedded in our practices and procedures. Lip service or tokenism when it comes to student voice doesn't mean a thing. This might be another example where for years we have strived to do things well for the children we teach but have often failed to follow through with the same principles for the adults in our schools. We can ask all the questions but give very little time or space for conversation that leads to change. Knightsmith (2019) talks about the voice of every learner being heard and valued, and how important it is when considering their wellbeing. The same goes for us as staff.

If we want people to feel seen, we first have to see them. If we want people to feel heard, we have to listen . . . and even then, there's a difference between looking and seeing, listening and hearing. With both, one has more depth than the other. You can look and listen just on the outside. But seeing and hearing have more to do with the heart. First and foremost, Cowley (2019) talks about the importance of knowing your people. Don't lose sight of the people. Know them. Know what they love, and what they find difficult. Know what makes them tick. Know what they're good at and what they find difficult. Know something of their families and circumstances, not in a prying way, but because you genuinely care. Be a compassionate leader and an authentic one, one who has integrity, one who seeks to cultivate empathy. Cowley (2019) expands on key values for strategically building a school community where wellbeing is at the centre. He unpacks the importance of celebration, collaboration, respect, trust, support, perseverance, resilience, courage, empathy and time. We talk about values all the time. In some schools the words trip off our tongues quite easily, but sometimes we can still miss the point. They're values because they convey value. They communicate value. People feel valued (seen, heard, respected and safe) when they're in place, when they're embedded into practice. If we're building communities where values like these are the foundation that underpins everything else, then we're going a long way to building communities that counteract the effects of shame. There will still be the internal mind games and well-worn neural pathways that we have to face, but it's harder to maintain the unhelpful narratives (keeping up, no place for failure, you're on your own, be everything you need, compete, prove yourself, you're only valued for what you achieve not who you are, and the 'stuckness' of this is how it's always going to be), if you're in an environment that's working hard to say the opposite. Instead of it all being down to you, the message and practice goes, we do things together here. We have a shared purpose here. There is trust and support here. If as leadership and staff teams we can acknowledge the external pressures but seek to dance to a different tune, then at least we're not blindly reiterating the messages and exacerbating the shame that's in the system. This is the external and internal work we can do. Build healthy communities.

Asking Questions To Inform What We Build

So, what do you want people to feel in your school? That they belong? We know this is so important for all members of our school communities, adults and children alike (Glazzard & Bostwick, 2018). Do you want people to have a quiet confidence in who they are and what they bring to the table? Where there is compassion and kindness, support and trust and where respect is tangible? As well as values we might ordinarily be working towards, if we are to push against the shame that seeks to undo us, we have to be intentional about it in the way that we build our communities. If our common responses to shame are moving away, moving towards and moving against, how can we press into the opposing forces of connecting, openness and working together in the face of differences and anxiety?

Let's look a little closer and ask some more questions. If shame leaves us feeling alone, how can we connect and build a deep sense of community? Instead of competing, what could team look like in our settings? Not just team meetings, or sharing the workload within team planning, but how could our school ethos and practice create a sense of team where we genuinely feel we're being championed, where people have not just got our back but are rooting for us even when the pressure is on, where we can ask for help and say when things are hard and know that people are still for us, even when that might look like boundaries and training and accountability, as well as support? How could team be more than just treats or social events, which are fun and have their purpose, but the legacy of which can dissipate quickly when back in the classroom or staff room? How could the concept of team bring about increased vulnerability, connection, trust and honest conversations about what comes up for us when we feel like we're pitted against each other?

If shame condemns, how can we build up and encourage? Instead of raised eyebrows or behind-closed-doors criticism, what could affirmation look like in our settings? How could we not just create support, but build in kindness to each other, even in the daily crazy? How can we lean into people's giftings? How can we help staff teams to press into what they love? How can we open up creativity in our staff teams rather than shutting it down or not having time for it? Where is there intentional space for regularly sharing the good stuff of the day and not just the difficult stuff? How can we openly celebrate each other's successes? How easy do we make it for people to ask for help, and how guilt-free and genuine is the response of leadership when they do? Is there a sense of being inconvenienced by any request for help, or are conversations valued as an opportunity to develop practice and show compassion? How proactive are we in asking how people are, rather than waiting for things to decline to a level that requires more serious help? How much is asking for help seen as a strength for professional development rather than something to be held against us? Could our areas of development be viewed not just as a journey towards learning and best practice, but also towards a greater sense of wholeness and wellbeing? And could that simply have merit in itself? How can we listen to how people are doing and create safe spaces for people to be able to really say when things are difficult? How can we create environments where we can be honest about both our strengths and weaknesses, without fear of judgement? It's got to be both.

Instead of over-function how can we bring about more balance for staff teams and have clear boundaries as well as expectations around workload and recreation? How can schools and groups of schools ensure timelines for things being completed are not shifted in a way that squeezes people's capacity? How can large academy trusts still keep sight of the people so that people don't feel like they're just minions or cogs in a huge machine? How can the interconnectedness of our work and why we even do this thing called teaching be conveyed and understood so that we genuinely recognise the part we each have to play, and value what we all bring to our environments? Just Associates (2006) talk about the concept of power with, which has to do with finding common ground and building collective strength, power to, where everyone knows the part they play and power within, coming from a place of self-worth which enables you to respect others in the face of differences. Building a community where all these things are valued and practised can help deter a culture of over-function and shame.

Creating Safe Spaces

If shame has a tendency to silence, how can we safely speak up, speak out and bring things out into the open? We know how important it is for children and young people to feel safe

GARDEN MAKEOVER

What do you want to plant, nurture and see grow in your community? How could you go about doing this?

in our schools, and that it's only when they experience safety in their environment that they can begin to engage with the risky task of learning and challenge. We've already mentioned Maslow's famous hierarchy of needs (1943) which says safety is crucial before we can access the parts of our brains that are required for other things. So as adults we need to lean into this idea of safety too. What could that look like for us? Is it even possible to create safe spaces in which staff can share in confidence? Could additional funding be sought to facilitate this? Could this be not just in the form of seeking support from HR and Occupational Health teams or calling an emergency emotional and mental health helpline when someone hits crisis, but as an ongoing regular investment in the health of staff teams? Might that look like investing in coaching for staff or some kind of regular supervision for individuals from a therapeutic perspective, and could this be available to everyone, not just leaders? Oberholzer and Boyle (2023) argue that mentoring and coaching should be a part of everyone's professional learning journey throughout their career, not just at the start or when things are difficult. What about counselling? We value its place for students, but many adults can still shy away from even thinking about it as a resource to support their own wellbeing and mental health. Luxmoore (2013) talks about the vast array of relationships within schools and how counsellors can be a positive, integral part of school communities. What if there was no shame about seeking help and counselling or therapeutic training could be made more available for staff as well as students? How could we build enough trust within our school environments to consider these options? These are big and some might say pie-in-the-sky ideas. With already fraught budgets how could we even begin to entertain them? But if we value people, if we value each other, perhaps wider options have to be considered.

So many questions! So many things to think about. So many things to which we need to put our minds to the task. But for shame to have less free reign in our schools, wellbeing must be right at the heart of everything we do for the children and staff (Erasmus, 2019). In our communities, we have to keep our vision and values at the fore. We have to keep on communicating who we are and what we hold dear. It speaks of our shared purpose and builds connectedness. By putting in the hard work of asking and reflecting on these kinds of questions, we can seek to shape some of the externals of our school settings, to try to foster emotionally safer environments that support our wellbeing. The more aware we are of how all the not enoughs and too muchness of our jobs trigger our own shame, the more intentionally we can press in to calling it out and pushing against it individually and together. This will help create healthier, more sustainable school teams and communities, who know their gifts and areas of expertise, who lead with purpose out of their sense of calling and vocation, with a passion and sense of belonging that gets them through the hard things. This is the task to which we need to put our hands. Another is the ongoing work of growing in self-awareness.

Grow in Self-awareness

In the previous chapter we looked at some tools that help us develop our self-awareness. Growing in self-awareness is the internal work of wellbeing and leading bravely. It requires bravery and courage. The process opens opportunities for us to lean into becoming more

LOOK IN THE MIRROR

What do you do when you want to look good? What do you do when you want to be right? What do you do when you want to win? What do these behaviours look like for you? When do they crop up, and how might you want to see them change?

whole people. It brings about both internal and external work. It causes us to examine what we are thinking and feeling and why that might be. It causes us to ask how the ways we show up fit with our values. It brings things up for us and others, and the challenge is how do we personally respond to any anxiety it throws up? What do we do with fear when it surfaces? In awkward conversations, what work might we need to do internally to seek to show up in a way that is not defensive, where we can remain attentive to what is being said and remain present to the person who is speaking, whilst also acknowledging the anxiety we feel? If shame is in the mix, the likelihood is the atmosphere will feel charged, and we would rather be anywhere else than in that conversation at that time. It's a tough task, but there's something of gold even in the trying.

When people talk about personal growth it can all sound a bit introspective. A bit personal. But the truth is, it can lead to changes in us that impact others for the better. When we feel rooted, we can grow. We use the phrase 'to put down roots.' When we talk about our roots, we're talking about our identity and knowing who we are and what we're for. There's a sense of settled-ness, which is all to do with feeling safe and grounded. It communicates something of belonging and connection, somewhere that feels like home, in the best sense of the word. When you are rooted, you're able to draw up nutrients from the soil around you; you're able to draw up the goodness and what you need from the environment in which you are placed . . . and that, in time, produces growth. The internal work of personal growth and the conditions in which that takes place go hand in hand. You have to water, feed and care for a plant. The community around it has to tend to it, if it is to grow, thrive and flourish. Deep down we want to grow. We don't want to be static. We want to bear fruit, if you like. It's almost as if we sense there's something of a gap between who we are and who we want to be, or maybe even who we feel we were made to be. It's like there could be something more for us and in us that we could grow towards. A bit like plants reaching for the light. We also have this innate leaning towards connectedness, towards something beyond ourselves. When the World Health Organisation talks about health and wellbeing it speaks of people having the right and duty to participate in planning and implementing it, and that this is done both individually and collectively (WHO, 2023). We want to work productively and contribute to our communities. We want to be productive. We might not call it that. We're more likely to say that we want to make a difference. But there's something that comes from within us that we want to give to others, in order to see good things grow.

Instead of personal growth, in education contexts we tend to use less flowery language. The phrase we use more is personal development. Teacher development reforms in the UK in recent years have seen a major investment in the professional development of staff in schools, from training and supporting those in initial teacher training and their early careers all the way through to those in mid to senior leadership roles. The basis of this has been a 'golden thread of high-quality evidence underpinning the support, training and development available through the entirety of a teacher's career' (DfE, 2022). The aim has been that this will lead to strong professional development and improved quality of teaching that in turn will impact positively on improving pupil outcomes for all. Tomsett and Uttley (2020) talk about the importance of prioritising professional learning to support staff wellbeing.

The hope is that having a sustained and consistent approach to career development will attract people into the role and keep them in it beyond their first few years. In the policy's introduction it states that 'these reforms will help teachers . . . feel more confident and in control of their careers' (DfE, 2022). As teachers, we want to be confident, highly qualified, highly trained and highly supported, not just to be able to deliver the goods, achieve results or compete with other global education systems, but to personally thrive. If our wellbeing is in a good place, we're more able to thrive, and that's what the children will see. They'll see people who want to be in the classroom, people who are present to them, with them and for them, and that will positively impact their wellbeing. If schools are highly relational places of work and our roles are based on this complex interplay of relationships, then it's not enough to just get good at the teaching or leading stuff; we also have to get good at or at least get better at the relational stuff, and that includes noticing the place of shame and growing in self-awareness. If, using the DfE's words, I want to feel more confident and in control of my career, I also have to know that regardless of how well trained or supported I am, there will be times in school when I don't feel confident or in control, and then I need to know what to do when this is the case. Maybe school communities could mirror the 'learn that . . .' and 'learn how to . . .' language of statements we see in National Professional Qualifications around becoming an expert teacher, to include indicators around our self and relational awareness.

So, to the task. What can we do? What can we try? It's often said that we have to own our wellbeing. We have to intentionally start with ourselves before we can invite others into the task. If others see you trying to revisit a conversation in which you showed up in a way you didn't want to, if they see you trying to repair something you messed up or apologising for the way you blew everything up out of proportion, if you start noticing this about yourself and start doing the work of trying to show up differently, they're going to notice. These are the tasks. These are the tasks of seeking to repair the ruptures that we experience around us. The self-reflection and then seeking to show up differently in our conversations and interactions, the self-reflection and then seeking to show up differently in the way we plan things and what we hope to achieve. If you become aware that your long-term planning and target-setting is sometimes driven by a fear of failing or not doing enough, and you start to reset some of those targets, or have conversations around what that throws up for you, others are going to notice. Over time, people will begin to see your intention, your trying and your values . . . and it might even catch on.

Maybe a place to start could be to revisit your school wellbeing questionnaires and include elements around growing in self-awareness. Maybe you could start the practice of noticing using some of the tools shared in the last chapter, or by diving into some of the self-reflection activities. If it sounds like I'm not providing any answers and I'm just asking questions, it's in the asking of the questions that comes the equipping and the empowering. That's where our self-awareness grows. It's in the asking of questions that we have to grapple with all the murky stuff that's stirred up and lean into change. The asking of the questions is a way we can start to get unstuck, because it brings hidden things out into the open. The only solution, if you like, is to commit to go on the journey . . . and to know there will be resistance. You will feel it, and so will others. So, use the reflection questions in each chapter. Use them to examine yourself. Take a good look . . . and grow.

And then, as part of the growing, though it starts with us, it can only go so far if we remain on our own. If we are to push against the work of shame, the third vital task is to find our people.

Find Your People

In a world where we are so adept at individuality and superficiality, our hearts were made for community, and we find ourselves longing for deep connection. It's strange, how we can be surrounded by people at work, at play and in our own homes and families, and still at times feel lonely. We're connected in so many ways yet often still don't really feel seen. Or known. And whilst we deeply long for this, we also shy away from it. We have this tendency to hide, to put up our guard, to pretend. We say, 'I'm good' ('fine' would be too much of a giveaway) when we're not; we avoid conversations that feel awkward; we tuck our pain and fear away. For if I really told you how I sometimes feel, would it be too much? Would I be too much? Would I not be enough for you to stick with me? And we fear being pushed away. It's part of our human condition. This is the reality of shame in action. It keeps us separate from each other. Relationships can be one of the most life-giving things on earth, but they can also be where we're most wounded. So, we're wary . . . and yet, we want to feel deeply seen, heard, known and to experience the safety of that space. In that vulnerable space we want to find that we are enough. When we get a glimpse of this, it grounds us, it does something in our souls.

When my grandparents were alive, maybe there was more of a sense of community about the way people lived. The cliches say that people back then wouldn't think twice about knocking on a neighbour's door to ask for something if they'd run out of it, and they'd wile away the hours nattering at the front gate, while the kids kicked a tin can up and down the road with jumpers for goalposts. Even with all of that going on, loneliness was still probably a thing. Now, our communities can look like online spaces and chats as well as being in the same physical space with people. We feel the joys as well as the frustrations of doing life with others, but even with busy diaries and hectic headspaces we can still sometimes feel like we're on our own. During the isolation of the pandemic, when normal life was curtailed and things looked very different for a while, many communities worked hard to build some level of connection with others, especially looking out for those who were on their own. We noticed loneliness as a stark reality. Now, in some ways we're back to how life was before. But even with more attention being paid to wellbeing and mental health, it can still feel like loneliness is something that is hard to mention. Because how can we be (or at least look) so connected and yet sometimes feel so alone at the same time?

Neuroscience says connection with others is good for us. Indeed, from the moment we are born we seek it out and depend upon it for our survival. Research states that connection with others impacts our wellbeing for the better and social connection has positive effects on our health (Robson, 2025). Studies show that people with a strong sense of belonging are more likely to report good health (Killam, 2026). Friendships really do matter. They have a measurable influence on our health and wellbeing (Dunbar, 2022). Don't have in mind the sometimes cheap and loosely coined BFF ('best friends forever') phrase but think more of life-giving friendships that speak of mess, blood, sweat and tears and really do stand the test of time. Brown (2021) likens connection to an anchor that steadies us when we feel adrift. She talks about the importance of courage, compassion and connection in our relationships with others and speaks of the intentional work of trying to live wholeheartedly (Brown, 2022).

When it comes to the depth or quality of our relationships, the remarkable thing is that if we can find just a few people we can deeply trust and with whom we can voice our more hidden things, where we can be authentic and try for a moment to do away with the hiding, it frees us in surprising ways. It's like a breath of fresh air. Have you ever read a really good book, and part of its joy was the whole breadth of the story that was told, the intricacies of the characters and their flaws, the roads they walked, the hardships they faced, the perseverance they showed? By the time you turn the last page you feel like you almost know them. There's something powerful about telling our whole stories. There's something powerful in the telling and the listening. It can almost feel like sacred ground . . . because we long to be fully known. Have you ever come to the end of an evening with friends – you've said your goodbyes and they've headed out the door – and you just sit on the sofa and pause a while and know that that was a good night? Maybe you shared something of the good things and hard things together, and it felt meaningful, real. It's that kind of feeling. You know you're better off for having them in your life. They're people you know you can turn to when the wheels are falling off; they're people where you can say it how it really is; you trust them and you know they're for you. You are known by them. They're your people. With all the unravelling that can happen in us and around us at school, and these things we're beginning to notice and feel within ourselves, it's good to go somewhere with that. We don't have to breach confidentiality, but we can still speak deeply about what is going on for us with those we trust. Intentionally pursuing connection with others is a way to stand, even in the face of things that feel hard. Connection pours balm on wounds, binds up what feels broken and bandages the deepest of fractures.

When we say 'could do better' about wellbeing, finding your people is a 'doing better' practice. We do well to do it. Instinctively we want to hide our weaknesses and sense of lack, but in telling our whole stories what we find is it builds us up. Where shame says stay silent, find people with whom you can safely speak up. Where shame says withdraw, press into being with the right people. People whose opinions matter. Where shame says you're no good or not enough, spend time with people who know you and with whom you know your worth. We need to find people with whom we can be vulnerable and take down our masks, with whom

FACE THE FEAR

What are you fearful of (really worried about) right now? Rate them on a scale of 1–5. Who could you talk to about this?

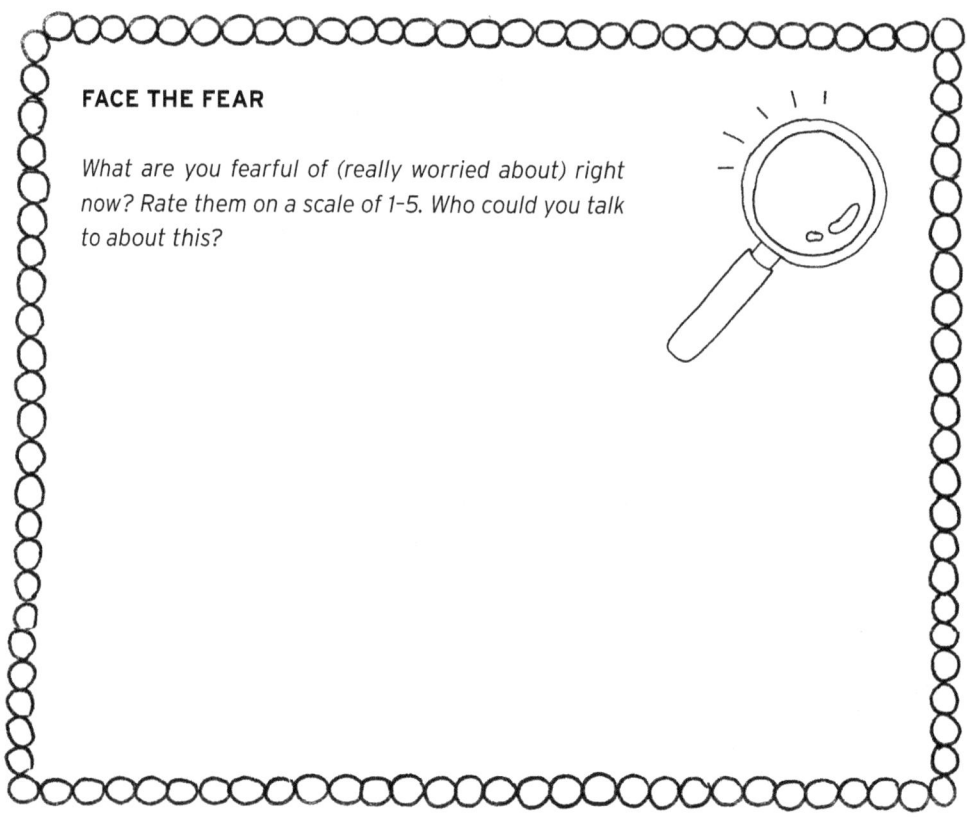

we can dare to be brutally honest. I say brutal, because sometimes it can feel that way. It's hard to say 'I feel so undone when this happens.' It's hard to say 'I still feel so anxious when I'm in that situation,' and even though we've talked about it before, it's still not going away. It takes courage to say you feel like you're spiralling and you're not sure when it will stop. We need to seek out people we can say these kinds of things to. People who will walk with us, cheer us on and want the best for us, those who will love us, even when that looks like holding up a mirror and saying perhaps uncomfortable truths, those who will keep us accountable to how we want to grow and be more whole. We don't need fixing. But we do want to be seen, heard and known. We want a place where it's safe to just be. Be vulnerable. Belong. Finding your people might be your partner or spouse, or someone in your family or close friends. What matters is that you connect deeply. Because connecting deeply with others stands in the face of everything shame wants to unravel in you. When we're vulnerable, something happens in that space. Something of our courage strikes a chord with others, and opens up something in them . . . and often, instead of the rejection we fear, what we experience in that space is compassion and connection . . . and we find we are not alone.

But finding our people is something we have to work at. Trusted friends don't just rock up out of nowhere one day. Forming deep friendships is hard, it can feel risky and it takes time.

There are no shortcuts to the process. Hall (2019) researched the time it takes for friendships to deepen to different levels. We have to put in the hours. That makes sense of course, because giving someone our time communicates something about value. We give quality time to those we love and care about. We've mentioned already how time is a valuable commodity, and we particularly notice when it is lacking. Everyday phrases nod to the value we place on investing time in relationships. There are those to whom we won't give the time of day, and others who we'll give all the time in the world to. Giving time to intentionally lean into connection and develop deep friendships counteracts the work of shame and supports our wellbeing. It is a worthy task to put our mind to, a task to put our hearts to and to prioritise with our time. So, what could a next step be for you when it comes to investing in friendship? What could a simple task be for you this week? Try that one thing.

There's a kindness about all three of these things – building connection as we build community, growing in self-awareness and vulnerability and experiencing the safety of being known in finding your people. When it comes to bettering our wellbeing, the way ahead is to press into all three so that we can lead bravely in our schools. All three aspects help us with the hard things and stand against the forces of shame . . . because at the end of the day, what makes a difference to all the young people we work with is us – you and me. You have value. You make a difference.

And . . .

***** Rest*****

Task and Try One Thing

PATTERN CHALLENGE

What ways do you see people relating to each other in your setting or team? What positives do you see? Are there any patterns in the way that colleagues interact with each other that you would like to see change? Why? What could be a next step towards this?

IN THE FOG

How able are you to admit that sometimes you just don't know what to do next or how to do it? What do you need to become clearer? What are you finding difficult to see about the way ahead? Who could you talk to, to help bring some clarity?

THE TORTOISE AND THE HARE

What would you like to fix quickly but you know is a long, slow, hard race? What kind of course do you need to take and why?

CRUSTY OLD HEART

What are some of the ugly ways in which you interact with others if you feel a bit threatened? (Do you do any of these? - give the silent treatment, turn the screw, it's my way or no way, take the moral high ground, shout louder, get busy, shut down etc. . . .) What impact do you think these have on those around you? What would you like to see change?

ICE CREAM PARLOUR

What tastes sweet to you right now in school? What sweet flavours are you seeing emerging within your teams?

POETRY PRACTICE

Robert Frost, the American poet, once said 'Education is the ability to listen to almost anything without losing your temper or your self-confidence' (1960). What do these things look like for you?

DIY

Do you ever feel like you'd be better off just doing a particular job yourself? When do you notice these kinds of thoughts? Why do you think you might have come to this conclusion? How do you feel when things are solely down to you? Who could you talk with about this?

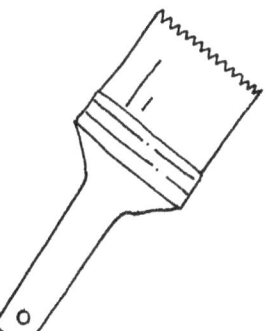

OUT OF CONTROL

When do you feel out of control? What do you tend to do when you feel like this and how do your responses impact on those around you?

WHEN THE STAKES ARE HIGH

When it comes to work, what feels like high stakes to you (where it feels like there's a lot riding on something)? Why might you be thinking this and who could you talk to about it?

THE END OF THE WORLD

When facing feelings of anxiety, where might you sometimes catastrophise about what might happen? In the face of these feelings, can you speak with someone to help you get the thinking part of your brain working around what might realistically happen?

REARVIEW MIRROR

How easy do you find it to ask for help, or to admit that you could have done something better? If you make a mistake, how do you look back over it and go about cleaning it up, or hope to approach it differently next time?

EXTERMINATE!

What do you want to do away with right now? Why? What could you do instead?

LOUD AND CLEAR

How aware are you of your shame voice (that voice of self-criticism that leaves you feeling a bit shrivelled and stuck)? What kinds of things does it say? Who could you talk to about it?

MONSTER UNDER THE BED

That thing that you're most fearful of – what is it? How real is it? How big is it? What can you do to deal with it/cope with the fear/ bring it out from lurking in the shadows?

RELAX

How do you best unwind? How can you be intentional about creating time and space for this in your week? What could that look like and what benefits might you see?

BRAIN DUMP

What are you thinking What are you feeling

YOU MAKE A DIFFERENCE

References

Brown, B. (2018). *Dare to lead: Brave work. Tough conversations. Whole hearts. Daring greatly and rising strong at work* (pp. 11, 12). Vermilion. Penguin Random House.

Brown, B. (2021). *Atlas of the heart: Mapping meaningful connection and the language of human experience*. Vermilion.

Brown, B. (2022). *The gifts of imperfection* (10th Anniversary ed.). Hazelden Publishing.

Cowley, A. (2019). *The wellbeing toolkit: Sustaining, supporting and enabling school staff* (pp. 31, 33). Bloomsbury Education.

Department for Education. (2022). *Delivering world-class teacher development (policy paper)* (pp. 4, 5). https://assets.publishing.service.gov.uk/media/62850bddd3bf7f1f433ae149/Delivering_world_class_teacher_development_policy_paper.pdf

Dunbar, R. (2022). *Friends: Understanding the power of our most important relationships*. Abacus.

Erasmus, C. (2019). *The mental health and wellbeing handbook for schools: Transforming mental health support on a budget*. Jessica Kingsley.

Evans, K. (Ed.). (2021). *The big book of whole school wellbeing*. Corwin Ltd, Sage Publications.

Glazzard, J., & Bostwick, R. (2018). *Positive mental health: A whole school approach*. Routledge.

Hall, J. A. (2019). How many hours does it take to make a friend? *Journal of Social and Personal Relationships, 36*(4), 1278–1296. Sage Publications.

Just Associates. (2006). *Making change happen: Power; concepts for revisioning power for justice, equality and peace*. https://justassociates.org/wp-content/uploads/2020/08/mch3_2011_final_0.pdf

Killam, K. (2026). *The art and science of connection: Why social health is the missing key to living longer, healthier, and happier*. Piatkus.

Knightsmith, P. (2019). *The mentally healthy schools workbook: Practical tips, ideas, action plans and worksheets for making meaningful change*. Jessica Kingsley.

Luxmoore, N. (2013). *School counsellors working with young people and staff; A whole school approach*. Jessica Kingsley.

Maslow, A. H. (1943). A theory of human motivation. *Psychological Review, 50*, 370–396. http://doi.org/10.1037/h0054346

Morrison McGill, R. (2015). *Teacher toolkit: Helping you survive your first five years*. Bloomsbury Education.

Oberholzer, L., & Boyle, D. (2023). *Mentoring and coaching in education: A guide to coaching and mentoring teachers at every stage of their careers*. Bloomsbury.

Ratcliffe, S. (Ed.). (2016). *Oxford essential quotations* (4th ed.). Oxford University Press. eISBN: 9780191826719, Readers Digest, April 1960.

Roberts, F. (2020). *For flourishing's sake: Using positive education to support character development and wellbeing*. Jessica Kingsley.

Robertson, B. (2020). *The teaching delusion. Why teaching in our schools isn't good enough (and how we can make it better)* (p. 141). John Catt Educational.

Robson, D. (2025). *The laws of connection: 13 social strategies that will transform your life*. Canongate Books.

Tomsett, J., & Uttley, J. (2020). *Putting staff first: A blueprint for revitalising our schools*. John Catt.

Waters, S. (Ed.). (2021). *Cultures of staff wellbeing and mental health in schools: Reflecting on positive case studies*. Open University Press.

World Health Organisation. (2023). *WHO framework for meaningful engagement of people living with noncommunicable diseases, and mental health and neurological conditions* (p. iv). https://iris.who.int/bitstream/handle/10665/367340/9789240073074-eng.pdf?sequence=1

Conclusion

If you checked in here first, hello. Some of us like to know something of the ending before we get stuck into a book. We want to know if there's a happily ever after, or at least to know that things end well. So here goes. The journey is looking brighter. We've still a way to go, but we've already come so far. Wellbeing is now seen as important, and commitments have been made to keep it that way. So now it's just a case of doing better with it all.

When it comes to working in a school, you might not always think that you make a difference, but you do. You might not always think that you matter, but you do. You might not always think that you're worth remarking on or taking note of, but the truth is you are remarkable. You might not always think that you are valued, but you are of such great worth. You might not always think that you are seen or heard, but your heart and the work of your hands is seen by each child who has ever stood in front of you, and you seeing them and them knowing that they have been seen by you is the most important thing you do. You might not always think that you are enough, but enough of that. You might sometimes think you are on your own, but we are in this together.

These are the truths we are to hold on to if we are to do better with our wellbeing. These are the truths we need to be reminded of when we find ourselves under pressure on so many fronts. These statements are not some kind of self-help mantra that is somehow all on you, that if you somehow say them enough or believe them hard enough, they'll somehow manifest into being. My hope is that as you do the work of this book, you would somehow know deep in your soul that these things are true about you. That you would be able to grasp hold of them tightly as deeply held truths, even when circumstances seem to say otherwise.

The climate in which we work can sometimes feel like such a challenge, with so much expected of us, yet with so few resources at our disposal. Having to do so much with so little for so long is hard. Do it long enough and it can sometimes leave you feeling like you're not really valued or that you don't really matter. Sometimes it's hard to see how much you matter when it feels like things around you say you don't. What we often find is that for a while we rally and press on, but over time it can all leave us feeling that we're lacking. That we're somehow not enough. And before we know it shame joins in and plays like a broken record, round and round, putting us all in a bit of a spin. So, it's important we reset the balance of who we are and what we do. It's important we go through the process to remind ourselves. Remember and reimagine the good stuff of why we do this thing after all, examine ourselves and look at the evidence of how things are going and how things can feel not just on the surface but deep down in our bones and in the environments in which we work, then to venture into safely speaking up and sharing about these things we have found, the good stuff and the hard stuff and becoming equipped and empowered to try things and do the next task of doing better.

Maybe as we do these things, we can lean into changing the tone of some of the less helpful messages we might feel are inherent in the system around us. Perhaps we could reframe them and in so doing reframe our responses to them. What if keeping up could be more like a celebration of keepy-uppies? Like when you're cheering on someone who keeps on going and keeps the ball bouncing. Look what you've done! Look what you've achieved! Well done! Maybe there's no place for failure can become, remember it doesn't all fall on you, we're not all leaning on you and there is space for us all to learn. What if when it comes down to it, you're on your own becomes when it comes down to it, you're not alone, remember your team and those who are for you. Instead of be everything you need, what if you knew you didn't have to do things alone and that you really could ask others to help, to walk alongside, to do it together, and what's really needed might just be you in that moment, not everything else? What if compete becomes but that won't make you complete. It's not going to fulfil you if you try to fill all the gaps yourself. You don't have to earn your value here. What if prove yourself becomes an assurance of don't worry, you have proven yourself time and again, so rest assured, settle down, we know you, we trust you? What if you're only valued for what you achieve, not who you are, becomes no look at who you are! Look what you bring to the room. Look what you bring to the people around you. And what if this is how it's always going to be becomes yes, you're going to keep on seeing something amazing in all those children before you, you're going to keep on seeing them when they feel all at sea and just want to be seen?

Maybe this book has been something of a discovery for you. Maybe you had little idea of how shame can wiggle its way into our thinking and damage our view of ourselves and others. Maybe you didn't know how it can inch its way into normal everyday interactions and cause so much havoc. With a growing awareness of shame and its tricks, my hope is that you've been able to notice and think and then pick up some tools with which you can act, in light of all you are discovering about yourself and your school community.

Wellbeing is a collective journey but also a very personal one. We are in this together and need to look out for each other along the way, but we also journey in our own heads and minds and bodies. So, build community, grow in self-awareness and find your people as ways to do things better . . . as ways to feel more seen, safe and secure. My hope is that by using this book to reflect, you can revisit it time and again to reset vision, inspire hope and equip you to carry on. If it's helpful to go further with any of the themes or things that might have come up for you, more resources and additional avenues of support are included at the end.

Remember and Reimagine. Examine and Evidence. Safely Speak Up and Share, Be Equipped and Empowered, and then get to the Task and Try One Thing. It doesn't matter how big or small that one thing is. RESET.

*****

A year or two before, we were sitting at the table in a pub. Me and that same friend from the beginning of the book, the one we were remembering in the wellbeing garden. That same friend who wanted to do things well and wanted for us to be well in the doing of them. Spring felt like it could be on its way but hadn't quite arrived just yet and people were still wrapped up in big woolly jumpers, covered up against the cold. I've started writing another book, I said. And as I tried to unpack my early ideas, she listened hard. There's a need for this out there, she said. She knew it. Not just because she knew it for herself, but because she knew it for others ... all those others she'd worked with over the years. And all the while I wanted her to grasp a sense of her own value and how different things can begin to feel when you feel seen and safe and secure. Not that I've got it all down, of course, but because I'm on the self-same journey. We may not be able to bring about any big change in the system as we go on this journey together, but maybe we could learn something that could bring about change for us? In us?

This is not just about being in the job for the long haul or avoiding burnout, I said. Nor is it about surviving and scraping through by the skin of our teeth. It's about still having hope and passion and those very reasons that we went into teaching still being alive in us as at the end of the day. It's a matter of our wellbeing and our hearts being held; it's about bravery and courage and hard things and good things; it's about us learning and growing and caring. It's about us doing better. Because we could.

ADDITIONAL RESOURCES

Anna Freud Guidance on Supporting Staff Wellbeing in Schools
https://www.annafreud.org/resources/schools-and-colleges/supporting-staff-wellbeing-in-schools/

DfE Education Staff Wellbeing Charter
https://assets.publishing.service.gov.uk/media/6194eb37d3bf7f0551f2d1a5/DfE_Education_Workforce_Welbeing_Charter_Nov21.pdf

DfE Guidance - Promoting and Supporting Mental Health and Wellbeing in Schools and Colleges
https://www.gov.uk/guidance/mental-health-and-wellbeing-support-in-schools-and-colleges

DfE Workload Reduction Toolkit
https://improve-workload-and-wellbeing-for-school-staff.education.gov.uk/workload-reduction-toolkit/

Education Support
https://www.educationsupport.org.uk

Education Support Helpline
08000 562 561

Education Support Resources
https://www.educationsupport.org.uk/resources/

Education Support Staff Wellbeing Audit Tool
https://www.educationsupport.org.uk/resources/for-organisations/guides/staff-wellbeing-audit/

Hub of Hope
https://hubofhope.co.uk/

Mentally Healthy Schools
https://www.mentallyhealthyschools.org.uk

MIND
https://www.mind.org.uk/workplace.

MindEd
https://mindedhub.org.uk/

NHS Every Mind Matters
https://www.nhs.uk/every-mind-matters/

What Works Centre for Wellbeing
https://whatworkswellbeing.org/

INDEX

Note: Page numbers in *italics* indicate a figure on the corresponding page

accountability 1, 50, 55, 112-113, 193, 197
achievement 3, *11*, *24*, 87, 106, 144-145
action plan 2, 38, 86, 109, 111, 136
additional needs *see* Special Educational Needs and Disability (SEND)
Adverse Childhood Experiences 79, 146
adversity 131, 134, 162
affirmation 137, 145, 176, 198
anxiety 44, 55, 173-174, 197, 202, *214*; in children 142, 144; increase of 136, 164, 166, *184*; lowering of 12; and shame *140*, 146
aspirations 75, 144
assessment 46, 113, 143
attachment 73, 132
attainment 84, 104-106
autopilot 166

behaviour 78-80, 82, 111, 136, 193, *201*; challenging 35, 84, 142-143; and emotional regulation 170; management of 48, 73, 86, 131; and shame 145-146
belonging 55, 78, *108*, 132, 176, 200-205
boundaries 50, 137, 145, 173-174, 176, 197-198; professional 76-77
Brown, B. 131, 135, 143, 163, 193-195, 205

capacity 106, 134, 136-137, 174, 195, 198
celebration 2, *11*, 50, 78, 197, 222
circle of control 175
coaching 43, 86, 200
collaboration 1, 197
commitment 1, 13, 50,107, 131, 178
community 9, 40, 55, 104, 167, 204; building 138, 177-178, 192, 195-199, 202, 207; and connection 13, 78, 132; local 36, 80-83, 86, 171; school 15, 42, 44, 48-50, 113, 222
compassion 3, 84, 147, 173, 197-198, 205-206; fatigue 80; self 175-176
competence 40, 84, 86, 141, 165

competition 80, 109-111
confidence 45-46, 71, 134, 163, 197, 200; self 212
connection 80, 132, 174, 177, 198, 204-207; and neuroscience 13; and relationship 113, 165, 202; and shame 144, 146
counselling 200
courage 138, 143, 163, 197, 200, 205-206
creativity 9, 39, 42, 50, 172-173, 198; and resilience 131
culture 42, 104-106, 136, 147, 192-195, 198; of deficit 33, 172; and wellbeing 89, 115

data 8, 52, 55, 87, 113, 145; inputting 39; tracking 47
defence mechanisms 141

early intervention 83, 147
Education Inspection Framework 55
Education Staff Wellbeing Charter 1
emotion 3, 60, *107*, 165-170, *179-180*
empathy 147, 197
empowerment 144, 163, 177-179, 203, 222-223
encouragement 52, 113, 193, 198; of children 8, 16, 78, 83
engagement 82-83, 145
ethos 104, 145, 192, 197
expectation 71, 89, 105, 113, 136, 168; children's 73-74; of colleagues 83-85, 198; of community 80-82; of government 45, 87, 162; of leadership 34, 49-50, 85-87, 173, 193; parental 74-76, 80, 144; personal 71-73

failure 105-106, 114, 143-144, 197, 222
friendship 7, 73, 76, 135, 205-207
funding *see* resources

gratitude 13-14
growth mindset 105
guilt 131-132, 198

identity 78, 137, 176, 202
imposter syndrome 66, 141
inclusion 35, 111, 145-146
isolation 2, 204

Johari Window 164-165

kindness 7, 175, 198, 207

leadership 85-86, 192-199; senior 35, 43, 110, 141, 202
limitations 174-175, *186*
loneliness 204

Maslow, A. H. 35, 200
mental health 2-3, 83-84, 89, 175, 200, 204; children's 35, 44-45, 55, 79, 146, 170; and Ofsted 55; and shame 132
mentor 43, 73, 84, 86, 144, 200
moderation 50, 141-142
motivation 2, 145

neuroscience 13, 205
nurture 79, *117*

Ofsted 1, 13, 53-55, 82, 109, 162

passion 11, *24*, 52, 54, 143; children's 7, 9, 16, 172; and resilience 131, 173, 177, 200, 223
perfectionism 137, *140*
performance 13, 80, 106, 144; management 50, 55, 86; tables 82
perseverance 197, 205
power 2, 86, 145, 163, 172-173, 198; of learning 8; positions of 49
professional development 86, 198, 202
progress 47, 80, 84, 104-106, 109, 177; children's 54, 87, 111, 143
provision 42, 44-46, 82-83, *117*; specialist 147, 171
PSA 48
pseudo family 77-79

recruitment 43
rejection 176, 206
relationship 1, 13, 73, 164-167, 171-173, 203-207; in school communities 76-81, 113, *121*, 145-147, 192-195, 200

reputation 40, 44; in community 54, 82, 87, 109-110, 144
resilience 47, 86, 106, 131, 193; children's 7, 50, 111, 173; development of 11; factors 132; and shame 147; and values 197
resources 2-3, 41-42, 55, 71, 87, 221; and community 83, 171; and school environments 42, 109; and self-care 170, 178; and SEND 45-46, 113, 147
respect 49-50, 142, 173, 192, 195, 197-198; mutual 193
responsibility 1, 76, 79-80, 83, 105, *179*; area of 86, 178; and safeguarding 79, 107; sense of 50, 168
rest *41*, 175, *187*, 207
retention 43

safeguarding 79-80, 83, 107, 131, 175
scarcity 33, 46, 83
self-awareness 163-165, 170, 177-178, 200-203, 207, 222
self-esteem 12, 144, 147
self-reflection 167, 203
self-regulation 165, 170-171
shame 106, 131-134, 141-143; and competition 110-112; cycle 143-149; and stress 134-140
Special Educational Needs and Disability (SEND) 44-45, 76, 82, 146, 171
standards 1, 45, 53, 87, 193; teachers' 105
stress 39, 43-44, 131-135, 143-146, 173, *185*; relief 61; stressors 80, 134, 166, 170-172
supervision 3, 178, 200

Teacher Wellbeing Index 1-2, 87
time 2-3, *17*, 33-34, 55, 147, 173; and administration 39-41; and children's needs 35-36, 44; and curriculum 34-35; and friendship 205-207; and self-compassion 175-176, 197; and training 36-39, 43; and trust 76, 111
The Timpson Review 79
training 43, 46, 83, 85-86, 136, 178; and accountability 193, 197; initial teacher 72, 202; and mental health 79, 175; therapeutic 200; and time 36-39
trauma 79-80, 132, 145-147
trust/Trust 39, 47-53, 111-112, 193, 197-198; Academy 38, 85-86, 109, 112, 141; build 9, 73-74, 82, 138, 195; and learning 35, 79, 146; and Ofsted 53-55; parental 76-78; position of 86

values 71, 84, 105, 132, *154*, 202-203; and vision 192-195, 197, 200; young people's 74
vision 113, 192, 200, 222
vulnerability 83, 105, 177, 195, 198, 207; and courage 143, 163; and failure 79; and learning 79

Working Lives of Teachers and Leaders survey 39
workload 48, 174, 193, 197-198; high 39; and Ofsted 53, 55; and stress 131, 145

ABOUT THE AUTHOR

Pippa McLean has spent much of her life being a teacher and SENDCO (Special Educational Needs and Disability Coordinator). She found her feet teaching where she grew up, in the London Borough of Newham in East London, before moving on to other primary schools across the South East.

She loves investing in others and has a heart to see people thrive and connected in community. Her love for people over the years has been seen in her commitment to school communities and other local community projects. Pippa is author of *The Pocket Diary of a SENCO: An Honest Guide to the Aspirations, Frustrations and Joys of Championing Inclusion in Schools.*

She continues to love a good book, a good walk and a good meal around a table with friends and family.

She and her husband have three older children and now also a much-loved dog.

hello@pippamclean.com